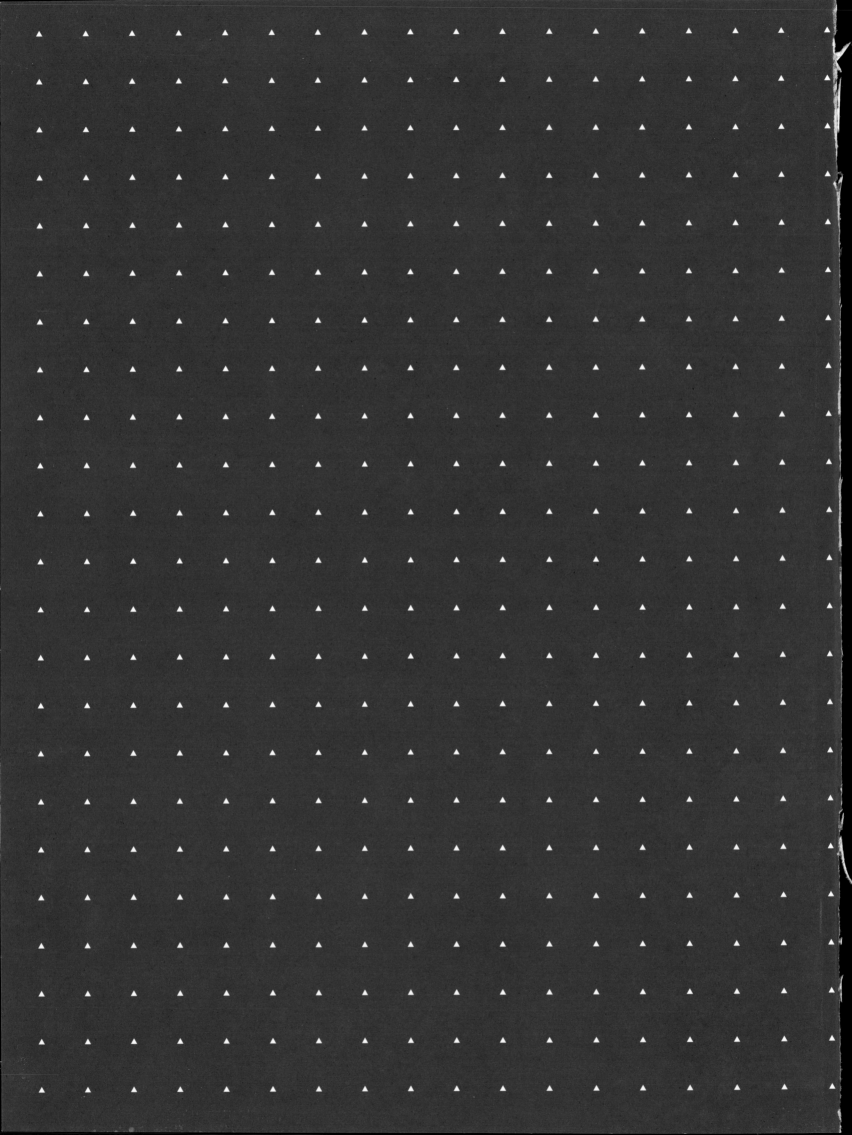

G R A P H I S   D E S I G N   9 7

GRAPHIS DESIGN 97
. . . .

THE INTERNATIONAL ANNUAL OF DESIGN AND ILLUSTRATION

DAS INTERNATIONALE JAHRBUCH ÜBER DESIGN UND ILLUSTRATION

LE RÉPERTOIRE INTERNATIONAL DU DESIGN ET DE L'ILLUSTRATION

EDITED BY • HERAUSGEGEBEN VON • EDITÉ PAR:

B. MARTIN PEDERSEN

PUBLISHER AND CREATIVE DIRECTOR: B. MARTIN PEDERSEN

BOOK PUBLISHER: CHRISTOPHER T. REGGIO

EDITORS: CLARE HAYDEN, HEINKE JENSSEN

ASSOCIATE EDITOR: PEGGY CHAPMAN

PRODUCTION DIRECTOR: VALERIE MYERS

PHOTOGRAPHER: ALFREDO PARRAGA

GRAPHIS INC.

(OPPOSITE) ILLUSTRATION BY GUY BILLOUT

COVER/UMSCHLAG/COUVERTURE: PHOTOGRAPY: CRAIG CUTLER STUDIO • DIGITAL IMAGING: CHROMART

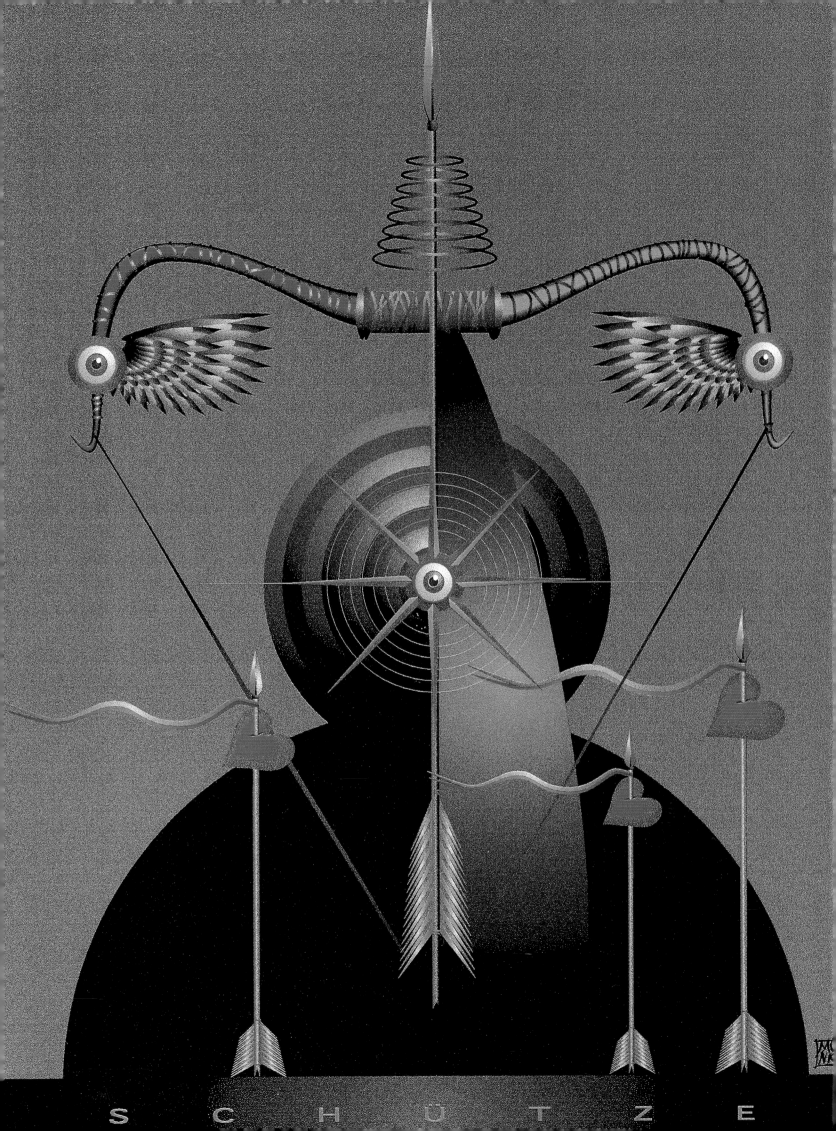

SCHÜTZE

CONTENTS

INHALT

SOMMAIRE

REMARKS

ANMERKUNGEN

ANNOTATIONS

WE EXTEND OUR HEARTFELT THANKS TO CONTRIBUTORS THROUGHOUT THE WORLD WHO HAVE MADE IT POSSIBLE TO PUBLISH A WIDE AND INTERNATIONAL SPECTRUM OF THE BEST WORK IN THIS FIELD.

ENTRY INSTRUCTIONS FOR ALL GRAPHIS BOOKS MAY BE REQUESTED FROM:
GRAPHIS INC.
141 LEXINGTON AVENUE
NEW YORK, NY 10016-8193

UNSER DANK GILT DEN EINSENDERN AUS ALLER WELT, DIE ES UNS DURCH IHRE BEITRÄGE ERMÖGLICHT HABEN, EIN BREITES, INTERNATIONALES SPEKTRUM DER BESTEN ARBEITEN ZU VERÖFFENTLICHEN.

TEILNAHMEBEDINGUNGEN FÜR DIE GRAPHIS-BÜCHER SIND ERHÄLTLICH BEIM:
GRAPHIS INC.
141 LEXINGTON AVENUE
NEW YORK, NY 10016-8193

TOUTE NOTRE RECONNAISSANCE VA AUX DESIGNERS DU MONDE ENTIER DONT LES ENVOIS NOUS ONT PERMIS DE CONSTITUER UN VASTE PANORAMA INTERNATIONAL DES MEILLEURES CRÉATIONS.

LES MODALITÉS D'INSCRIPTION PEUVENT ÊTRE OBTENUES AUPRÈS DE:
GRAPHIS INC.
141 LEXINGTON AVENUE
NEW YORK, NY 10016-8193

(OPPOSITE) ILLUSTRATION BY SIEGMAR MÜNK

This book is dedicated to the memory of Saul Bass, Walter Herdeg, Roberto Sambonet, Bradbury Thompson and Gérard Miedinger. Their talent and contributions to the field of graphic design shall not be forgotten. ■ Dieses Buch ist dem Andenken von Saul Bass, Walter Herdeg, Roberto Sambonet, Bradbury Thompson und Gérard Miedinger gewidmet. Ihre Begabungen und ihre Leistungen auf dem Gebiet des Graphik-Designs werden uns unvergessen bleiben. ■ Cet ouvrage est dédié à Saul Bass, à Walter Herdeg, à Roberto Sambonet, à Bradbury Thompson et à Gérard Miedinger. Leur talent et leurs réalisations dans le domaine du design graphique resteront à jamais gravés dans nos mémoires.

GRAPHIS TOP TEN IN DESIGN

ALAN CHAN DESIGN COMPANY
CHARLES S. ANDERSON DESIGN COMPANY
KOEWEIDEN POSTMA ASSOCIATES
MIRES DESIGN
NIKE, INC.
PENTAGRAM DESIGN
SANDSTROM DESIGN
SOCIO X
VANDERBYL DESIGN
VSA PARTNERS

COMMENTARIES

KOMMENTARE

COMMENTAIRES

JOHN GORHAM

I recently read an interview with Chris Krage, the deputy art editor of THE TIMES, in which he said "It's possibly an unfashionable thing to say in the mid-nineties, but I like ideas. If it's a clever enough idea it will penetrate the subconscious and people will remember it and can talk about it years later." He was talking about illustration, but I think the same also applies to graphic design. □ When I started out as a young graphic designer in the 1960s, I remember seeing the work of Alan Fletcher, Colin Forbes, and Bob Gill and being immediately struck by their approach to graphic design. What I loved about it was the originality of thought. Bob Gill explains it better than I can in his book FORGET ALL THE RULES ABOUT GRAPHIC DESIGN. Paraphrasing him a little, he says, "An ordinary problem can lead to surprising, original, graphic solutions, provided the designer is prepared to let go of any preconceptions about how the design is supposed to look." I have tried to adhere to and practice this sound advice. I am very saddened by the attitude of the 1990s in rejecting "idea" graphics and replacing it with "style" graphics. • For the past twenty-nine years my passion has been "idea" graphics. I prepare all my own mechanical artwork in a handcrafted way and, when necessary, I enjoy handlettering and illustration. I don't have a computer and recently produced a poster proclaiming that my only gizmo was the back of an envelope, with its mouse being the stump of a pencil. I refuse to be pressured into having a computer just because it's fashionable to do so. I prefer my ideas to come from my mind, not a machine. I was encouraged to read that Michael Dempsey of Carrol, Dempsey & Thirkhill has said, "If I can do a job conventionally, then I do. It seems silly to use a computer." The only time I get involved with an Apple Mac is when I need to do some typesetting, or if I have to put my artwork on disk. This is done for me by an outside operator. • I was somewhat taken aback to read in a design journal that an "Apple Mac designer" stated that he was sorry design groups practicing "idea" graphics still exist—in his view they were nothing more than "dinosaurs." Unfortunately, I don't think he is alone in this opinion, especially amongst art colleges and the students graduating from them. They

seem to think the Mac is some sort of god and anyone working in a different way is as dead as the dodo. • I consider it ridiculous to dismiss "idea" graphics in this rather silly and arrogant manner, particularly as I think the first duty of a designer is to understand a problem and solve it in the most simple, direct, and imaginative way. Otherwise all you end up with is "wallpaper" design. • Good "idea" graphics can have a timeless appeal. When I show art students my work, they often express surprise that some of it was designed twenty or so years ago, as it still looks fresh. I very much doubt that the same will be said of the majority of computer design now being done. • Michael Johnson, who knows a lot more about computers than I do, believes that computer ownership allows designers to get away with limited idea input because technology can do so many tricks. He also feels that there are people who turn on their computers and turn off their brains. • I am pleased to say that there are still design groups, such as The Partners, producing great "idea" graphics and continuously winning awards for it. In fact, The Partners are first in the top 100 award-winning design consultancies. I think that they will be around when most of the "style" designers have disappeared. It is these "style" designers who shall surely inherit the term "dinosaurs."

JOHN GORHAM IS A SELF-TAUGHT GRAPHIC DESIGNER BORN IN GREAT BRITAIN IN 1937. HE HAS WORKED FOR THE INTERNATIONAL PRINTING CORPORATION, *THE SUNDAY TIMES* AND CASSONS ADVERTISING AGENCY. SINCE 1967 HE HAS RUN HIS OWN DESIGN STUDIO. HE WAS A PART-TIME TUTOR AT THE ROYAL COLLEGE OF ART FROM THE MID-1970S TO THE EARLY 1980S. HE IS A MEMBER OF THE *ALLIANCE GRAPHIQUE INTERNATIONALE* AND HAS WORK IN THE PERMANENT POSTER COLLECTION OF THE MUSEUM OF MODERN ART IN NEW YORK. HE IS A RECIPIENT OF THE D&AD'S PRESIDENT'S AWARD AS WELL AS MANY OTHER NATIONAL AND INTERNATIONAL AWARDS.

Kürzlich las ich ein Interview mit Chris Krage, dem stellvertretenden Art Editor der *Times*, in dem er sich wie folgt äusserte: «Mitte der neunziger Jahre mag es altmodisch klingen, aber mir gefallen Ideen. Wenn die Idee intelligent genug ist, dringt sie ins Unterbewusstsein, und die Leute werden sich noch Jahre später daran erinnern und darüber reden.» Er sprach über Illustration, aber ich glaube, das gleiche gilt auch für Graphik-Design. ■ Ich erinnere mich, in den sechziger Jahren, als ich gerade begonnen hatte, als Graphik-Designer zu arbeiten, graphische Arbeiten von Alan Fletcher, Colin Forbes und Bob Gill gesehen zu haben, die mich tief beeindruckten. Was mir daran so gefiel, war ihre Originalität. In seinem Buch *Forget All the Rules about Graphic Design* erklärt Bob Gill es besser, als ich es vermag. Er sagt darin in etwa folgendes: «Ein gewöhnliches Problem kann zu überraschenden, originellen graphischen Lösungen führen, vorausgesetzt, der Graphiker ist bereit, alle vorgefassten Vorstellungen dessen, wie das Design aussehen sollte, über Bord zu werfen.» Ich habe immer versucht, mich an diesen vernünftigen Rat zu halten, und mir macht es zu schaffen, dass Ideen heute kaum mehr zählen und stattdessen Stil im Graphik-Design dominiert. ■ In den vergangenen 29 Jahren habe ich mich für Graphik begeistert, die auf Ideen aufbaut. Ich mache alle Reinzeichnungen für meine Entwürfe auf die herkömmliche Art und habe Freude daran, Buchstaben von Hand zu entwerfen und Illustrationen zu machen, wenn das gewünscht wird. Ich habe keinen Computer. Kürzlich habe ich ein Plakat gemacht, in dem ich

erkläre, dass meine Werkzeuge nicht Bildschirm und Maus, sondern Rückseite eines Umschlags und ein Bleistiftstummel sind. Ich weigere mich, einen Computer zu benutzen, nur weil das der Trend ist. Ich ziehe es vor, Ideen zu haben, die im Kopf entstehen und nicht in einer Maschine. Folgende Worte von Michael Dempsey von Carrol, Dempsey & Thirkhill haben mir Mut gemacht: «Wenn ich einen Job auf konventionelle Weise machen kann, dann tue ich es. Es erscheint mir unsinnig, einen Computer zu benutzen.» Nur wenn ich mit Satz zu tun habe oder meine Entwürfe auf Diskette haben muss, komme ich mit einem Apple Mac in Berührung, aber das macht jemand für mich ausser Haus. ■ Es hat mich erstaunt, in einer Design-Zeitschrift zu lesen, dass ein «Apple Mac Gestalter» geäussert habe, er bedaure, dass Graphik-Büros, die Ideen-Graphik machen, noch immer existieren – seiner Meinung nach seien sie nichts als «Dinosaurier». Leider muss ich annehmen, dass er mit seiner Ansicht nicht allein ist, wobei ich insbesondere an die Kunstschulen und ihre Absolventen denke. Sie scheinen zu glauben, der Mac sei eine Art Gott und jeder, der anders arbeitet, sei schon längst tot. ■ Für mich ist es lächerlich, «Ideen-Graphik» auf solch dumme und arrogante Art abzutun, zumal ich der Meinung bin, dass es die Pflicht eines jeden Gaphikers ist, ein Problem zu begreifen und es auf möglichst einfache, direkte und phantasievolle Art zu lösen. Wenn nicht, kommt nichts als Tapetengraphik dabei heraus. ■ Kürzlich wurde mir erzählt, wie ein junger Graphiker auf die Ausstellung eines der führenden Computer-Graphiker unseres Landes reagiert hatte. Als das erste Dia gezeigt wurde, dachte er «wie aufregend», dann kam das nächste Dia, und er dachte «hmmm». Im Laufe der Präsentation bekam er mehr und mehr das Gefühl, dass alles gleich aussah. ■ Gute «Ideen»-Graphik kann zeitlos sein. Wenn ich meine Arbeiten Studenten zeige, sind sie oft überrascht, dass einige schon vor ca. 20 Jahren entstanden sind und noch immer frisch aussehen. Ich bezweifle sehr, dass sich das auch vom heutigen Computer-Design sagen lassen wird. ■ Michael Johnson, der viel mehr über Computer weiss als ich, glaubt, dass der Besitz eines Macs es den Graphikern erlaubt, mit viel weniger Ideen auszukommen, weil die Technologie viele Tricks möglich macht. Er befürchtet, dass viele den Computer einschalten und ihren Kopf dabei ausschalten. ■ Es freut mich, sagen zu können, dass es noch immer Graphikfirmen gibt, wie zum Beispiel The Partners, die grossartige «Ideen-Graphik» machen und dafür auch fortlaufend Preise bekommen. The Partners sind übrigens die Nummer Eins auf der Liste der preisgekrönten Top-100-Designfirmen in Grossbritannien. Ich glaube, es wird sie noch geben, wenn die meisten der «Stil-Graphiker» längst verschwunden sind. Letztere sind es, die die Bezeichnung «Dinosaurier» verdienen.

John Gorham, 1937 in Grossbritannien geboren, ist Autodidakt. Er hat u.a. als Graphiker für die International Printing Corporation, *The Sunday Times* und Cassons Advertising Agency gearbeitet. Seit 1967 betreibt er sein eigenes Design-Studio. Von Mitte der siebziger bis Anfang der achtziger Jahre unterrichtete er am Royal College of Art. Er ist Mitglied der *AGI* und mit seinen Arbeiten in der Sammlung des Museum of Modern Art, New York, vertreten. Zu den vielen nationalen und internationalen Auszeichnungen gehört auch der D&AD President's Award, der im 1993 verliehen wurde.

Récemment, j'ai lu une interview de Chris Krage, rédacteur artistique adjoint au *Times*, lequel déclarait: «Cela peut paraître démodé à notre époque, mais je dois avouer que j'aime les idées. Si une idée est intelligente, elle s'immisce dans l'inconscient, les gens s'en souviennent et en parlent encore bien des années plus tard.» Il évoquait l'illustration, mais je crois que ses propos s'appliquent aussi au design graphique. ▲ Alors que je débutais dans la profession comme designer graphique, je me rappelle avoir vu dans les années 60 des travaux graphiques d'Alan Fletcher, de Colin Forbes et de Bob Gill, qui m'ont fait une vive impression, surtout en raison de leur approche originale. Dans son livre *Forget All the Rules about Graphic Design*, Bob Gill l'explique – mieux que je ne pourrais le faire – en ces termes: « Un problème ordinaire peut déboucher sur des solutions graphiques aussi surprenantes qu'originales, à condition toutefois que le graphiste soit disposé à jeter par-dessus bord toutes les idées préconçues que l'on peut se faire sur l'apparence du design.» J'ai toujours essayé de respecter scrupuleusement ce conseil et j'ai beaucoup de peine à accepter qu'en matière de design graphique, le style prime aujourd'hui sur les idées. ▲ Au cours des 29 dernières années, je me suis consacré avec passion au graphisme conceptuel. Je prépare tous mes travaux dans la plus pure tradition, soit de façon «artisanale», et, si nécessaire, j'ébauche des caractères à la main ou je fais des illustrations. Chez moi, l'ordinateur n'a pas voix au chapitre. Il y a quelque temps, j'ai conçu une affiche qui proclamait que mes instruments de travail se résument au dos d'une enveloppe et à un bout de crayon de papier plutôt qu'à un ordinateur et à une souris. Je me refuse à utiliser un ordinateur seulement parce que c'est la mode. Je préfère voir naître les idées dans ma tête et non pas dans une machine. Les propos de Michael Dempsey de Carrol, Dempsey & Thirkhill m'ont mis du baume au cœur: «Si je peux exécuter un travail de façon conventionnelle, je le fais. Je trouve que c'est insensé d'utiliser un ordinateur.» Les seules fois où l'ordinateur s'impose, c'est lorsqu'il s'agit de composer un texte ou que je dois avoir mes productions artistiques sur disquette. En fait, c'est un opérateur externe qui fait ce travail pour moi. ▲ J'ai été surpris de lire dans un magazine spécialisé les déclarations d'un

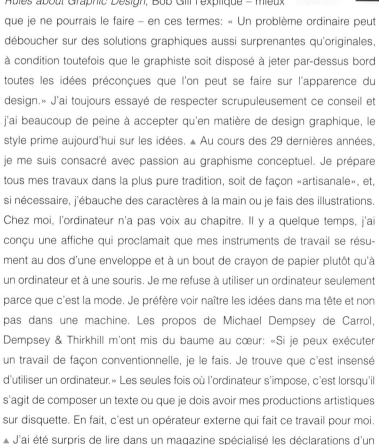

COLIN BLAKELY · DAVID SUCHET
RED MONARCH
DAVID PUTTNAM · CHARLES WOOD · GRAHAM BENSON
CARROLL BAKER · JACK GOLD

concepteur qui travaille sur Mac, lequel regrettait qu'il existe toujours des agences de graphisme dont le travail repose en premier lieu sur la recherche d'idées. Selon lui, ces personnes sont des «dinosaures». Malheureusement, je dois reconnaître qu'il n'est sans doute pas le seul à partager cet avis – je pense avant tout aux écoles d'art et à leurs diplômés. Ils vénèrent leur Mac telle une divinité et croient que quiconque travaille avec d'autres outils n'a aucune chance. ▲ Je trouve stupide et ridicule de condamner avec autant d'arrogance le graphisme conceptuel, surtout que chaque graphiste se doit de comprendre un problème, de le résoudre de façon aussi simple, directe et pertinente que possible. Sinon, le résultat est tout juste bon pour faire office de tapisserie. ▲ Il y a quelque temps, un graphiste m'a raconté qu'il était allé voir une exposition consacrée à l'un des meilleurs graphistes du pays qui travaillent sur ordinateur. En voyant la première diapo, il s'est dit «C'est fascinant!», à la deuxième, il a pensé «M'ouais...» et, au fur et à mesure de la présentation, il avait de plus en plus l'impression que tout était coulé dans le même moule. ▲ Un graphisme avec de bonnes idées peut être intemporel. Quand je montre mes travaux à mes étudiants, ils sont souvent surpris d'apprendre que certains d'entre eux datent d'il y a 20 ans et qu'ils aient conservé une telle fraîcheur. Je doute que l'on en dise un jour autant de la conception assistée par ordinateur. ▲ Michael Johnson, dont les connaissances informatiques sont plus étendues que les miennes, estime que les graphistes qui possèdent un ordinateur peuvent se permettre d'avoir moins d'idées parce que la technologie fait le reste. Il pense qu'en enclenchant leur ordinateur, ils mettent en même temps leur cerveau en veilleuse. ▲ Je suis heureux de constater qu'il existe toujours des agences de graphisme comme The Partners, qui ont des idées géniales et pour lesquelles elles remportent constamment de nouveaux prix. D'ailleurs, l'agence occupe la première place sur la liste des 100 agences les plus couronnées de Grande-Bretagne. Je crois que ces agences seront toujours là lorsque les graphistes qui ont pour seul souci le style auront disparu depuis longtemps. Et ce sont ces derniers que l'on taxera à coup sûr de «dinosaures».

John Gorham, né en 1937 en Grande-Bretagne, est un designer graphique autodidacte. Il a travaillé pour l'International Printing Corporation, *The Sunday Times* et l'agence publicitaire Cassons. Depuis 1967, il a sa propre agence de design. Depuis le milieu des années 70 jusqu'au début des années 80, il a enseigné au Royal College of Art. Il est membre de *l'Alliance Graphique Internationale*, et ses travaux sont exposés dans la collection du Museum of Modern Art à New York. Il s'est vu décerner de nombreux prix nationaux et internationaux, dont le D&AD's President's Award. (Opposite page) "Helvetica Snow," Christmas poster created for Typeshop. Designer: John Gorham. ● (This page) "Red Monarch," a film poster designed for Enigma/Goldcrest. Art Director: John Gorham. Designers: John Gorham, Howard Brown.

SCOTT MIRES

Today's graphic design industry is changing at a dizzying pace. Typesetting has given way to QuarkXpress, airbrushing to Photoshop, stripping to digital files. From stripping and color separations to typesetting, air-brushing and retouching, what was once done out-of-house, is now all done in-house. The speed at which we communicate has created a demand for instant gratification, an industry-wide expectation of "ideas while you wait." In this ever-evolving world where technology and graphic communications meet, what now constitutes good design? □ The most important thing we deliver to clients are ideas—ideas that ignite interest, move products, and build brands. As long as clients value our ability to create compelling communications, it doesn't really matter what final form these take. In printed, broadcast or online media, it's the message, not the medium, which is most important. Good design, however, takes commitment not just to an idea and

project, but to the creative process. The designer must orchestrate both clients' needs and demands and his own personal insight and interpretation. It's getting the most out of the hand that's dealt to you. Good design requires taking all of the variables within a project and getting them to add value to the final piece. It also requires seeing each potential obstacle as a challenge to make the job better. It means neither getting discouraged by defeat, nor becoming enamored with success. • Good design requires an atmosphere of growth and camaraderie, of respect and fun. Good design happens only when people who enjoy their jobs work together to bring a project to fruition. It takes a workplace in which what one thinks and feels makes a difference in the project on which one works. Truly successful design is much more than the sum of its parts. It has a life of its own, born

of human insight and the need to communicate. It is not only a visual commentary, but also feeling, defining, fulfilling, expanding, enlightening and uplifting. It has heart and soul. • To create, we need a certain amount of friction and restraint. An open canvas and pocketbook do not necessarily make for the perfect project—our best work is created within a defined set of boundaries and rules. To me it's like working on a puzzle for which there are only a few pieces. The solver must find the rest of the pieces by defining and creating them. The challenge isn't really to create something out of nothing. It is to take what is there and add significantly to it. • Is it good design if it doesn't work, is over budget and two weeks late, or can't be produced? Is it good design if the designer hates it or if no one will work with him again? Is it good design if it makes the client a lot of money or it wins every award

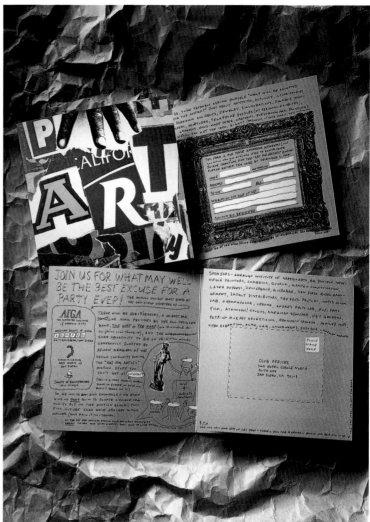

on the planet? Is it good design if it is beautiful, ugly or illegible? Is it good design if Massimo Vignelli likes it? If David Carson likes it? If a gas station attendant likes it? ● Good design is the appropriate solution to the design problem the client presents. Good design comes from the ability to ask questions of ourselves, of our clients, and of each other. The endless desire to answer those questions keeps us coming back day after day.

Scott Mires is founder and creative director of Mires Design in San Diego, California. His creative team has earned national and international awards for design and marketing excellence. Mires Design clients have included Intel, Nike, Pepsi, Hewlett Packard and the California Center for the Arts, among others.

Die Graphik-Design-Branche verändert sich heute in atemberaubendem Tempo. QuarkXPress hat den Schriftsatz verdrängt, Photoshop die Airbrush-Technik, digitale Datensätze die Montage. Wir haben all diese Funktionen ohne fremde Hilfe übernommen, und die Geschwindigkeit, mit der wir kommunizieren, hat dazu geführt, dass sofortige Erfüllung erwartet wird, eine branchenweite Haltung nach dem Motto: «Ideen, während Sie warten.» Was versteht man heute in dieser sich ständig weiterentwickelnden Welt, in der Technologie und graphische Kommunikationen aufeinanderstossen, unter gutem Design? ■ Das Wichtigste, was wir Kunden liefern, sind Ideen. Ideen erzeugen Interesse, bewegen Produkte, bauen Marken auf. Solange Auftraggeber unsere Fähigkeit schätzen, überzeugend für sie zu kommunizieren, ist es egal, in welcher Form das geschieht. Am wichtigsten ist die Botschaft, nicht das Medium. ■ Gutes Design erfordert jedoch Engagement, und zwar nicht nur in bezug auf eine Idee und ein Projekt, sondern auf den kreativen Prozess. Der Gestalter muss die Bedürfnisse und Forderungen des Auftraggebers mit seinen persönlichen Einsichten und Interpretationen in Einklang bringen. Das bedeutet, dass man das Optimale aus einer Sache herausholen muss. Gutes Design verlangt, dass man den Spielraum innerhalb eines Projektes zum Vorteil des Endproduktes nutzt. Dazu gehört auch, jedes mögliche Hindernis als Herausforderung zu betrachten, die Aufgabe noch besser zu lösen. Das heisst, sich weder von Niederlagen entmutigen noch von Erfolgen blenden zu lassen. ■ Gutes Design verlangt ausserdem eine Umgebung, die von Wachstum, Kameradschaft, Respekt und Spass geprägt ist. Gutes Design entsteht nur, wenn Leute, die ihre Arbeit lieben, zusammenarbeiten, um ein Projekt optimal fertigzustellen. Dazu gehört ein Arbeitsplatz, auf den man sich jeden Morgen freut und wo das, was man denkt und fühlt, für das Projekt, an dem er oder sie gerade arbeitet, von Bedeutung ist. ■ Wirklich erfolgreiches Design ist viel mehr als nur die Summe seiner Teile. Es hat ein eigenes Leben, geboren aus menschlichen Einsichten und dem Bedürfnis zu kommunizieren. Es ist nicht nur ein visueller Kommentar, sondern auch Gefühl, Umschreibung, Ausführung, Erweiterung, Erleuchtung und Erhebung. Es hat Herz und Seele. ■ Um etwas zu erschaffen, brauchen wir ein gewisses Ausmass an Reibung und Einschränkung. Freie Hand in der Gestaltung und genug finanzielle Mittel bedeuten nicht unbedingt einen perfekten Auftrag – die besten Arbeiten entstehen innerhalb bestimmter Grenzen und Regeln. Für mich ist das wie ein Puzzle, zu dem man nur wenige

Teile hat. Der Löser der Aufgabe muss den Rest der Teile finden, indem er sie selbst definiert und erschafft. Die Herausforderung besteht nicht wirklich darin, etwas aus dem Nichts zu schaffen, sondern etwas schon Vorhandenes in die Hand zu nehmen und etwas Wichtiges hinzuzufügen. ■ Ist es gutes Design, wenn es nicht funktioniert oder das Budget überschreitet oder zwei Wochen zu spät abgeliefert wird? Ist es gutes Design, wenn es sich in der Produktion nicht umsetzen lässt oder wenn der Auftraggeber nie mehr mit dem Designer zusammenarbeiten wird? Ist es gutes Design, wenn Sie es verabscheuen? Ist es gutes Design, wenn es den Auftraggeber reich macht und ihm alle Auszeichnungen der Welt einbringt? Ist es gutes Design, wenn es schön, hässlich oder unleserlich ist? Ist es gutes Design, wenn niemand in der Designfirma mehr mit dem betreffenden Designer zusammenarbeiten will? Ist es gutes Design, wenn es Massimo Vignelli gefällt. Oder David Carson? Oder einem Tankwart? ■ Gutes Design ist eine angemessene Lösung für ein Design-Problem, das der Auftraggeber vorlegt. Gutes Design hat mit der Fähigkeit zu tun, sich selbst, dem Kunden und einander Fragen zu stellen. Der unablässige Drang, Antworten auf diese Fragen zu finden, lässt uns Tag für Tag zurückkehren.

Scott Mires ist Gründer und Creative Director von Mires Design in San Diego, Kalifornien. Sein Team von 11 Mitarbeitern hat für hervorragende Leistungen im Design und Marketing nationale und internationale Auszeichnungen erhalten. Zu den Kunden von Mires Design gehörten u.a. Intel, die Lebensmittelgruppe LA Gear, Harcourt Brace & Co., Rubio's Restaurants, Nike, Pepsi, Hewlett Packard und das California Center for the Arts.

Le design graphique évolue aujourd'hui à un rythme effréné. Le QuarkXPress a évincé la composition, le Photoshop, l'aérographie, et les fichiers numériques ont remplacé le montage. Autant de techniques que nous avons appris à maîtriser et grâce auxquelles nous exécutons désormais nous-mêmes des travaux que nous avions l'habitude de déléguer. Compte tenu de la rapidité des nouveaux moyens de communication, les clients exigent que nous répondions immédiatement à leurs attentes et ils considèrent le slogan «Des idées pendant que vous attendez» comme le nouveau mot d'ordre de notre profession. Dans ce monde en constante mutation, marqué par la synergie de la technologie et de la communication graphique, qu'entend-on par design de qualité? ▲ Ce que nous fournissons d'essentiel aux clients, ce sont les idées. Des idées qui éveillent l'intérêt, permettent de développer des produits et donnent naissance à de nouvelles marques. Tant que les clients apprécient l'efficacité des supports de communication que nous inventons, peu importe la forme sous laquelle ceux-ci se présentent. C'est le message qui prime et non le média utilisé. ▲ Reste que le design de qualité suppose de l'engagement, et ce pas seulement pour une idée ou un projet, mais aussi pour le processus de création. Le concepteur doit parvenir à faire converger les besoins et les exigences du client avec sa propre façon de penser, tout l'art étant d'utiliser au mieux la marge de manœuvre impartie. Examiner toutes les options possibles dans le cadre d'un projet et trouver la constellation qui donnera le meilleur produit final, telle est la clef du design de qualité. Il faut également savoir tirer parti des obstacles qui surgissent au profit d'un résultat encore meilleur. En la matière, le découragement face à l'échec n'est pas plus de mise que l'aveuglement face à la réussite. ▲ Le design de qualité ne peut prendre naissance que dans un vivier d'idées favorisé par la camaraderie, le respect et le plaisir ambiants. Il ne peut être que l'œuvre de designers passionnés par leur métier qui lui impriment la mar-

que de leur personnalité et de leurs réflexions au cours d'un travail d'équipe. ▲ Et le design de qualité atteint son summum lorsque, loin de se limiter à la somme de ses composantes, il s'anime d'une vie propre que lui ont insufflée la pensée humaine et le besoin de communiquer. Dépassant le stade de simple commentaire visuel, il devient alors tout à la fois sentiment, description, accomplissement, prolongement, illumination et élévation. Et c'est ce qui lui donne une âme. ▲ Difficultés et contraintes stimulent la création. Le concepteur qui a carte blanche et qui dispose de moyens financiers suffisants n'est pas forcément celui qui réalisera le projet le plus pointu. Les meilleurs travaux sont issus d'un cadre de règles et de réglementations bien définies. A mes yeux, ce processus s'apparente à un puzzle dont on ne posséderait que quelques pièces. Pour trouver la solution, il convient d'identifier les pièces manquantes et de les créer soimême. A cet égard, la gageure n'est pas tant de faire sortir quelque chose du néant que de compléter judicieusement ce dont on dispose déjà. ▲ Peut-on parler de design de qualité quand le but n'est pas atteint, que le budget est dépassé, que le délai n'est pas tenu et que la production s'avère impossible? Peut-on parler de design de qualité quand le concepteur n'est pas satisfait de son travail ou que plus personne ne veut avoir affaire à lui par la suite? Peut-on parler de design de qualité quand, grâce au projet, la fortune du donneur d'ordre est assurée et qu'il se voit décerner tous les titres honorifiques du monde? Peut-on parler de design de qualité quand le résultat est magnifique, affreux ou indéchiffrable? Peut-on parler de design de qualité quand la réalisation est saluée par Massimo Vignelli? Ou par David Carson? Ou par un pompiste? ▲ Le design de qualité est la réponse adéquate aux attentes du client. Il naît de toutes les questions que se posent le designer, son client ou toute autre personne. Et de ce besoin irrépressible d'en rechercher jusqu'au bout la solution avec opiniâtreté.

Scott Mires est fondateur et directeur de la création de Mires Design à San Diego, Californie. De nombreux prix nationaux et internationaux sont venu couronner les excellents travaux de son équipe créative dans les domaines du design et du marketing. Parmi les clients de Mires Design figurent, entre autres, Intel, le groupe LA Gear (industrie alimentaire), Rubio's Restaurants, Nike, Pepsi, Hewlett Packard et le California Center of Arts.

GRAPHIS

DESIGN

NINETY-SEVEN

1

2

3

4

5

6

6

(OPPOSITE) 1 **H S A** *DF&R Restaurants, Inc.* □ 2 **N I K E ,   I N C** *(IN-HOUSE)* □ 3 **R O G E R   F E L T O N**
A S S O C I A T E S *Centec* □ *(THIS PAGE)* 4 **J O H N   B R A D Y   D E S I G N   C O N S U L T A N T S   I N C .** *Greater Pittsburgh Council*
5 **V S A   P A R T N E R S ,   I N C .** *Harley-Davidson, Inc.* □ 6 **U R B A N   O U T F I T T E R S ,   I N C .** *(IN-HOUSE)*

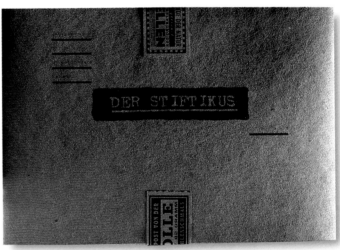

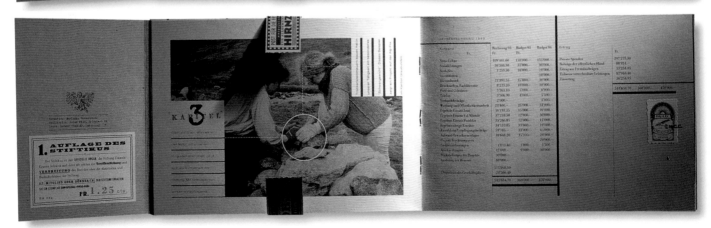

7 **WILD & FREY** *STIFTUNG UMWELTEINSATZ*

(OPPOSITE) 8 **LEIMER CROSS DESIGN CORPORATION** *NINTENDO CO, LTD*

Nintendo World

Look around. Nintendo is in more places... more ways...than ever before. In homes in Japan, via satellite. In the USA, play head-to-head by phone line on the XBAND system. 30,000 feet above the ocean, in your airline seat. 3,000 miles away from home, your hotel room. Even in the health club, your Life Fitness Exertainment Cycle. And in touch 24 hours a day, via our consumer service center...or on line at the Nintendo Power Source web sites and chat rooms. The applications are diverse. But our focus remains singular: real life research and development dedicated to learning how to make even better what is already the world's favorite form of electronic interactive entertainment.

Online: nintendo@aol.com. or www

The first three dimensional moving pictures for your home. The first interface... around your face. An- other way. Another world.

To Our Shareholders: Fiscal 1995 was an outstanding year for Adaptec. We posted record revenues as we continued our worldwide leadership in the critical input/output (I/O) market. We expanded our portfolio of innovative IOware solutions. We made significant progress in applying our core competencies to take advantage of the worldwide growth of the PC market. We made significant investments to ensure Adaptec's participation in new markets that will grow rapidly in the next few years. ⇨

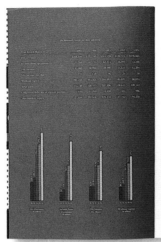

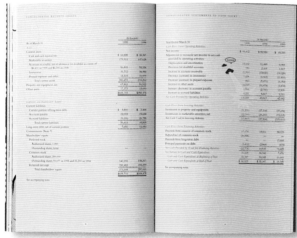

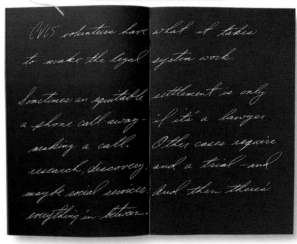

9 **CAHAN & ASSOCIATES** *ADAPTEC, INC.*　　　　10 **VSA PARTNERS, INC.** *CHICAGO VOLUNTEER LEGAL SERVICES*

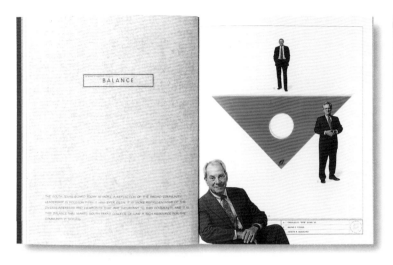

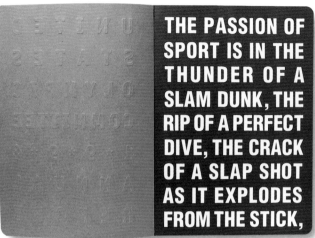

THE PASSION OF SPORT IS IN THE THUNDER OF A SLAM DUNK, THE RIP OF A PERFECT DIVE, THE CRACK OF A SLAP SHOT AS IT EXPLODES FROM THE STICK,

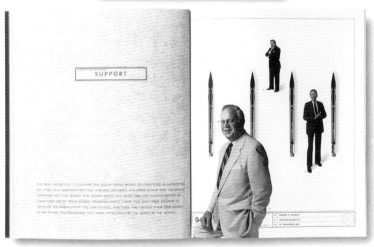

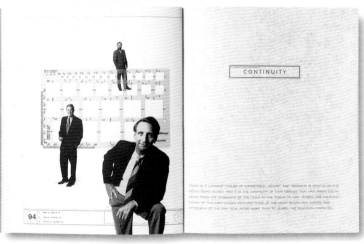

11 **GEER DESIGN, INC.** *South Texas College of Law*

12 **SIBLEY/PETEET DESIGN** *United States Olympic Committee*

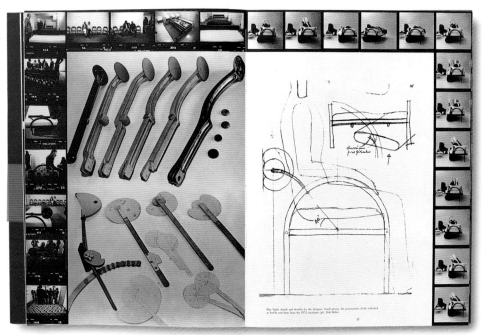

(THIS SPREAD) 13 **LAMBDA SRL** *Driade S.P.A.*

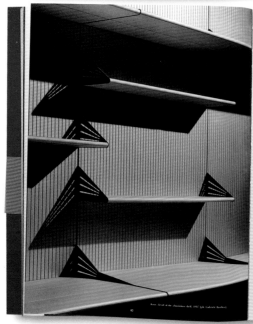

THE DESIGNER INDUSTRY

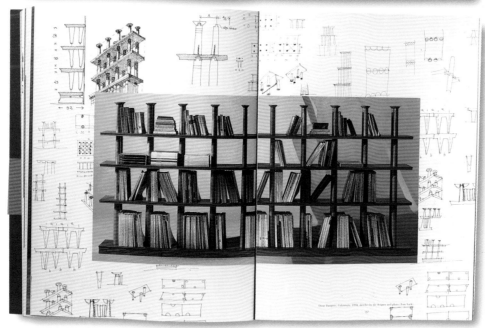

14 **SHINZO GRAPHICA & ASSOCIATES** *Felissimo*

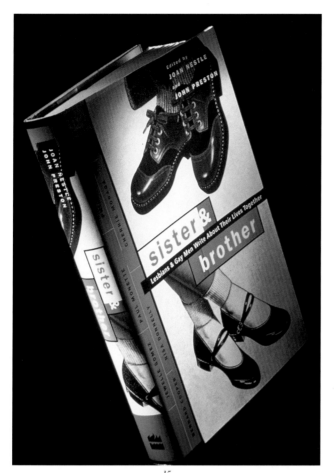

15

16

17

18

The PaineWebber ArtCollection

Introduction by Jack Flam

Commentaries on the plates by
Monique Beudert and Jennifer Wells

Foreword by Donald B. Marron

RIZZOLI

Clemente   Murray   Diebenkorn
Guston
Baselitz
Johns   Smith
Richter   Chia
Cragg
Flavin   Kline
Long

The PaineWebber Art Collection

Intro
duc
tion

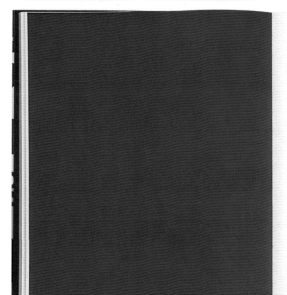

20

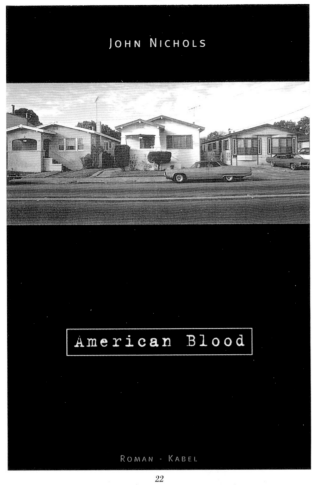

21

22

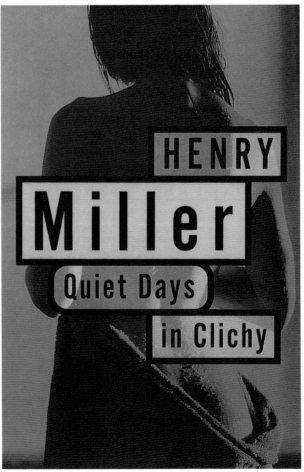

23

20 **HANS-HEINRICH SURES** *(STUDENT PROJECT)* □ 21 **MICHAEL SCHWAB STUDIO** *HYPERION/DISNEY*
22–23 **GROVE/ATLANTIC** *(IN-HOUSE)*

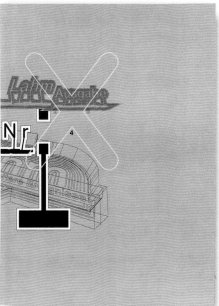

24 **LAHM** *INSTITUT FÜR BUCHGESTALTUNG AN DER STAATLICHEN AKADEMIE DER BILDENDEN KÜNSTE STUTTGART*

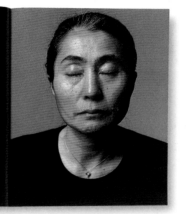

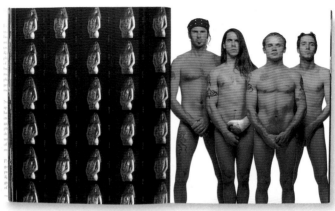

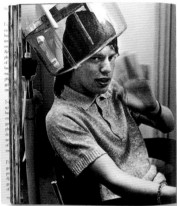

Celebrities in our cul-
that their souls will
camera or in the pho-
in so many words,
losing their souls and
machine, however
have sought the
public eye. They
portant images are
more to the point,
however hard they
fully be able to
control that power.

IN PORTRAITS of quiet moments
we can sense the explosive drive within
artists. And as we stand in awe of their
impressive might onstage, we remember
the resonant images of their quieter
selves. Often photographs are also private moments made public, with all the
contradictions such a description suggests. In seeming isolation, the artist is,
in fact, twice being observed, first by the
photographer, then by us. To the degree
that the artist conspires in the shaping
of the shoot, there may even be three
levels of observation, with the first taking place in the artist's imagination.

(THIS SPREAD) 25 **FRED WOODWARD** *LITTLE BROWN*

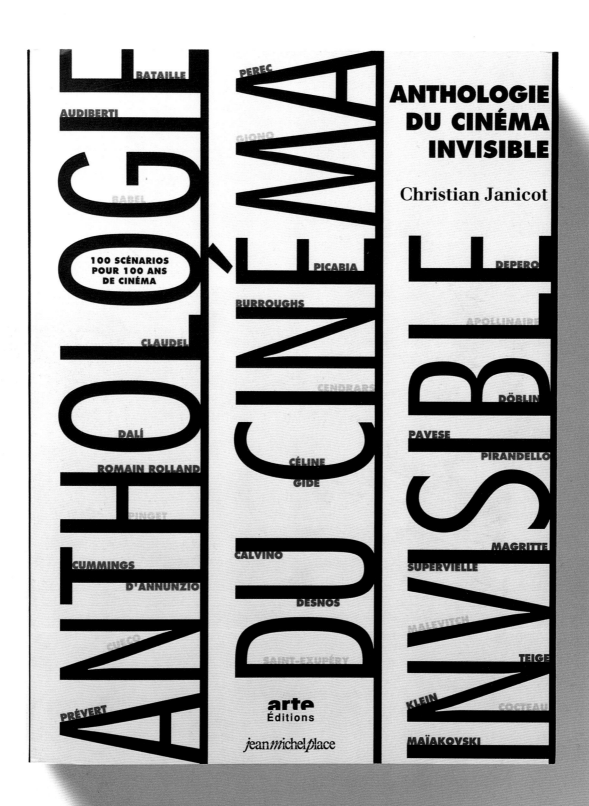

(ABOVE) 26 **BULNES & ROBAGLIA** *Editions Arte* □ *(OPPOSITE)* 27 **THOMAS S. SCHAER VISUELLER GESTALTER SGV SGD** *Nemesis Verlag Pierre Farine* 28 **MTV OFF-AIR CREATIVE** *Melcher Media/Pocket Books* □ 29 **K/PLEX** *Brotmuseum Ulm*

27

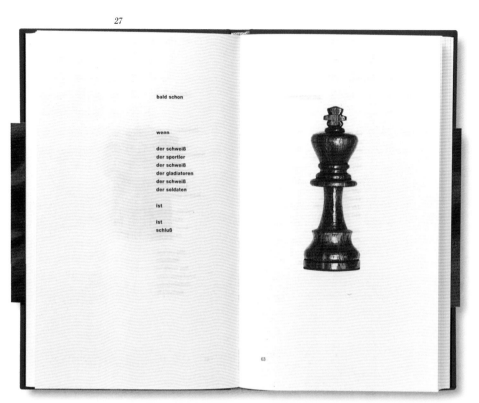

28

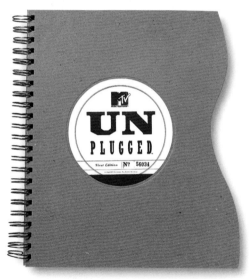

29

30

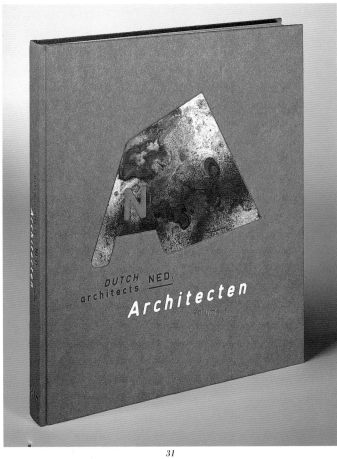

31

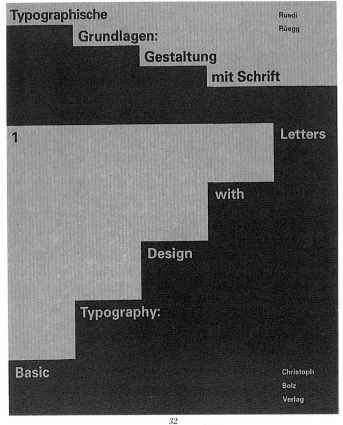

32

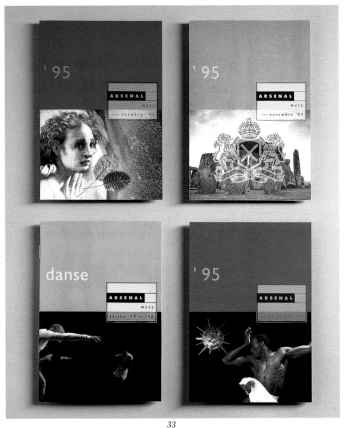

33

30 **DESIGN GUYS** *CONSORTIUM BOOK SALES* □ 31 **KOWEIDEN POSTMA ASSOCIATES** *BIS PUBLISHERS* □ 32 **CHRISTOPH BOLZ** *SFGB SCHULE FÜR GESTALTUNG* □ 33 **LE PETIT DIDIER** *ARSENAL* □ (OPPOSITE) 34 **MICHAEL MABRY** *CHRONICLE BOOKS* 35 **PENCIL CORPORATE ART** *GUSTAV LÜBBE VERLAG GMBH* □ 36 **THE MIT PRESS DESIGN DEPARTMENT** *MIT PRESS*

34

35

36

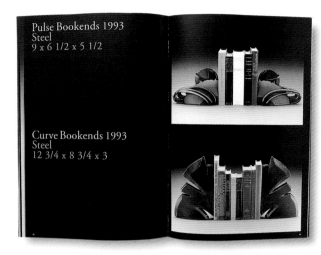

Pulse Bookends 1993
Steel
9 x 6 1/2 x 5 1/2

Curve Bookends 1993
Steel
12 3/4 x 8 3/4 x 3

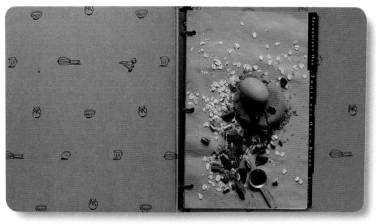

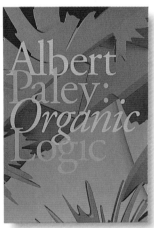

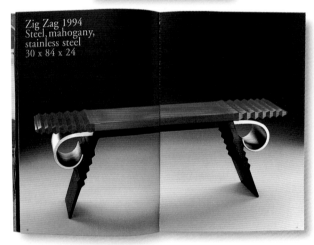

Zig Zag 1994
Steel, mahogany,
stainless steel
30 x 84 x 24

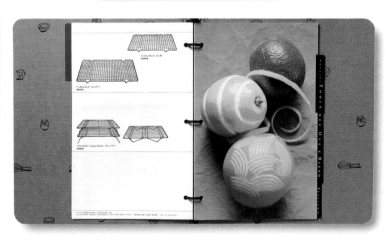

Sideboard 1993
Steel, glass
46 x 80 x 22 1/2

37 **PENTAGRAM DESIGN** *Peter Joseph Gallery*

38 **TULINO DESIGN, INC.** *B. Via International Housewares, Inc.*

Color can indicate the place in which we live. It can imply the types of natural materials we relate to both ethnically and culturally. It is synonymous with the distilled demands of our activities in the context of the images, trends and current design thinking chosen to

Color

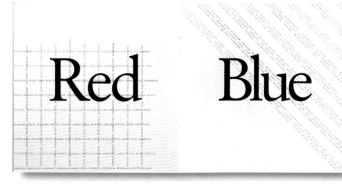

Red Blue

Purple Green

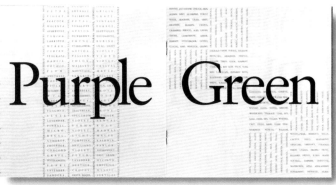

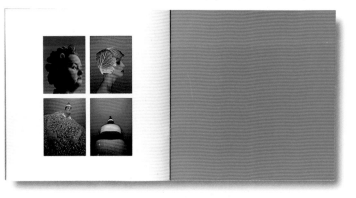

39 **PENTAGRAM DESIGN** *PALLAS TEXTILES*

40 **BROADBENT CHEETHAM VEAZEY** *SHED FILMS*

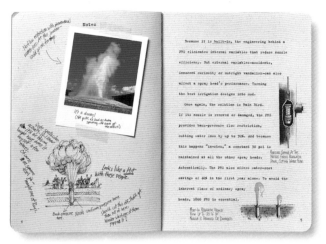

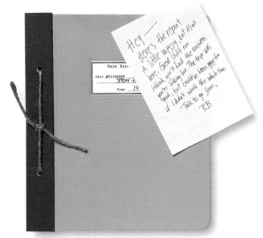

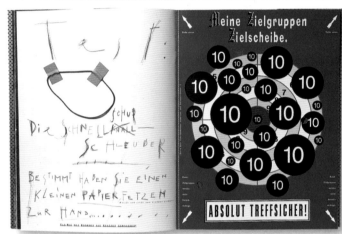

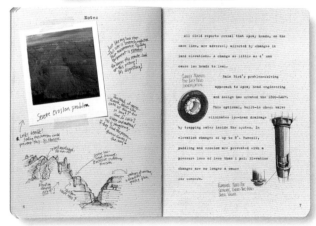

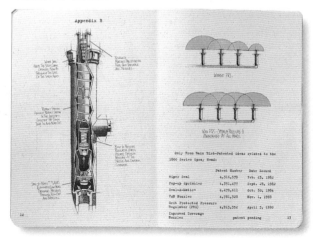

41 **NORDENSSON LYNN ADVERTISING** *Rain Bird*

42 **HEBE WERBUNG & DESIGN** *(IN-HOUSE)*

[JACK MACHOLL]

As a marketer of financial services over the past 14 years, I've worn many hats. I've been a strategic planner, a manager of people, a product developer; I've overseen the creation of new corporate identities, comprehensive marketing/public relations programs and campaigns.

My experience positions me well to be a contributor to the long-term success of a progressive, innovative company.

Jack Macholl

[JACK MACHOLL]

I'm looking for a position in which I can contribute to business success – a place to hang my hat long-term.

I'm eager to meet face-to-face to discuss my background and opportunities to make a difference for a dynamic organization.

Thank you for your consideration.

43 **VSA PARTNERS, INC.** *JACK MACHOLL*

44

45

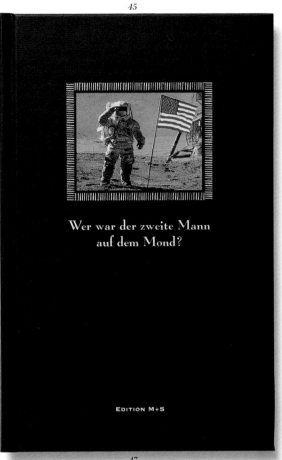

Wer war der zweite Mann
auf dem Mond?

EDITION M+S

46

47

Parallèle

Notre mission consiste à créer, dans le cadre d'une relation de confiance établie dès les premiers instants, des instruments de communication qui suscitent une perception positive et durable de nos clients, de leurs produits et de leurs services. Notre force repose sur des ressources humaines et techno- logiques de haut calibre, qui œuvrent de concert à l'atteinte des objectifs de nos clients, à l'intérieur de deux disciplines fusionnées dans un processus unique:

la **communication-design**.

(THIS PAGE, TOP AND OPPOSITE) 54, 56 **GOODBY SILVERSTEIN & PARTNERS** *BELL HELMETS*
(THIS PAGE, BOTTOM) 55 **SQUIRES & COMPANY** *LOS RIOS ANGLERS*

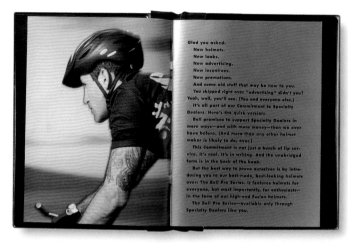

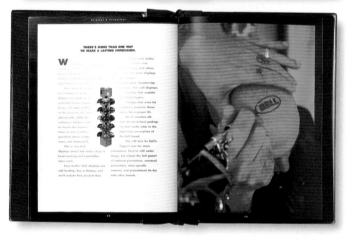

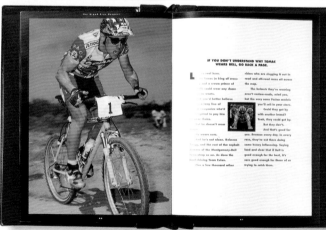

56

57 **AZONE + ASSOCIATES** *BIN OFUSA*   58 **THE DESIGNORY, INC.** *LEO BURNETT USA/OLDSMOBILE*

REFINED

CLASSIC

FINE

BALANCED

HONORED

ROBERT TALBOTT
NECKWEAR REMAINS
THE MOST ELEGANT OF
GENTLEMEN'S ACCESSORIES:
HANDSOME, WELL-MADE AND QUITE
AFFORDABLE. THE UNSURPASSED QUALITY OF
ROBERT TALBOTT NECKTIES BESPEAKS TRADITION
AND REFINEMENT: A QUIET ASSURANCE WITH REMARKABLE
POWERS OF SUGGESTION. FROM THE SPIRITED CLASSICS OF THE
BEST OF CLASS COLLECTION TO THE AUDACIOUS PRINTS OF OUR
EXCLUSIVE LIMITED SERIES, TALBOTT OFFERS AN ARRAY OF NOTED

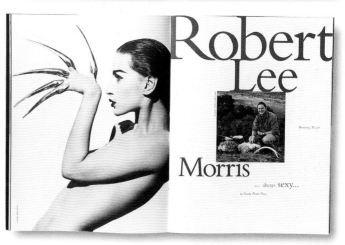

DISCREET

SMART

WITTY

PERFECT

PRIZED

59 **VANDERBYL DESIGN** *ROBERT TALBOTT, INC.*   60 **PENTAGRAM DESIGN** *COUNCIL OF FASHION DESIGNERS OF AMERICA*

61

Brooklyn Academy of Music

1995
Next
Wave
Festival

BAM's 1995 Next Wave
Festival is sponsored by
Philip Morris Companies Inc.

62

João Machado

Cartazes

63

Missouri

MO

MANY ORBITS · MANY OPTIONS

University of Missouri-Columbia   1995-96

64

PATI NÚÑEZ

61 **PENTAGRAM DESIGN** *BROOKLYN ACADEMY OF MUSIC* ☐ 62 **JOÃO MACHADO** *(SELF-PROMOTION)*
☐ 63 **THE NORTH CHARLES STREET DESIGN ORGANIZATION** *THE UNIVERSITY OF MISSOURI-COLUMBIA, OFFICE OF PUBLICATIONS*
64 **ESTUDI PATI NÚÑEZ** *(IN-HOUSE)*

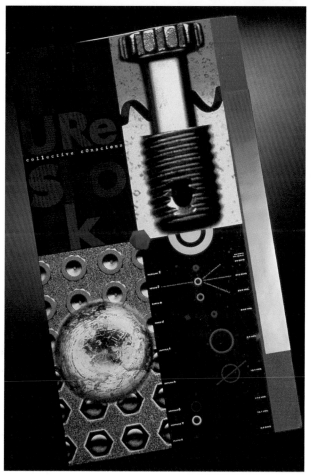

65 **LOUEY/RUBINO DESIGN GROUP, INC.** *LITHOGRAPHIX, HOPPER PAPER CO.*

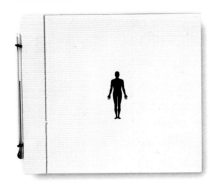

THE **PENGUIN** IS ADMIRABLY SUITED FOR **WET, COLD** WEATHER.

In product design, form and function are totally integrated; one does not follow the other. All materials have a special nature; some are malleable, such as glass or steel, and some are not, such as marble. With some materials, such as plastics, one can obtain precise details; with others, such as china and porcelain, one cannot. All materials, however, reflect or absorb light according to their surface finish. Light is the master of form. It shapes the contours of an object, and distinguishes hard from soft, and transparent from opaque.

In designing products for everyday use, we sense the importance of a user's perception and we articulate the products to achieve deliberate connotations– since whatever is perceived is retained and analyzed in one way or another.

Designed by Lella and Massimo Vignelli: "The Halo" A Swiss Watch made by Pierre Junod

HUMANS DO.

BE OUR GUEST IN THE PENGUIN HOUSE AT THE CENTRAL PARK WILDLIFE CENTER. 830 FIFTH AVE. (AT 64TH ST.) ON TUESDAY, MAY 9TH AT 6:00 P.M. TO WELCOME STORM-F.I.T.™ FABRIC – THE NEWEST MEMBER OF THE PERFORMANCE LINE OF NIKE F.I.T. FABRICS – INTO THE WORLD. PLEASE R.S.V.P. TO LIZ FLYNN AT 212.505.9494.
(WARM CAPS WILL BE PROVIDED.)

Our basic concept was to transform the watch into a transparent, weightless object. To achieve this effect, we designed a frame that covers the case and expands the glass of the face into a subtly colored interchangeable "halo."

PENGUINS DO **NOT** REQUIRE **PRO- TECTION** FROM RAIN·SLEET. SNOW. **OR** THEIR OWN PERSPIRATION.

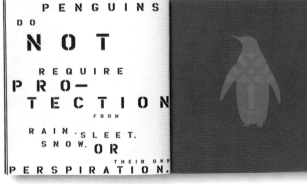

66 **NIKE, INC.** *(IN-HOUSE)*

67 **VIGNELLI ASSOCIATES** *PIERRE JUNOD WATCHES*

prénom du roi mage Melchior. Et merci aux autres Mas, Joseph, Jean et Jean-Pierre, les fils de Pierre, le taupier. Merci à Guillaume Moisset qui a laissé le buron de son père pour forger l'acier et à Pierre Raffy, le fils de Joseph, l'instituteur. Merci à Auguste Valmy, venu de Saint-Geniez d'Olt, à Joseph Pagès et à Berthe, sa veuve et à tous ses ouvriers, les Rigal, les Cure, les Benel, les Seguis. Merci à eux parce que ce sont eux, tous ensemble qui ont fait le Laguiole à Laguiole et qui ont donné son âme à ce couteau-là ! ■

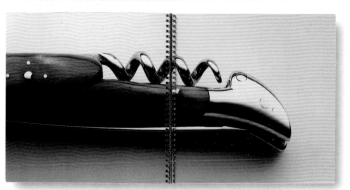

68 **PHILLIPE SAGLIO** *LAGUIOLE*

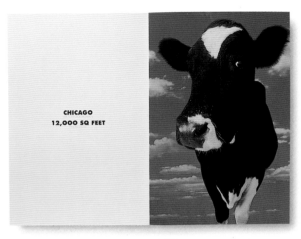

CHICAGO
12,000 SQ FEET

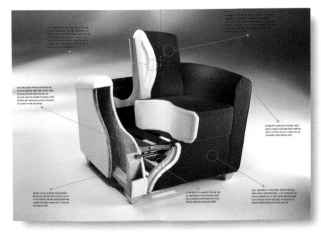

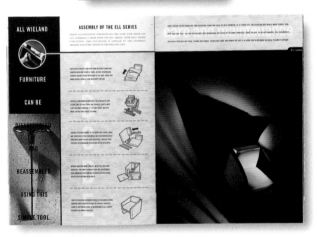

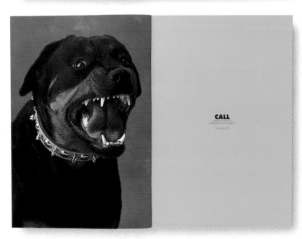

CALL

69 **LISKA + ASSOCIATES** *Steve Grubman Photography*   70 **DUFFY DESIGN** *The Wieland Furniture Company*

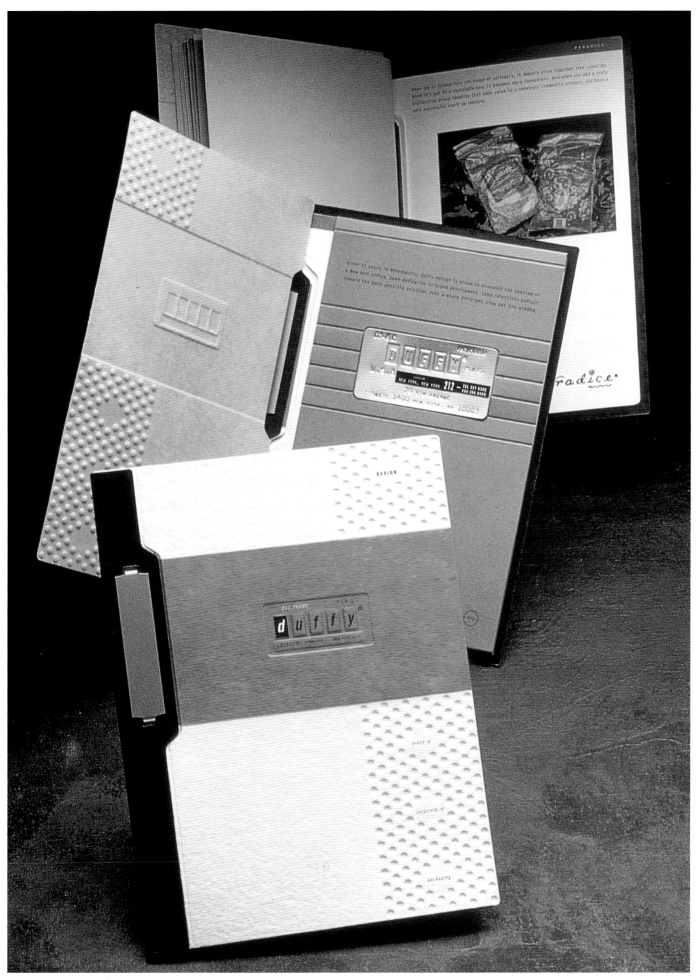

71 **DUFFY DESIGN** *(IN-HOUSE)*

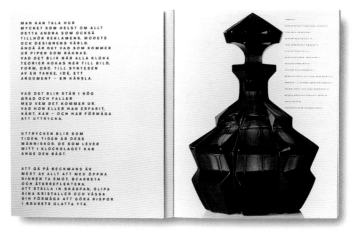

MAN KAN TALA HUR
MYCKET SOM HELST OM ALLT
DETTA ANDRA SOM OCKSÅ
TILLHÖR REKLAMENS, MODETS
OCH DESIGNENS VÄRLD.
ÄNDÅ ÄR DET VAD SOM KOMMER
UR PIPEN SOM RÄKNAS.
VAD DET BLIR NÄR ALLA KLOKA
TEORIER KOKAS NER TILL BILD,
FORM, ORD, TILL SYNTESEN
AV EN TANKE, IDÉ, ETT
ARGUMENT – EN KÄNSLA.

VAD DET BLIR STÅR I HÖG
GRAD OCH FALLER
MED VEM DET KOMMER UR.
VAD HON ELLER HAN ERFARIT,
KÄNT, KAN – OCH HAR FÖRMÅGA
ATT UTTRYCKA.

UTTRYCKEN BLIR SOM
TIDEN. TIDEN ÄR DESS
MÄNNISKOR. DE SOM LEVER
MITT I KLOCKSLAGET KAN
ANGE DEN BÄST.

ATT GÅ PÅ BECKMANS ÄR
MEST ATT LÄRA ATT MED ÖPPNA
SINNEN TA EMOT, BEARBETA
OCH ÅTERREFLEKTERA.
ATT STÄLLA IN SKÄRPAN, SLIPA
SINA KRISTALLER OCH VÄSSA
SIN FÖRMÅGA ATT GÖRA RISPOR
I BRUSETS GLATTA YTA.

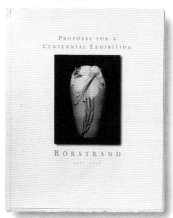

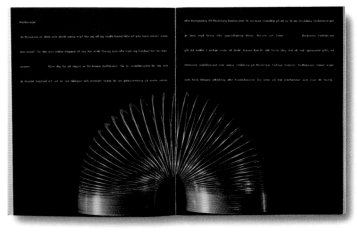

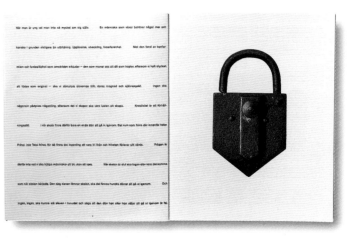

72 **SOCIO X** *Robert Schreiber*

73 **BECKMANS SCHOOL OF DESIGN** *(IN-HOUSE)*

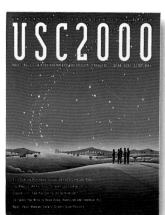

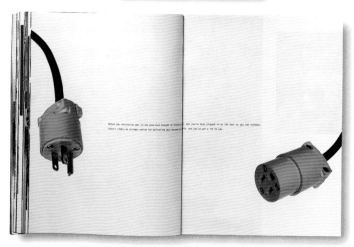

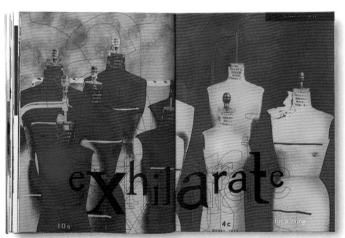

74 **REED AND STEVEN** *THE ART INSTITUTE OF FORT LAUDERDALE*   75 **PENTAGRAM DESIGN** *UNIVERSITY OF SOUTHERN CALIFORNIA*

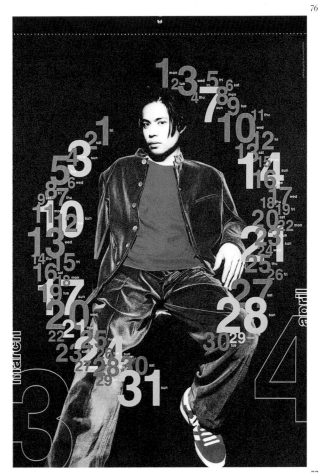

(TOP) 76 **B-BI STUDIO INC.** *Funky Jam Corporation*
(BOTTOM) 77 **SHISEIDO INTERNATIONAL MARKETING CREATIVE GROUP** *Shiseido Co., Ltd.*

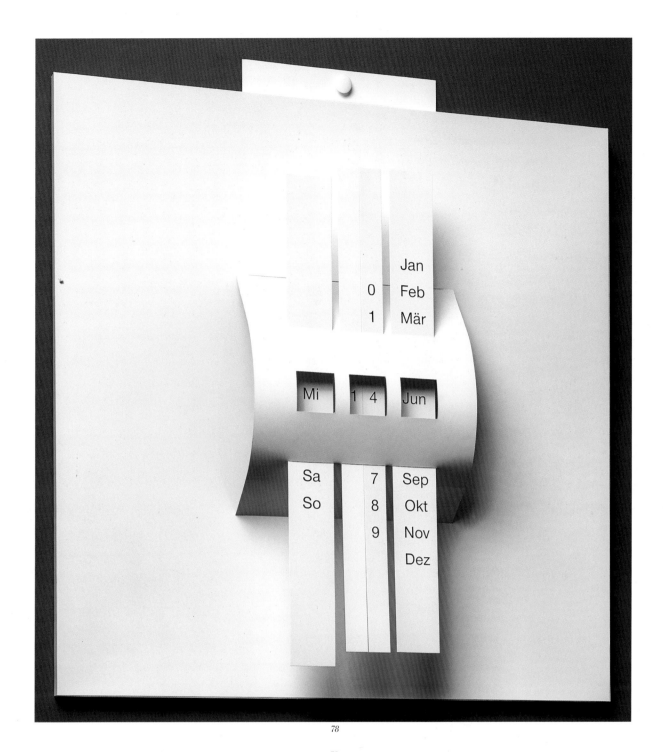

78

79

(TOP) 78 **ATELIER DERNBECHER** *(IN-HOUSE)*
(BOTTOM) 79 **FOSSIL DESIGN STUDIO** *FOSSIL, INC.*

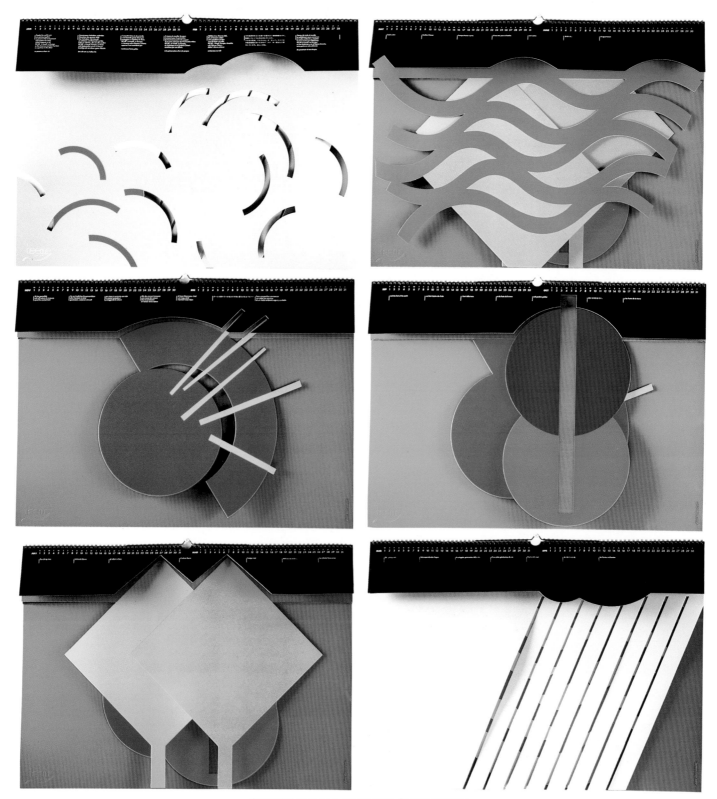

(OPPOSITE) 80 **RALF KLENNER** *Diploti Calendar*
(THIS PAGE) 81 **STUDIO REISINGER** *Iscar Hardmetal Tools Company Ltd.*

(THIS SPREAD) 82 **TAMOTSU YAGI DESIGN** *Tamotsu Yagi Exhibition, San Francisco Museum of Modern Art*

(ABOVE) 83 **ANTISTA FAIRCLOUGH DESIGN** *Ashland Petroleum*
(OPPOSITE) 84 **GEE + CHUNG DESIGN** *IBM Corporation*

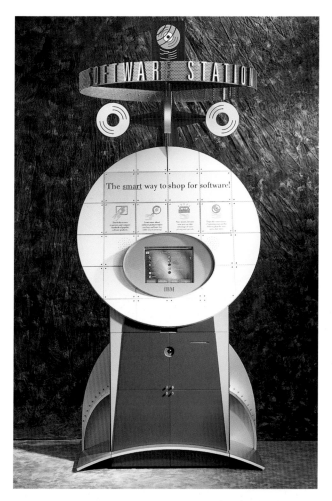

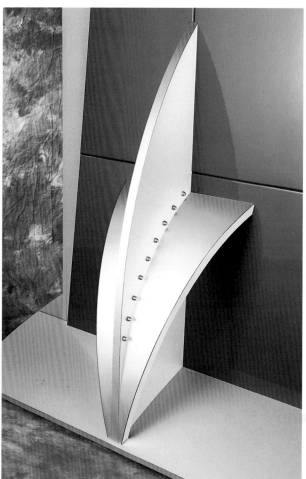

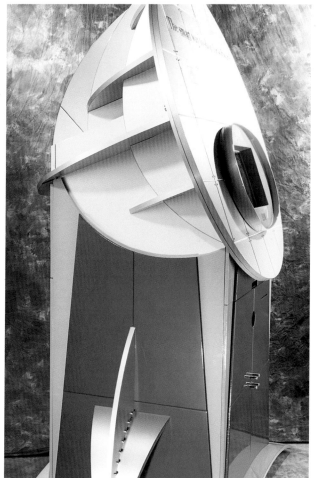

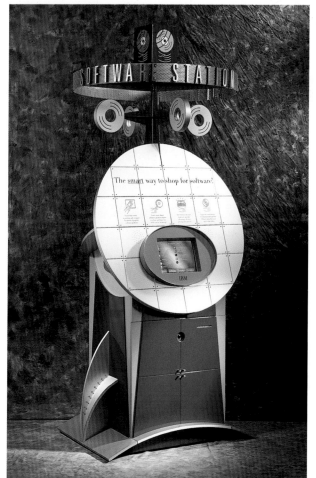

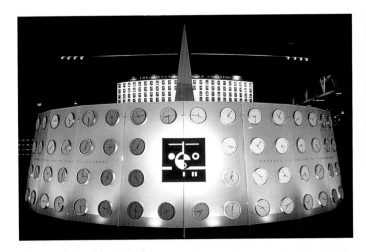

30' x 40' trade show exhibit for Duncan Aviation, a full service business jet maintenance company based in Lincoln, Nebraska.

Context:

The National Business Aircraft Association (N.B.A.A.) show is a high tech extravaganza of manufacturers showing their new aircraft. Across the asile from Duncan was some 22 million dollars of the latest Learjets. On the other side was an Italian helicopter.

(THIS SPREAD) 85 **MAUK DESIGN** *DUNCAN AVIATION*

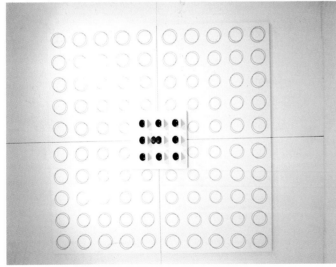

(THIS SPREAD) 86 **SHISEIDO CO. LTD** *(IN-HOUSE)*

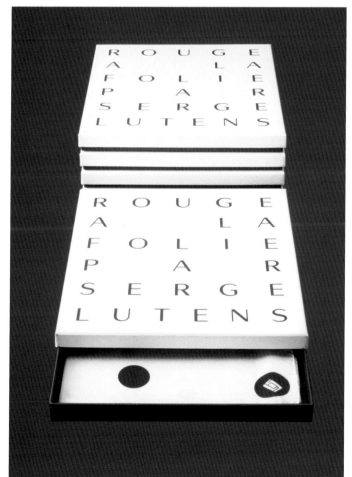

(OPPOSITE) 87 **DESIGN PARTNERSHIP** *METRO*

(ABOVE) 88 **MIRES DESIGN, INC.** *CALIFORNIA CENTER FOR THE ARTS*

(THIS SPREAD) 89 **THINKING CAPS** *GIANT INDUSTRIES*

(THIS SPREAD) 90 **LORENC DESIGN** *GEORGIA-PACIFIC CORP.*

(ABOVE) 91 **BJ KRIVANEK ART+DESIGN** *"THE VOICE OF THE HOMELESS" ORIENTATION ROTUNDA AT THE UNION RESCUE MISSION, LOS ANGELES, CALIFORNIA*
(OPPOSITE, TOP) 92 **HEWARDESIGN** *JAVA THE HUT* □ (BOTTOM) 93 **BNA DESIGN LTD** *HOYTS NZ LIMITED*

92

92

93

93

94 **PENTAGRAM DESIGN** *MINNESOTA CHILDREN'S MUSEUM*

95 **SANDSTROM DESIGN** *REEBOK INTERNATIONAL LTD.*

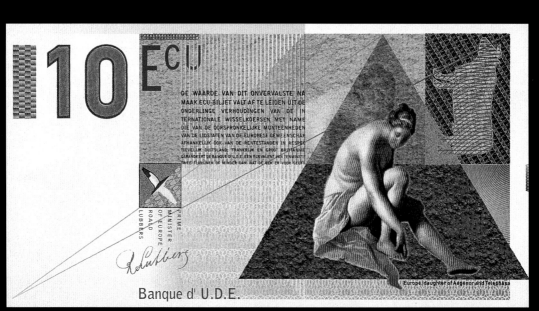

(OPPOSITE, TOP) 96 **MAX ROBINSON & ASSOCIATES** RESERVE BANK OF AUSTRALIA □ (OPPOSITE, BOTTOM) 97 **VORM VIJF** PROOST EN BRANDT
(ABOVE) 98 **MARTY SMITH TECHNICAL ILLUSTRATION** (IN-HOUSE)

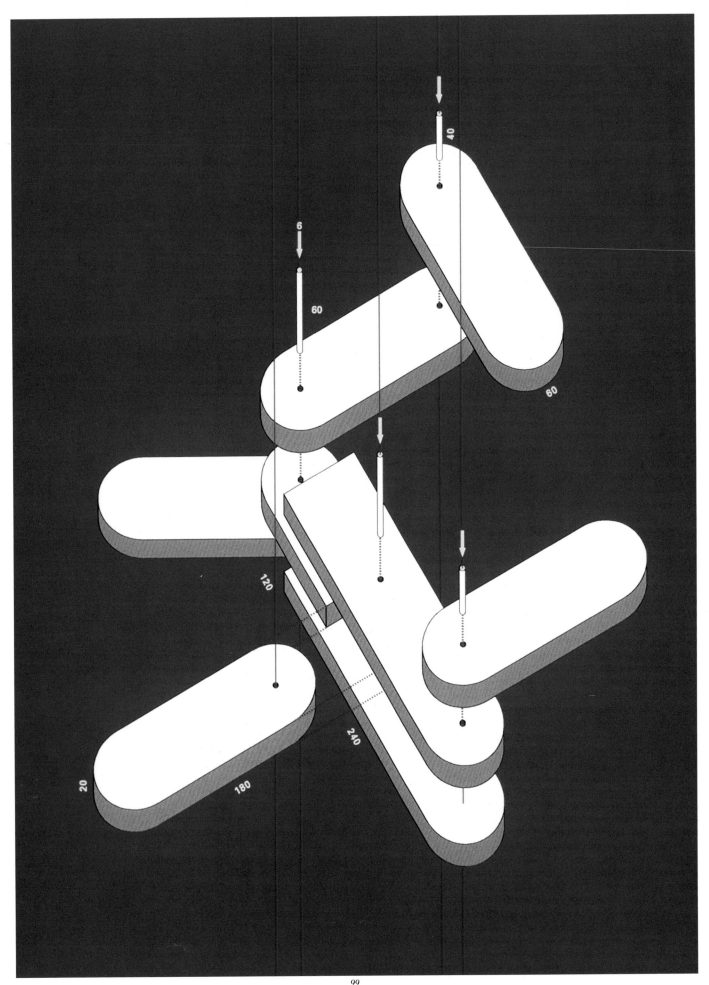

99

100

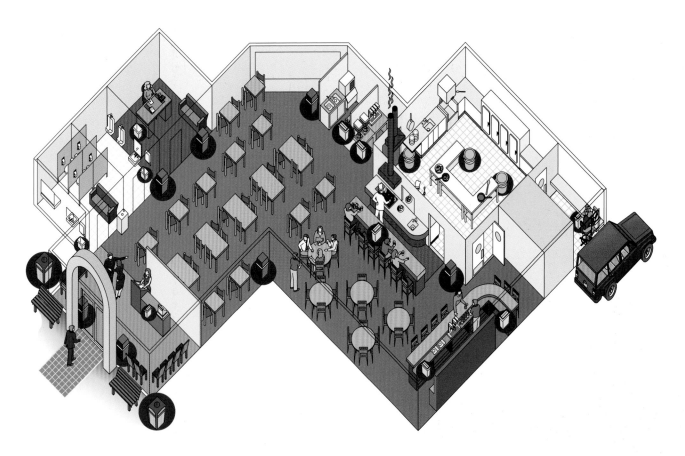

101

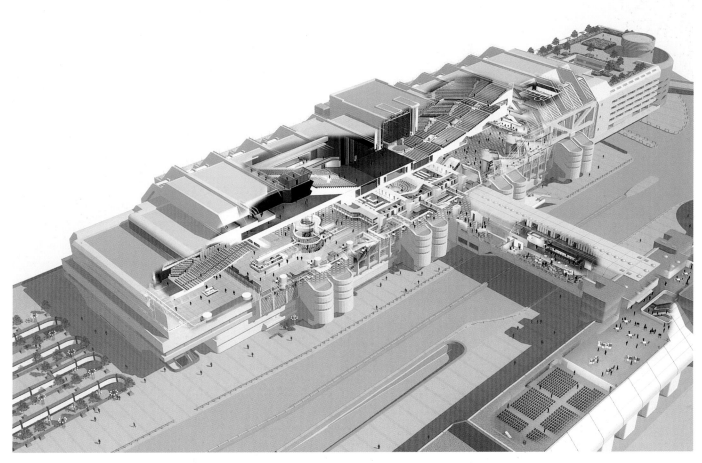

(OPPOSITE) 99 **RONNIE PETERS** *SIEMANS NIXDORF* □ *(THIS PAGE, TOP)* 100 **JEFFERY WEST** *PENNECO PACKAGING SPECIALTY PRODUCTS*
(THIS PAGE, BOTTOM) 101 **SCHRAMMS GRAFIK-DESIGN & DIGITAL MEDIA ART** *MESSE BERLIN GMBH*

WHITE LIGHT

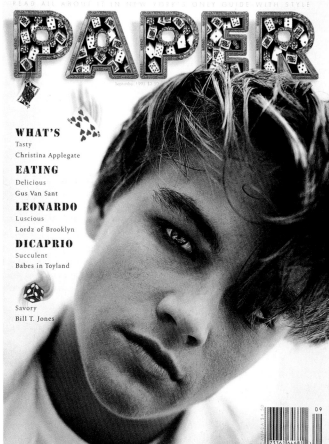

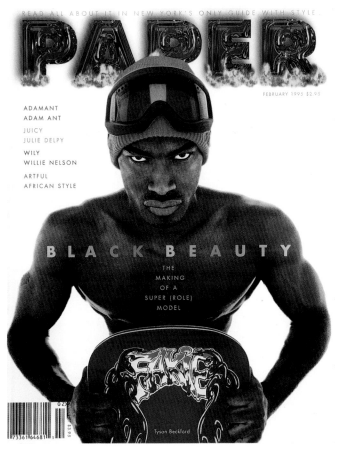

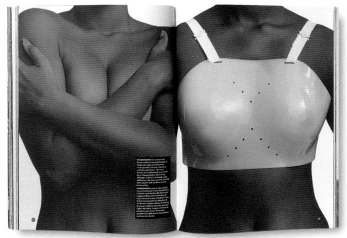

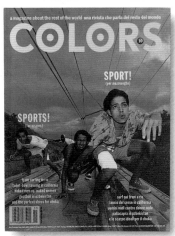

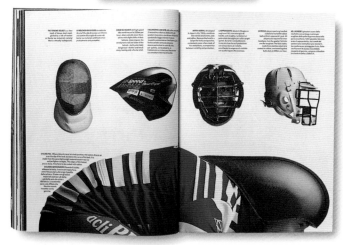

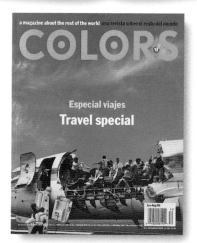

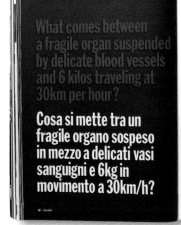

103 **TIBOR KALMAN, MARK PORTER** *Colors Magazine Srl*

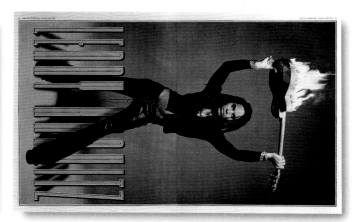

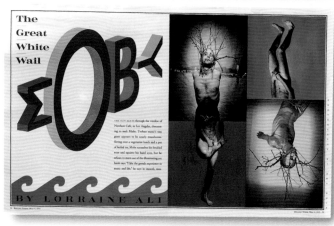

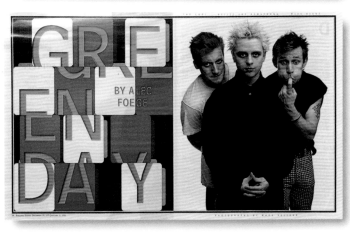

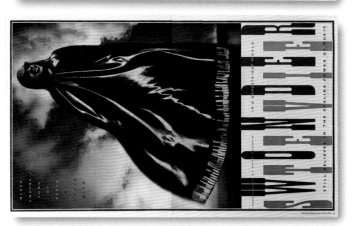

104 **FRED WOODWARD** *ROLLING STONE*

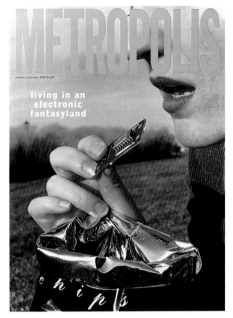

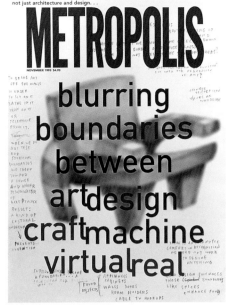

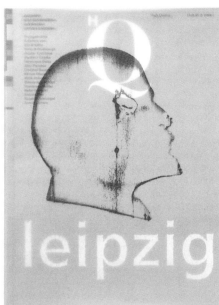

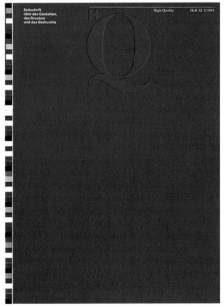

(THIS PAGE, TOP ROW) 105 **CARL LEHMANN-HAUPT, WILLIAM VAN RODEN** *METROPOLIS*
(THIS PAGE, MIDDLE & BOTTOM ROWS) 106 **BÜRO ROLF MÜLLER** *HIGH QUALITY*

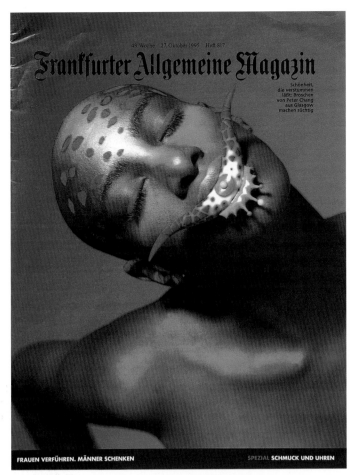

107 **PETER BREUL** *FRANKFURTER ALLGEMEINE MAGAZIN*

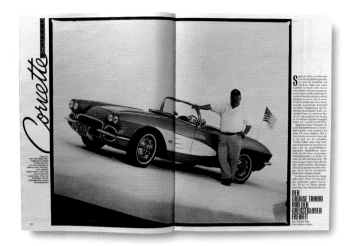

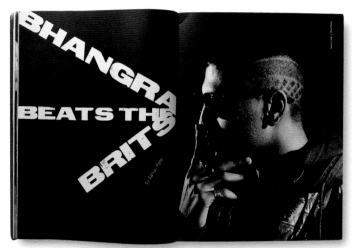

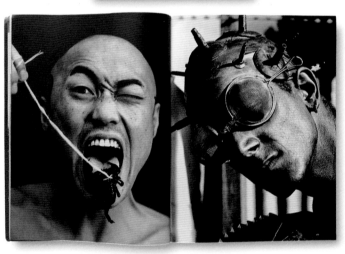

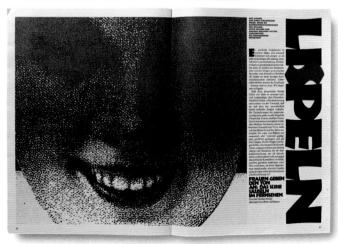

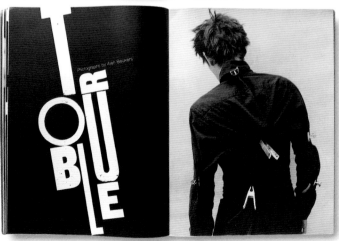

108 **PETER BREUL** *FRANKFURTER ALLGEMEINE MAGAZIN*

109 **FROST DESIGN** *BIG*

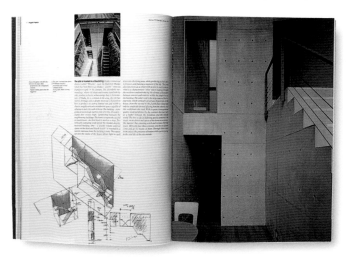

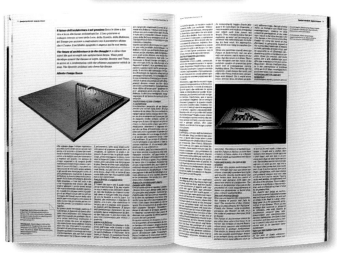

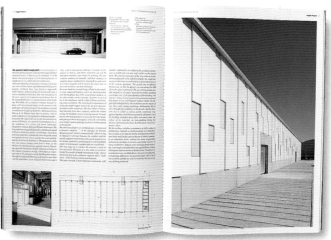

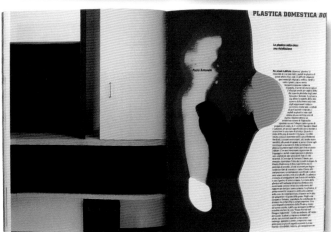

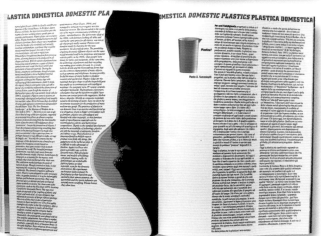

111

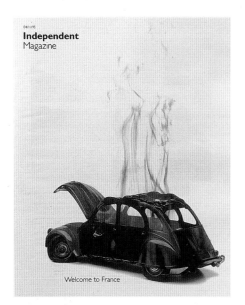

Independent
Magazine

Welcome to France

Independent
Magazine

Get out of jail free

Independent
Magazine

Burning with seasonal desires

112

80%
VAN DE
RECLAME IS
EEN
BELEDIGING
VOOR HET
PUBLIEK

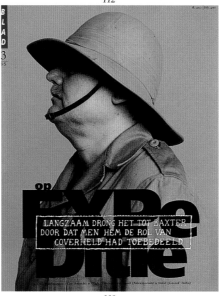

LANGZAAM DRONG HET TOT BAXTER
DOOR DAT MEN HEM DE ROL VAN
COVERHELD HAD TOEBEDEELD

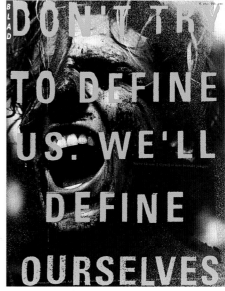

DON'T TRY
TO DEFINE
US. WE'LL
DEFINE
OURSELVES

113

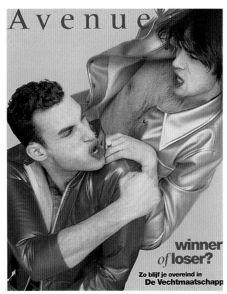

Avenue

winner
of loser?
Zo blijf je overeind in
De Vechtmaatschapp

Avenue

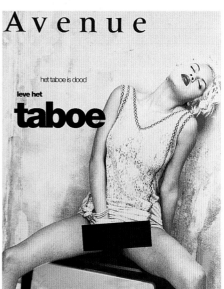

Avenue

het taboe is dood

leve het
taboe

(THIS PAGE, TOP ROW) 111 **FROST DESIGN** *INDEPENDENT MAGAZINE* □ (MIDDLE ROW) 112 **HANS WOLF** *BLAD MAGAZINE*
(BOTTOM ROW) 113 **RENÉ ABBÜHL** *AVENUE*

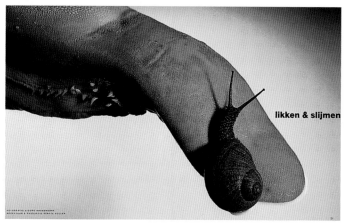

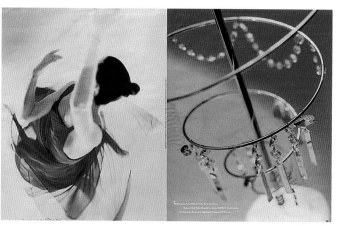

114 **RENÉ ABBÜHL** *AVENUE*

115 **JANET FROELICH** *THE NEW YORK TIMES MAGAZINE*

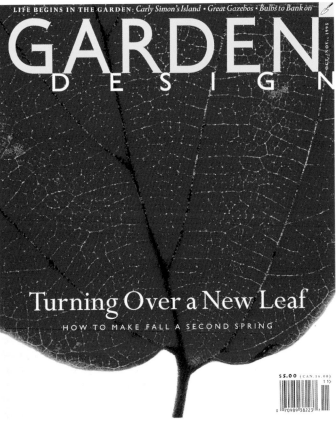

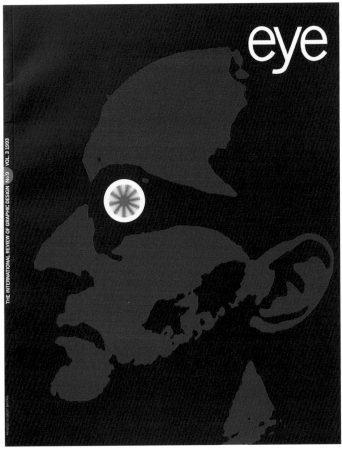

(TOP, LEFT) 116 **PENTAGRAM DESIGN LTD.** *POLAROID UK* □ (TOP, RIGHT) 117 **PAUL ROELOFS** *GARDEN DESIGN*
(BOTTOM, LEFT) 118 **TOKI DESIGN** *SEE: A JOURNAL OF VISUAL CULTURE* □ (BOTTOM, RIGHT) 119 **STEPHEN COATES** *EYE*

W i G

women · in · general

THREE
WOMEN'S
PSYCHES

HEAVY
SCULPTURE
POETRY
PHOTOGRAPHY
MUSIC BOX

SNOW-
BOARDING
BODY-
BOARDING
SKATE-
BOARDING

WOMEN

ART

SPORTS

premier

VOL. I ISSUE ONE $3.95

7 50644 87990 5

01 >

120 **DAWN KISH** *W.I.G. Magazine*

(TOP ROW) 121 **TOM FOWLER, INC.** *PFIZER*
(MIDDLE & BOTTOM ROWS) 122 **SASCHA WEIHS** *SELF-PROMOTION*

123 **VIA DESIGN INC** *AUDOBON SOCIETY OF NEW HAMPSHIRE*

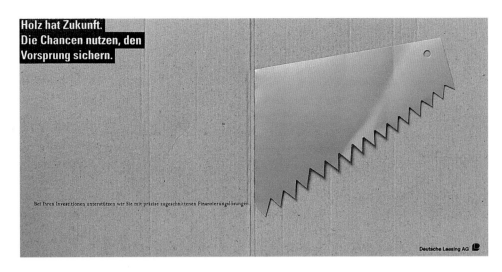

(TOP) 124 **DAILY ART** *DEUTSCHE LEASING AG* □ *(MIDDLE)* 125 **KUO DESIGN OFFICE** *SELF-PROMOTION*
(BOTTOM) 126 **BRAD & DEBI HOCHBERG** *PROMOTION* □ *(OPPOSITE)* 127 **VAUGHN WEEDEN CREATIVE** *(IN-HOUSE)*

(ABOVE) 128 **MILTON BRADLEY** *(IN-HOUSE)*
(OPPOSITE) 129 **CATHLEEN TOELKE**

129

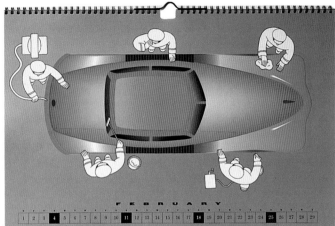

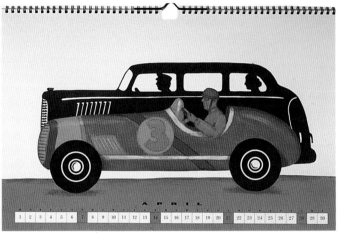

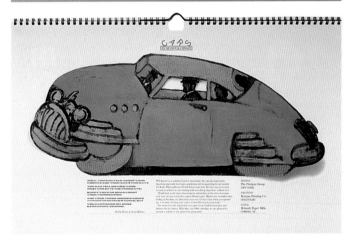

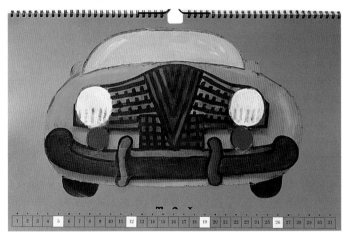

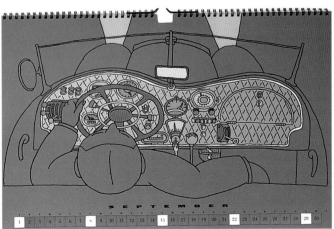

(THIS PAGE) 130 **SEYMOUR CHWAST** BERMAN PRINTING INC.
(OPPOSITE) 131 **PETER KRÄMER** FRANKFURTER ALLGEMEINE ZEITUNG GmbH

132

133

134

(OPPOSITE) 132 **ANDREA MCCANN** *Monterey Bay Aquarium* 133 **LUBA LUKOVA STUDIO** *The Living Theatre* □
134 **GARY BLAKELY** *Aitken & Blakely* □ (ABOVE) 135 **FRANK VIVA** *The Washington Post*

136 **JOHN SPRINGS** *SAMSUNG*

137

137

138

138

(TOP ROW) 137 **GUY BILLOUT** NEW JERSEY RESOURCES CORPORATION □ (BOTTOM ROW) 138 **GUY BILLOUT** COMPASS DEUTSCHLAND GMBH

(TOP) 139 **WIESLAW SMETEK** *EBURON-DELFT* □ (BOTTOM) 140 **IKU AKIYAMA** *TOKYO DIGITAL PHONE CO., LTD.*

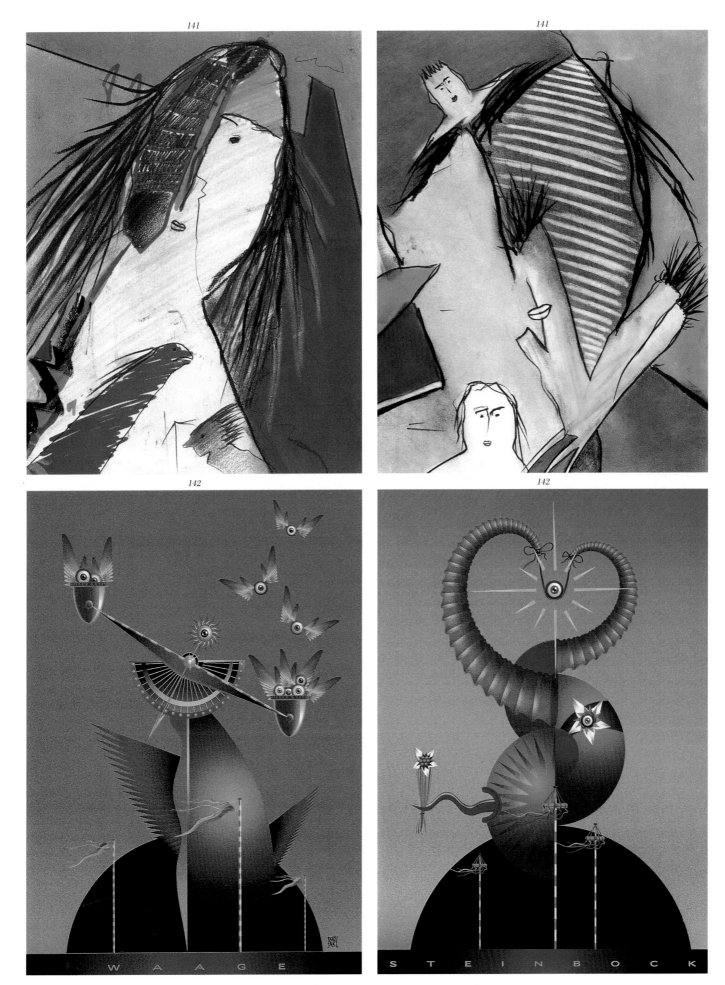

(TOP) 141 **PEDER STOUGÅRD** □ *(BOTTOM)* 142 **SIEGMAR MÜNK** *MÜNKILLUS*

143

144

145

146

147

148

149

150

(OPPOSITE PAGE) 143 **FABIO ISAYA** □ 144 **MIRKO ILIĆ** *THE NEW YORK TIMES* □ 145 **FRANCES MIDDENDORF** □
146 **DENNIS CORRIGAN** *CORRIGAN GALLERY OF HUMOROUS AND ROMANTIC ART* □ 147-148 **WIESLAW SMETEK** *ZUK RECORDS* □ *(THIS PAGE, TOP)*
149 **DENNIS CORRIGAN** *CORRIGAN GALLERY OF HUMOROUS AND ROMANTIC ART* □ *(THIS PAGE, BOTTOM)* 150 **LUDVIK GLAZER** *ZEIT MAGAZIN*

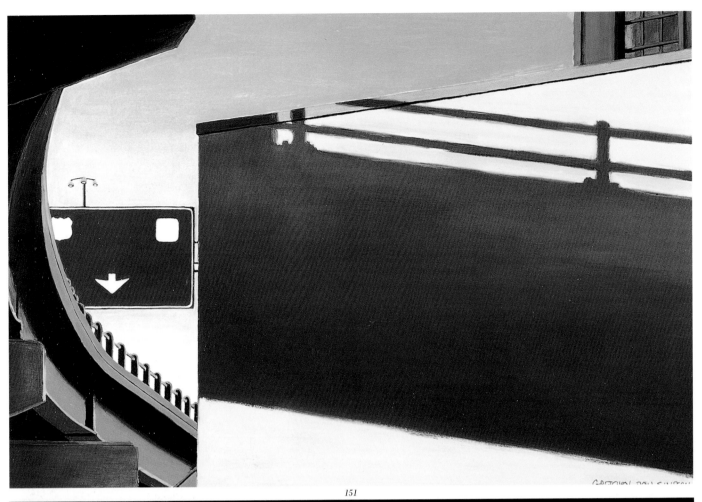

151

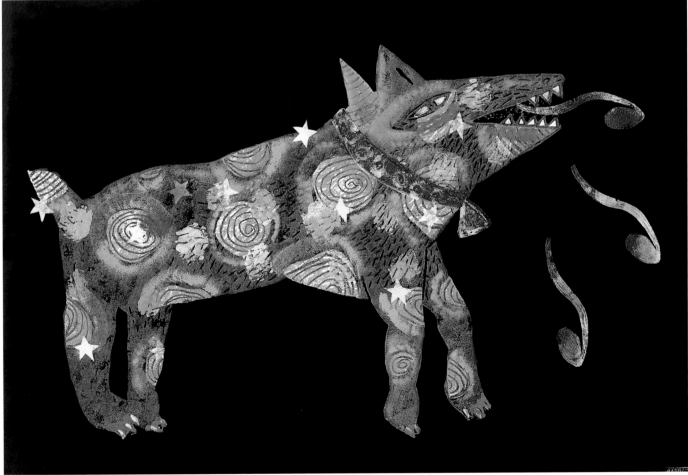

152

153

154

155

155

(OPPOSITE, TOP) 151 **GRETCHEN DOW SIMPSON** *Winross* □ (OPPOSITE, BOTTOM) 152 **DYGA DESIGN** □
(THIS PAGE) 153 **JEFF KOEGEL** *CS First Boston* □ 154 **NICHOLAS WILTON** *Donaldson, Lufkin & Jenrette* □
155 **CATHLEEN TOELKE** *One Great Hour of Sharing*

156

157

159

158

160

161

(OPPOSITE) 156 **CAWRSE & EFFECT** *Consider It Dunn* □ 157 **MADDOCKS & COMPANY** (*IN-HOUSE*) □ 158 **MORLA DESIGN** *San Francisco Production Group*
159 **FRANKFURT BALKIND PARTNERS** *Pantone, Inc.* □ (*ABOVE*) 160 **CRONAN DESIGN, INC.** *NewMedia Magazine* □ 161 **THE EDISON GROUP** (*IN-HOUSE*)

J.W. FRY PHOTOGRAPHY

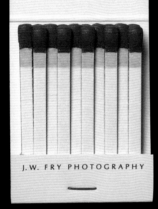

MATCH-MAKING

J.W. FRY PHOTOGRAPHY

BURN

BABY

BURN

162

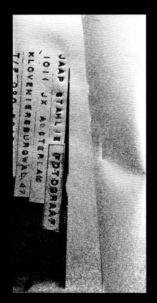

162

JAAP STAHLIE FOTOGRAAF
1011 JX AMSTERDAM
KLOVENIERSBURGWAL 47
T/F 020-6240109
BANKRELATIE ABN AMRO
REKENINGNR. 348705909

NIET VOUWEN!

163

164

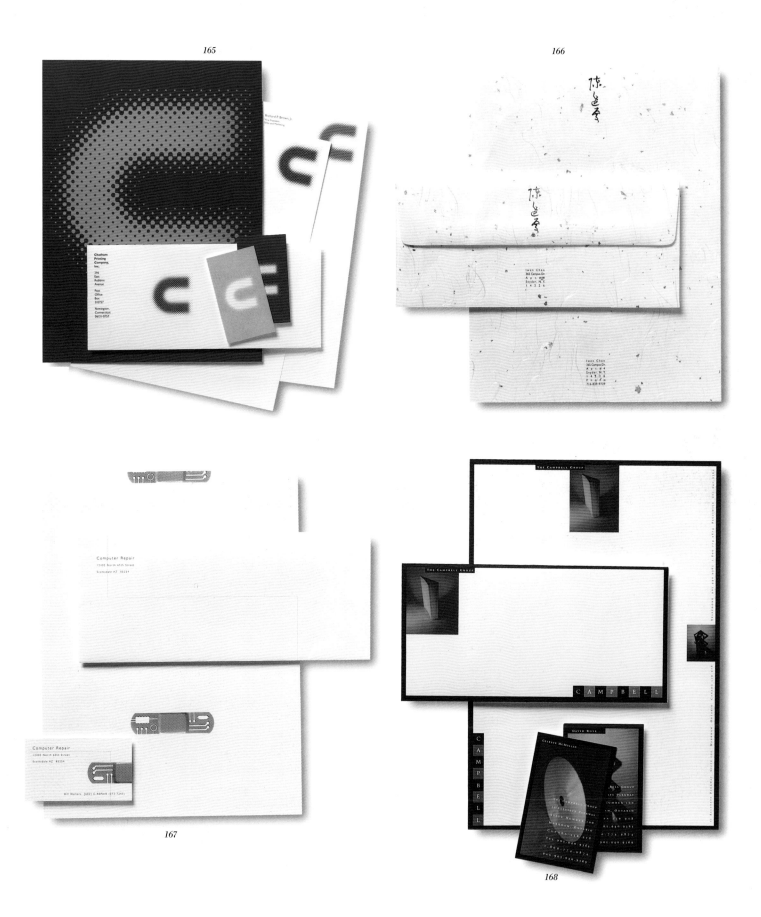

165

166

167

168

(OPPOSITE) 162 **YAMAMOTO MOSS** *J.W. FRY PHOTOGRAPHY* □ 163 **KOWEIDEN POSTMA ASSOCIATES** *JAAP STAHLIE* □ 164 **HORNALL ANDERSON DESIGN WORKS, INC.** *CAPONS* □ (THIS PAGE) 165 **CUMMINGS & GOOD** *CHATHAM PRINTING* □ 166 **IWEN CHEN** *SELF-PROMOTION* 167 **S.D. ZYNE** *COMPUTER REPAIR* □ 168 **VANDERBYL DESIGN** *CAMPBELL GROUP*

169

170

171

172

173

174

175

176

177

178

179

180

181

182

183

184

185

186

187

188

189

190

191

192

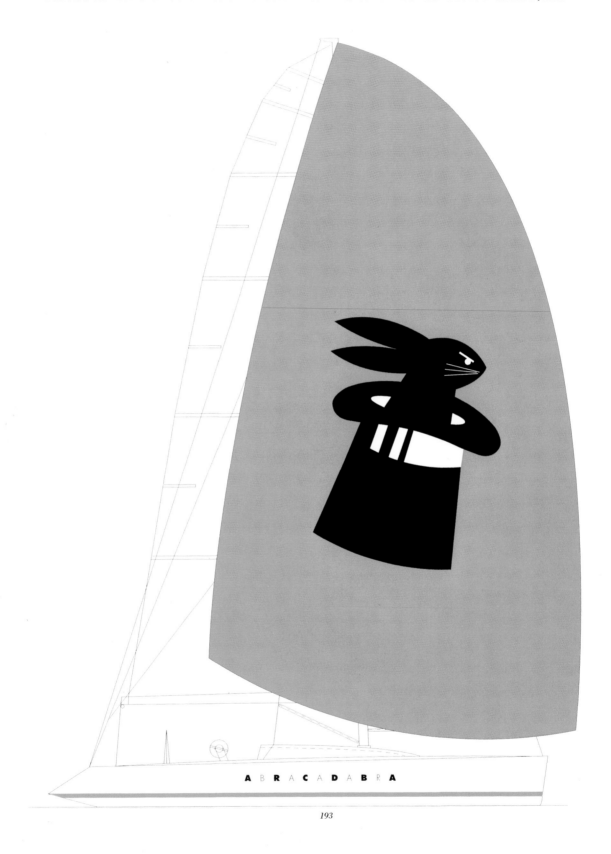

A B R A C A D A B R A

193

194

195

196

197

198

199

200

201

202

203

204

205

206

207

208

209

210

211

212

VANALT

213

214

215

216

217

218

219

COFFEE BAR

220

221

wood-fired steaks

222

223

219 **MALCOLM TURK** *PAPER MAGAZINE* □ 220 **PENTAGRAM LONDON** *GRANADA HOSPITALITY LTD* □ 221 **GEER DESIGN, INC.** *TIMES 3 PRODUCTIONS*
222 **MULLER & CO.** *J. GILBERTS* □ 223 **BNA DESIGN LTD** *HOYTS NZ LIMITED*

225

226

227

228

229

230

231

232

233

234

235

224 **MALCOLM GREAR DESIGNERS, INC.** *ATLANTA COMMITTEE FOR THE OLYMPIC GAMES* □ 225 **MIRES DESIGN, INC.** *INTEL CORP.* □ 226 **GIRAFFE GMBH** *ANDREAS LABES, PHOTOGRAF* □ 227 **RICKABAUGH GRAPHICS** *THE WALKER GROUP* □ 228 **ALAN CHAN DESIGN COMPANY** *HONG KONG SEIBU ENTERPRISE LTD.* 229 **VANDERBYL DESIGN** *WINDQUEST* □ 230 **PENTAGRAM LONDON** *GRANADA HOSPITALITY LTD* □ 231 **CHARLES S. ANDERSON DESIGN COMPANY** *HOW* □ 232 **SIBLEY/PETEET DESIGN** *CENTRAL & SOUTH WEST* □ 233 **GIRAFFE GMBH** *ROCKRADIO B* □ 234 **C. BOLZ** (*STUDENT PROJECT*) □ 235 **KYOSTI VARIS**

236

INTERACTIVE

SOFTWARE

VISUALIZATION

ANIMATION

237

238

239

240

241

242

243

244

236 **RICKABAUGH GRAPHICS** *GRANT MEDICAL CENTER* □ 237 **CRONAN DESIGN** *ENGINEERING ANIMATION, INC.*
238 **MADDOCKS + COMPANY** *AMERICAN CRAFT MUSEUM* □ 239 **JAGER DI PAOLA KEMP DESIGN** *HARVEST MARKET*
240 **FRAZIER DESIGN** *MAGICO* □ 241 **REED AND STEVEN** *BLUXO RECORDS* □ 242 **NIKE, INC.** *(IN-HOUSE)*
243 **SACKETT DESIGN ASSOCIATES** *FIREFIGHTERS IN THE SCHOOLS* □ 244 **VSA PARTNERS, INC.** *HARLEY-DAVIDSON, INC.*

245

246

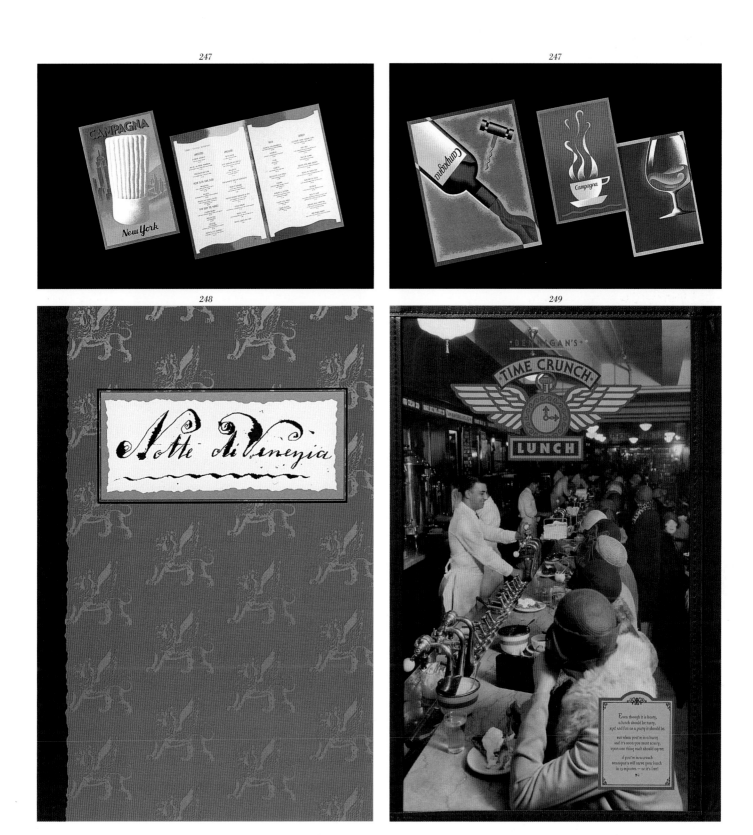

247

247

248

249

(OPPOSITE) 245 **RUBIN POSTAER AND ASSOCIATES** *California Pizza Kitchen* □ 246 **DAVID CARTER DESIGN ASSOCIATES**
Hyatt Regency, Osaka □ 247 **ROGERS SEIDMAN DESIGN TEAM** *Campagna Restaurant* □ 248 **GILES DESIGN** *St. Luke's Foundation*
249 **DENNARD CREATIVE, INC.** *Bennigan's Restaurants*

250

251

252

(OPPOSITE, TOP) 250 **MIRES DESIGN, INC.** *DEBORAH LIV JOHNSON* □ *(OPPOSITE, BOTTOM)* 251 **ART INDUSTRIA** *ATLANTIC RECORDS*
(ABOVE) 252 **ROBIN LYNCH, LAURIE GOLDMAN** *BLUE THUMB RECORDS* □ *(BELOW)* 253 **ALLEN WEINBERG** *SONY MUSIC*

253

254

255

254 **JEFFERY FEY** *Capitol Records, Inc.* □ 255 **CHRISTINA KRUTZ** *BMG Ariola Media GmbH* □ *(opposite page)* 256 **SAGMEISTER INC.** *Energy Records* □ 257 **MINATO ISHIKAWA ASSOCIATES INC.** *Edoya Records Ltd.* □ 258 **JAGER DI PAOLA KEMP DESIGN** *Q-Prime* 259 **DEBORAH NORCROSS** *Luaka Bob, Inc./ Warner Bros.*

256

257

258

259

260

261

(THIS PAGE) 260 **JEFFERY FEY** *CAPITOL RECORDS, INC* □ 261 **DEBORAH NORCROSS** *REPRISE RECORDS* □ (OPPOSITE) 262 **MARK BURDETT** *SONY MUSIC* □ 263 **MOMENTUM DESIGN** *John Moriarity Productions, Inc.* □ 264 **GREENBERG KINGSLEY, INC.** *Discovery Records* 265 **SOCIO X** *ISLAND RECORDS* □ 266 **MARK LINKOUS** *CAPITOL RECORDS, INC.* □ 267 **FELDER GRAFIK DESIGN** *Bib Band Club Dornbirn* 268 **SARA ROTMAN** *EPIC RECORD* □ 269 **BUTTGEREIT & HEIDENREICH KOMMUNIKATIONSDESIGN** *(SELF-PROMOTION)* 270 **ALEC BATHGATE** *FLYING NUN RECORDS* □ 271 **JEFFERY FEY/TOMMY STEELE** *CAPITOL RECORDS, INC.* □ 272 **SARA ROTMAN** *SONY MUSIC* 273 **MIRKO ILIĆ CORP.** *HELIDON*

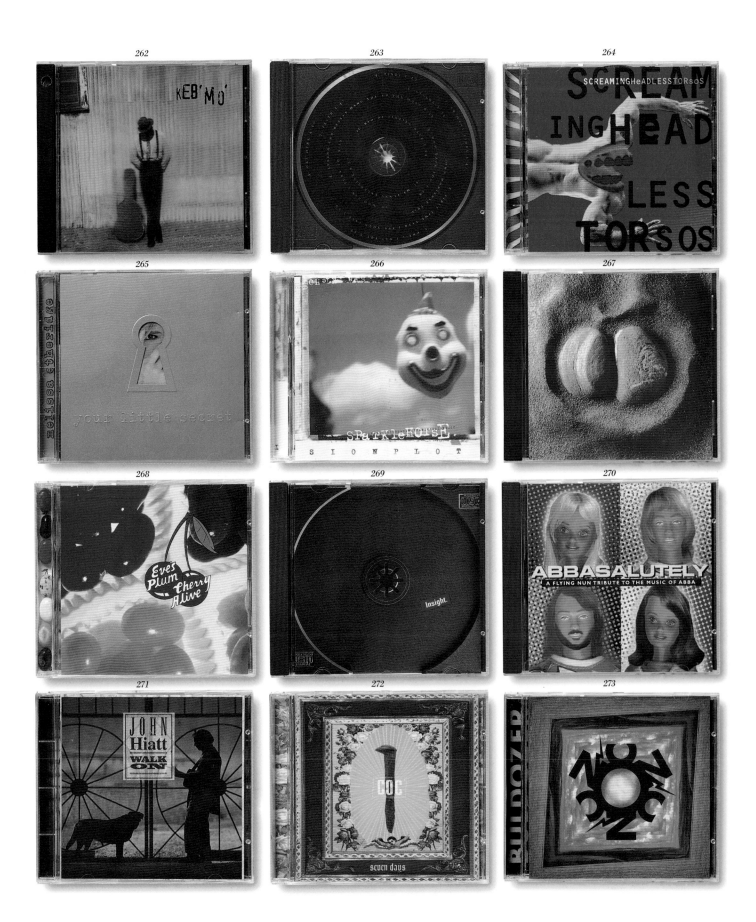

262

263

264

265

266

267

268

269

270

271

272

273

274

275

277

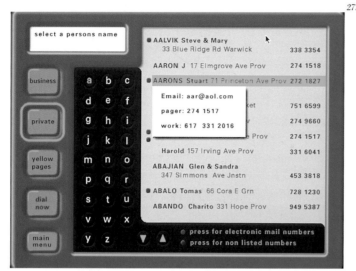

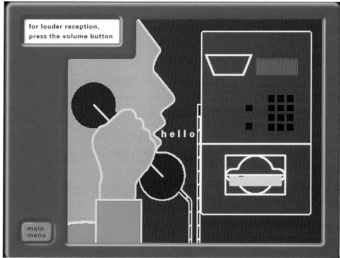

278

(PREDEDING SPREAD) 274 **PHILLIPS DESIGN GROUP** *Atlantic Technology* □ 275 **PROFILE DESIGN** *Ascend Communications, Inc.*
276 **STUDIO D DESIGN** *Concierge Software* □ (THIS PAGE) 277 **INFOGRAM** *Prototype Public Telephone Application*
278 **RONNIE PETERS** *WGBH* □ (OPPOSITE) 279 **THE DESIGN OFFICE OF WONG & YEO** *Digital Pictures* □ 280 **AKAGI**
REMINGTON *Opcode Music Systems* □ 281 **THE DESIGN OFFICE OF WONG & YEO** *Digital Pictures* □ 282 **DGWB ADVERTISING** *Qualcomm Inc.*

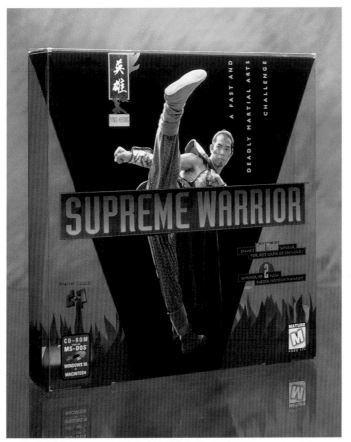

279

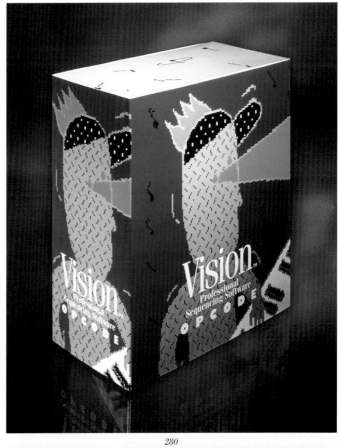

280

281

282

283

284

285

286

287

288

(PRECEDING SPREAD) 283 **MADDOCKS & CO.** SONY COMPUTER ENTERTAINMENT □ 284 **JENSEN DESIGN ASSOCIATES** CANON COMPUTER SYSTEMS, INC.
285 **FRAZIER DESIGN** XAOS TOOLS INC. □ (OPPOSITE, TOP) 286 **ZIMMERMANN CROWE DESIGN** ELECTRONIC ARTS
(OPPOSITE, BOTTOM) 287 **CFD DESIGN** PIRANHA INTERACTIVE □ (ABOVE) 288 **SIBLEY/PETEET DESIGN** NORTEL

289

(ABOVE) 289 **SANDSTROM DESIGN** *Tazo Tea Company* □ (OPPOSITE) 290 **BOLT, KOCH & KO** *Volg Konsumwaren AG* □ 291 **PACKAGE LAND CO, LTD.** *Arab Coffee* □ 292 **SANDSTROM DESIGN** *Tazo Tea Company* □ 293 **BOLT, KOCH & KO** *Volg Konsumwaren AG* □ 294 **LIDJI DESIGN OFFICE** *Aromance Home*

290

291

292

292

293

294

295

295 **TUCKER DESIGN** *Saddlers Creek Winery* □ *(Opposite)* 296 **DUFFY DESIGN** *Minute Maid* □ 297 **PACKAGING CREATE, INC.** *Gekkeikan*

296

296

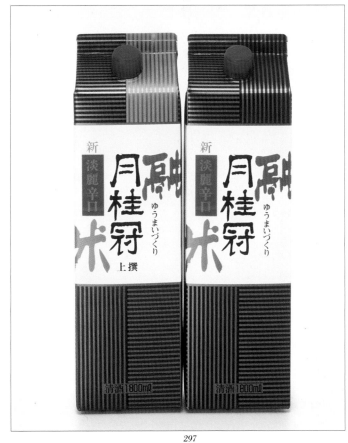

297

297

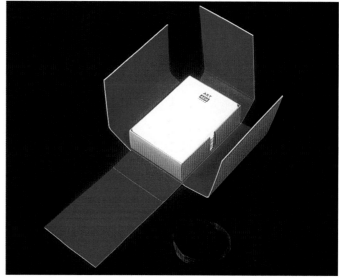

299 **JUN SATO DESIGN** *Gallery Interform*

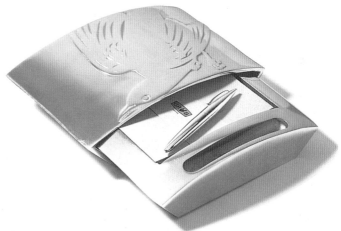

300 **BRD DESIGN** *Self-promotion*

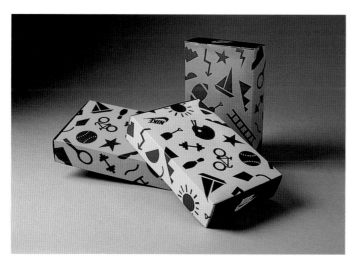

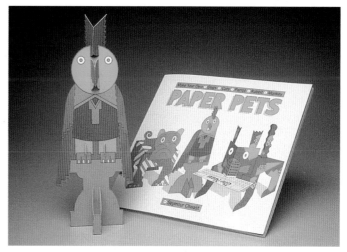

301 **NIKE, INC.** *Nike/Kids Foot Locker*

302 **PUSHPIN GROUP** *Harry N. Abrams*

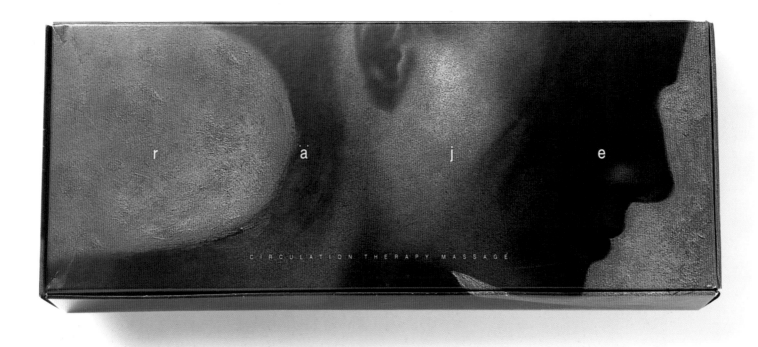

303

304

305

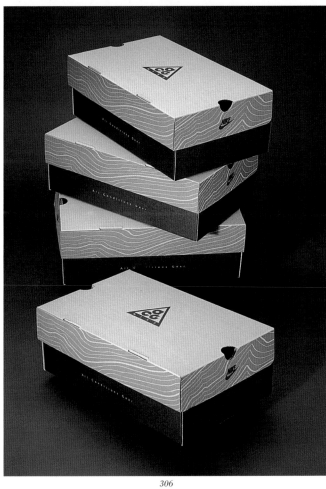

306

306

307

308

309

310

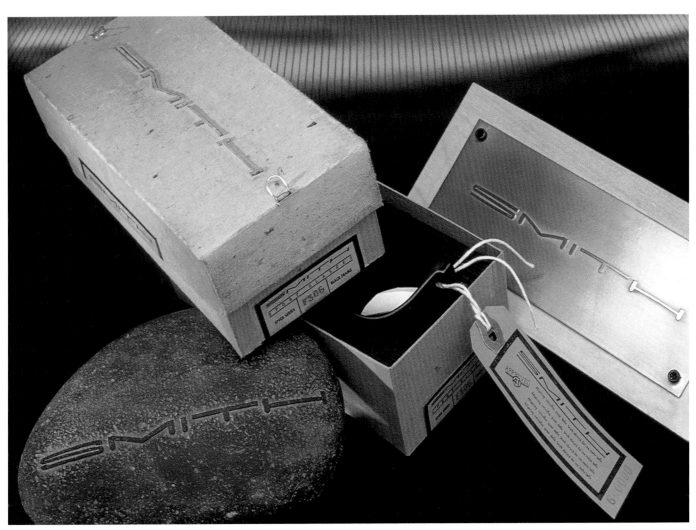

311

(OPPOSITE) 307 **PACKAGING CREATE INC.** *New Oji Paper Co., Ltd.* □ 308 **CHARLES S. ANDERSON DESIGN COMPANY** *Sierra Designs*
309 **DOOKIM DESIGN** *Utoo Zone* □ 310 **SIA CO., LTD.** *Cow Brand Soap* □ 311 *(ABOVE)* **HORNALL ANDERSON DESIGN WORKS, INC.** *Smith Sport Optics*

312

313

314

314

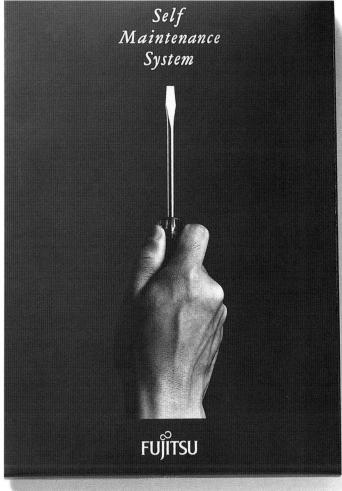

315

316

(THIS PAGE) 315 **DUFFY DESIGN** *Jim Beam* □ 316 **DIVISION** *Saku Brewery* □ *(OPPOSITE)* 317 **THORBURN DESIGN** *Millenium*
318 **HORNALL ANDERSON DESIGN WORKS, INC.** *William & Scott Company*

317

318

(THIS PAGE) 319 **ANTISTA FAIRCLOUGH DESIGN** ANHEUSER BUSCH, INC.

(OPPOSITE, TOP) □ 320 **DUFFY DESIGN** FLAGSTONE BREWERY □ (OPPOSITE, BOTTOM) 321 **CAHAN & ASSOCIATES** BOISSET USA

320

320

321

321

322

323

324

325

326

327

(OPPOSITE) 322 **CALDEWAY DESIGN** *Goosecross Cellars* □ 323 **TUCKER DESIGN** *Spicers Paper* □ 324 **TUCKER DESIGN** *Lactos Tasmania*
325 **TUCKER DESIGN** *Southcorp Wines* □ 326 **TUCKER DESIGN** *Lanzerac Country Estate* □ 327 **TUCKER DESIGN** *Southcorp Wines*
(THIS PAGE) 328 **TAKU SATOH** *Nikka Pure Malt Whiskey*

(THIS PAGE) 329 **CHARLES S. ANDERSON DESIGN CO.** FRENCH PAPER COMPANY
(OPPOSITE) 330 **BAILEY LAUERMAN & ASSOCIATES** WESTERN PAPER COMPANY

NOW OPEN

WESTERN PAPER'S NEW LINCOLN WAREHOUSE AT
5241 NORTHWEST 13TH STREET. WE'RE ALL MOVED IN AND
WE'RE READY FOR BUSINESS. READY TO CONTINUE THE
SERVICE THAT WE STARTED IN THIS TOWN 155 YEARS AGO.

STOP IN SOMETIME, AND SEE WHAT UNFOLDS.

western
PAPER

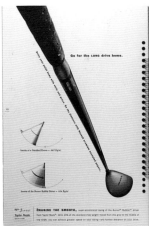
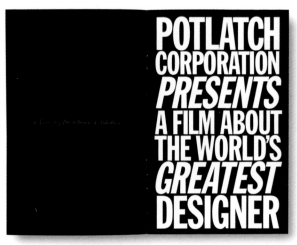

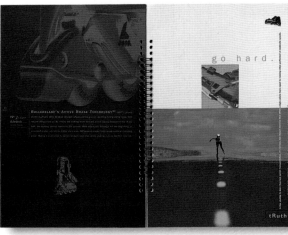

(ABOVE, LEFT) 331 **COPELAND HIRTHLER DESIGN + COMMUNICATIONS** *Neenah Paper* □ *(RIGHT)* 332 **VSA PARTNERS, INC.** *Potlatch Corporation*

(LEFT) 333 **PENTAGRAM DESIGN** *SIMPSON PAPER COMPANY* ☐ (RIGHT) 334 **SIBLEY/PETEET DESIGN** *Weyerhaeuser*

335

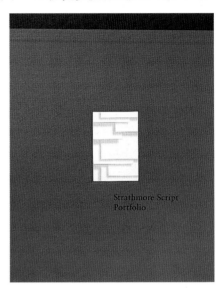

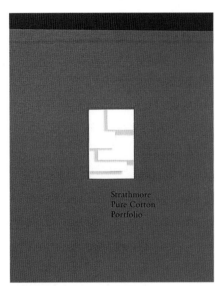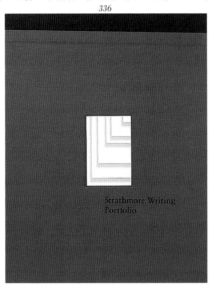

336

Strathmore
Pure Cotton
Portfolio

Strathmore Writing
Portfolio

Strathmore Script
Portfolio

337

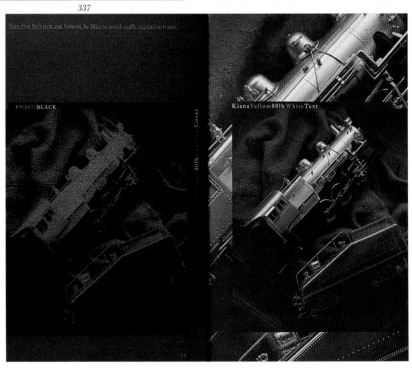

(TOP) 335 **PENTAGRAM DESIGN** *MOHAWK PAPER MILLS* □ *(MIDDLE)* 336 **DESIGNFRAME, INC.** *STRATHMORE PAPERS*
(BOTTOM) 337 **BESSER JOSEPH PARTNER** *HOPPER PAPER COMPANY*

338

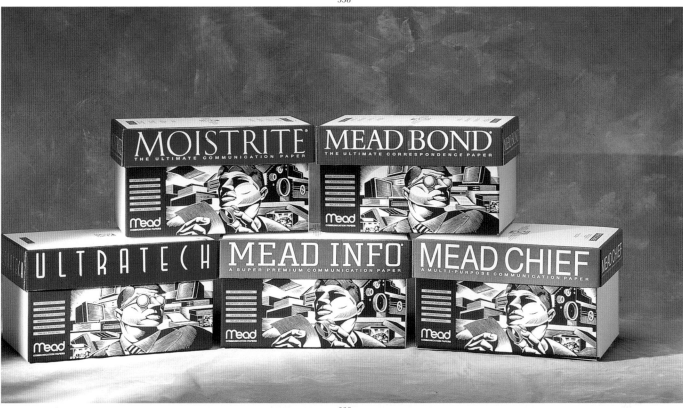

339

(TOP) 338 **NORTHLICH STOLLEY LAWARRE DESIGN GROUP** *MEAD COMMUNICATION PAPERS*
(BOTTOM) 339 **THORBURN DESIGN** *DOMTAR PAPER*

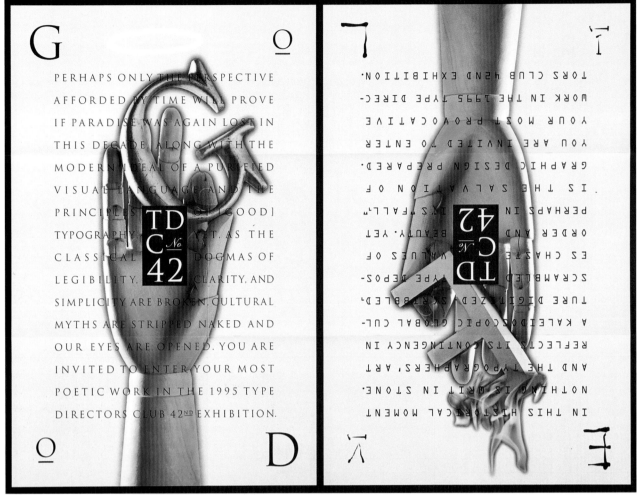

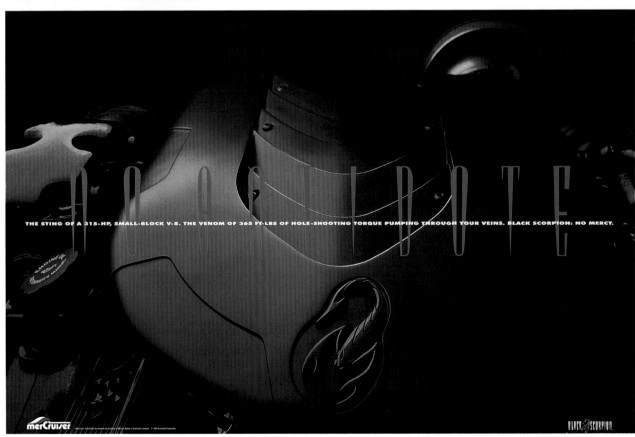

(TOP) 340 **VANDERBYL DESIGN** *TYPE DIRECTORS CLUB* □ (BOTTOM) 341 **SHR PERCEPTUAL MANAGEMENT** *MERCRUISER*
(OPPOSITE) 342 **HOLGER MATTHIES** *KULTURBEHÖRDE*

343

Warning: Amsterdam may seriously damage your sensitivity

344

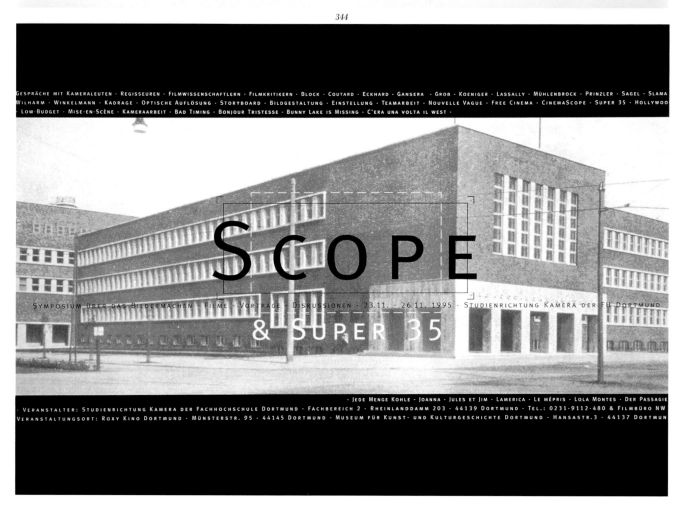

(TOP) 343 **KOWEIDEN POSTMA ASSOCIATES** *CREATIVE REVIEW MAGAZINE*
(BOTTOM) 344 **HANS-HEINRICH SURES** *FACHHOCHSCHULE DORTMUND*

345

(treat water with respect)

346

FRANÇOIS NOËL

(TOP) 345 **BATEY ADS** *Asian Pals of the Planet*
(BOTTOM) 346 **LE PETIT DIDIER** *François Noël*

Now that espresso
has come to Cincinnati,
Louise Fili has left her cappuccino
machine behind to venture west for an
evening's engagement at the Art
Directors Club of Cincinnati.
Cincinnati Art Museum.
September 20th.

347 **LOUISE FILI LTD.** *Cincinnati Art Directors Club*
(OPPOSITE) 348 **RBMM/THE RICHARDS GROUP** *Williamson Printing Company*

If the annual's late, the relationship's expired. We get it. Williamson Printing.

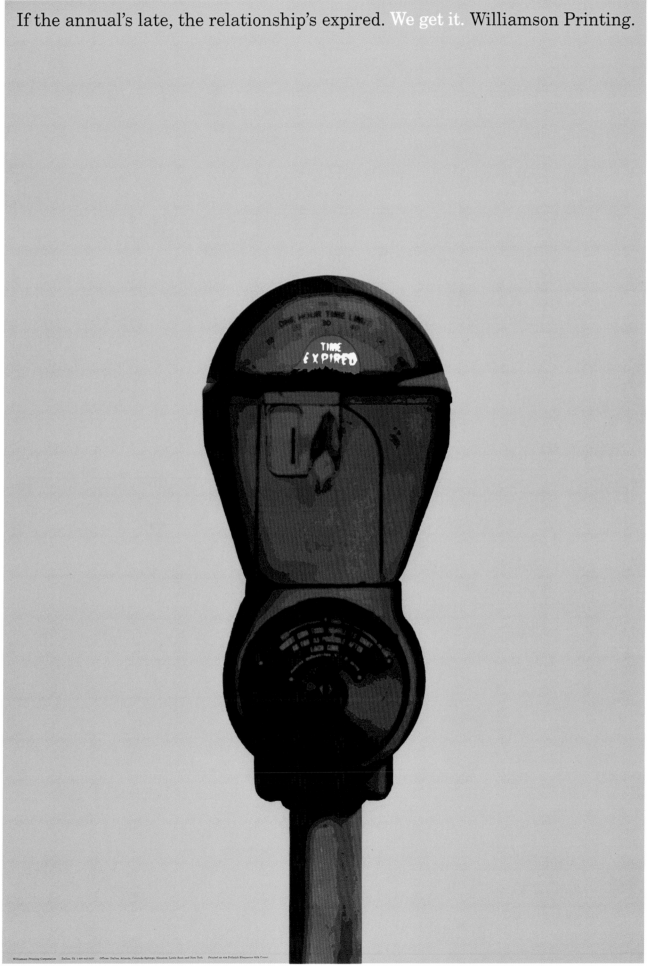

348

OLYMPIA WA *TO* ATLANTA GA

349 **YOUNG & LARAMORE** *KUBIN-NICHOLSON*

Or come to our creativity workshop with Tom Monahan.

350 **CLEVELAND CLARK INC.** *CREATIVE CLUB OF ATLANTA*

351

352

351 **GREENBERG KINGSLEY, INC.** *GUGGENHEIM MUSEUM* □ 352 **HALLMARK CARDS, INC.** *(IN-HOUSE)* □ *(OPPOSITE)* 353 **SMART DESIGN** *TIMEX, JOE BOXER*
354 **VIGNELLI DESIGNS, INC.** *PIERRE JUNOD WATCHES* □ 355 **ALAN CHAN DESIGN COMPANY** *ALAN CHAN CREATIONS* □ 356 **MICHAEL GRAVES ARCHITECT** *PROJECTS*

353

354

355

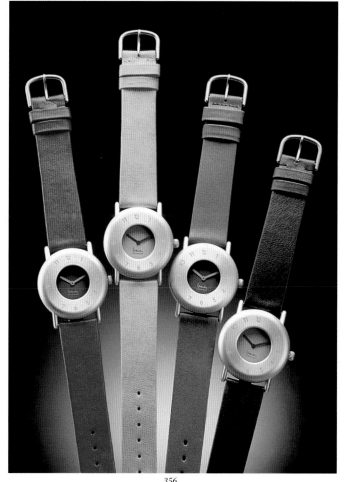

356

357

358

359

360

361

361

362

362

(OPPOSITE) 357 **SQUIRES & COMPANY** (IN-HOUSE) □ 358 **CLIFFORD SELBERT DESIGN COLLABORATIVE** *Spinergy, Inc.* □ 359–360 **CHARLES S. ANDERSON DESIGN COMPANY** *CSA Archive* □ (THIS PAGE) 361 **THE BURDICK GROUP** *Itoki Co. Ltd.* □ 362 **TODD BRACHER** (IN-HOUSE)

363

364

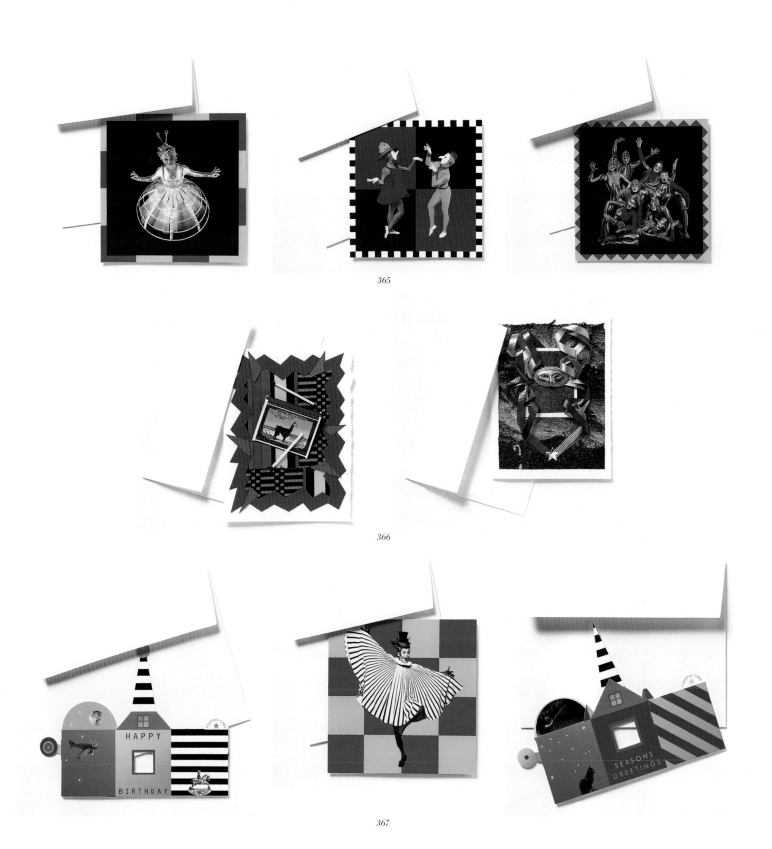

365

366

367

(OPPOSITE) 363 **MIRES DESIGN, INC.** *FOUNDSTUFF PAPERWORKS* □ 364 **PART STUDIO** *EGELY RESEARCH CO. LTD.*
135 *(THIS PAGE)* **PAPER HOUSE PRODUCTIONS** *(IN-HOUSE)* □ 366 **ROMEANTICS** *(IN-HOUSE)* □ 367 **PAPER HOUSE PRODUCTIONS** *(IN-HOUSE)*

Central Park, designed by Fredrick Law Olmsted and Calvert Vaux, is a masterpiece of 19th Century landscape architecture, and the most frequently used urban park in the United States. The Central Park Conservancy is dedicated to the care and upkeep of this treasured landmark, providing a permanent endowment for landscape maintenance as well as funding educational, recreational and volunteer programs for the Park's current and future visitors.

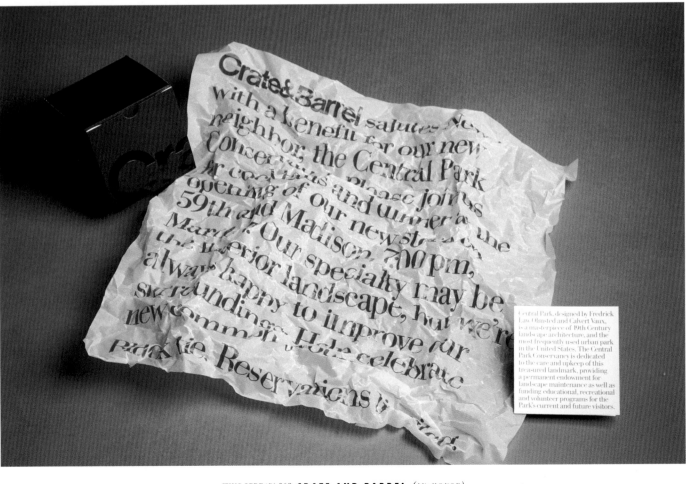

Crate&Barrel salutes New York with a benefit for our new neighbor, the Central Park Conservancy. Please join us for cocktails and dinner at the opening of our new store on 59th and Madison, 7:00 pm, March 7. Our specialty may be the interior landscape, but we're always happy to improve our surroundings. Help celebrate our new common ground. Reservations required.

Central Park, designed by Fredrick Law Olmsted and Calvert Vaux, is a masterpiece of 19th Century landscape architecture, and the most frequently used urban park in the United States. The Central Park Conservancy is dedicated to the care and upkeep of this treasured landmark, providing a permanent endowment for landscape maintenance as well as funding educational, recreational and volunteer programs for the Park's current and future visitors.

(THIS SPREAD) 368 **CRATE AND BARREL** *(IN-HOUSE)*

369

370

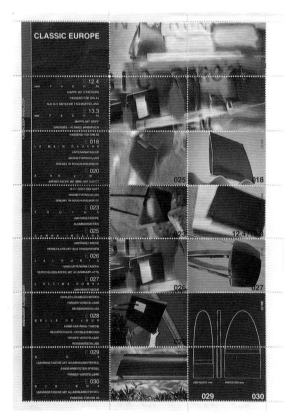

371

372

(THIS PAGE) 369 **WALLACE CHURCH ASSOCIATES, INC.** (IN-HOUSE) ☐ 370 **REED AND STEVEN** (IN-HOUSE) ☐ 371 **P.A.K. PLANUNG ARCHITEKTUR KONZEPTDESIGN** *ZETBE* ☐ 372 **THE MARLIN COMPANY** *Reckitt and Colman* ☐ (OPPOSITE) 373 **HUTCHINSON ASSOCIATES** *Dupli-Graphic*

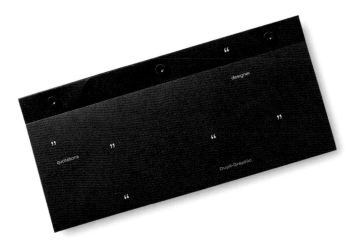

Charles Eames

Massimo Vignelli

"New design will come from new problems."

"Believe, express, and defend your responsibility
towards society
of not producing cultural trash."

Paul Rand

Josef
Müller-
Brockmann

"Trendiness is seductive, especially to the young and inexperienced,
for the principal reason that it offers no restraints, is lots of 'fun,'
permits unlimited possibilities for 'self-expression,' and doesn't
require conforming to the dictates of reason or aesthetics."

"The tauter the composition of elements
in the space available, the more effectively can
the thematic idea be formulated."

Hermann Zapf

Wolfgang
Weingart

"A typographers deepest service is rendered to author and reader
when the pages—all the pages—truly belong to each other,
no one of them given undue eminence."

"I am convinced that intensive investigation of
elementary typographic exercises is a pre-requisite
for the solution of complex typographic problems"

373

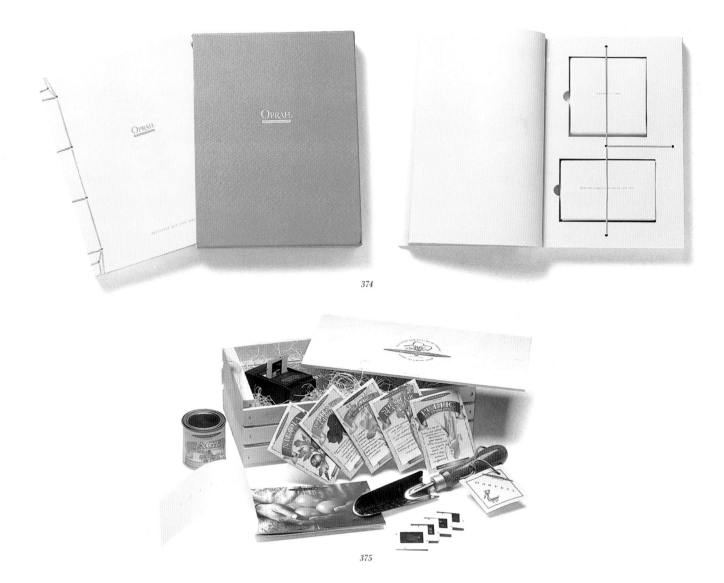

374

375

374 **VSA PARTNERS, INC.** *Harpo Productions, Inc.* □ 375 **STEWART HOLT ADVERTISING** *(in-house)* □ 376 **SANDSTROM DESIGN**
Levi Strauss & Co. □ *(opposite)* 377 **DESIGN GUYS** *Target Stores* □ 378 **SANDSTROM DESIGN** *California Marriott Hotels*

376

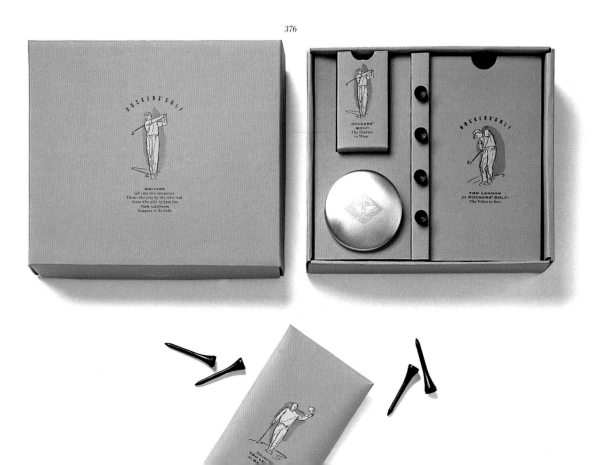

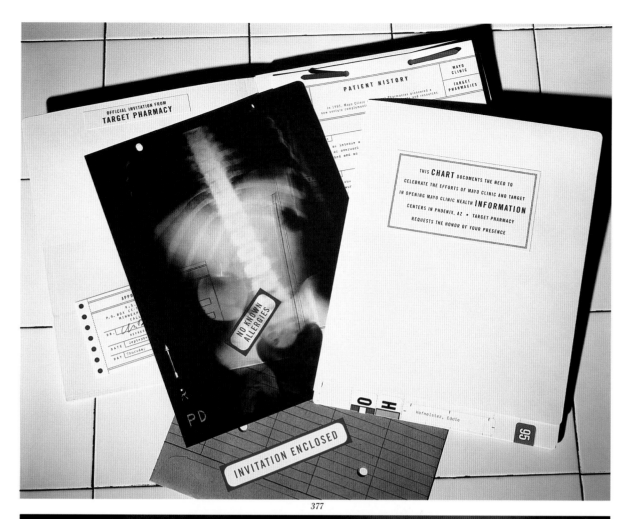

377

378

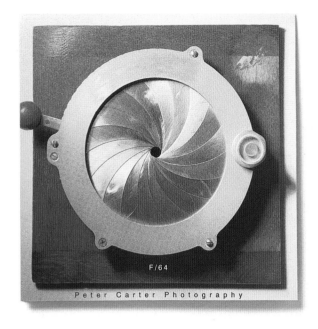

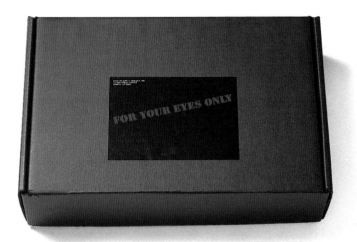

379 **BORGARDT SCHEIBEL & WHEATON** *PETER CARTER*

380 **RITTA & ASSOCIATES** *BMW OF NORTH AMERICA*

(OPPOSITE) 381 **CHARLES S. ANDERSON DESIGN CO.** *CSA ARCHIVE* □ 382 **HORNALL ANDERSON DESIGN WORKS, INC.**
MICROSOFT CORPORATION □ 383 **DUFFY DESIGN** *FLAGSTONE BREWERY* □ 384 **DUFFY DESIGN** *WIELAND FURNITURE COMPANY*

381

382

383

384

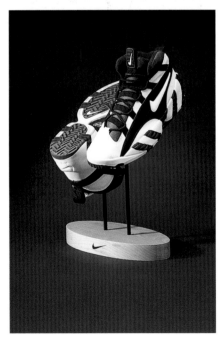

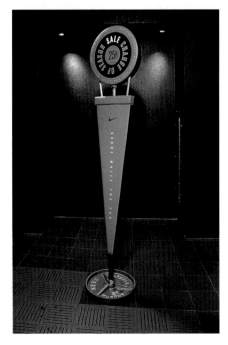

(THIS SPREAD) 385 **NIKE, INC.** *(IN-HOUSE)*

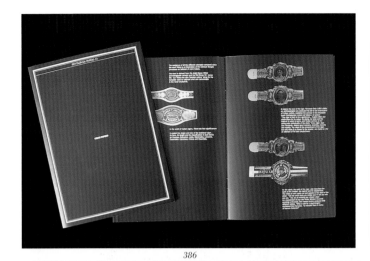

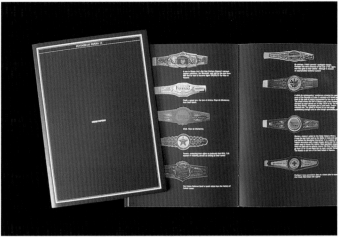

386

386

387

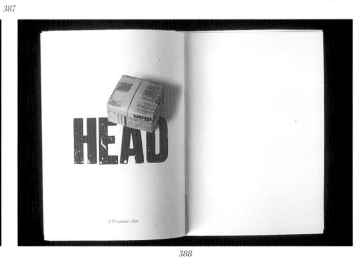

388

388

(THIS SPREAD) 386 **PENTAGRAM DESIGN** (IN-HOUSE) □ 387 **PENTAGRAM DESIGN** HONG KONG MANAGEMENT ASSOCIATION
388 **PENTAGRAM DESIGN** (IN-HOUSE) □ 389 **DESIGNERS COMPANY** HOOGHOUDT DISTILLERS □ 390 **TEMPLIN DESIGN** (IN-HOUSE)

389

390

(ABOVE) 391 **DOOKIM DESIGN** *SAMSUNG CORP.*

(OPPOSITE) 392 **ALAN CHAN DESIGN COMPANY** *DAVINCI CO. LTD.*

(ABOVE) 393 **ATELIER HAASE & KNELS** *Boutique Evelyn*
(OPPOSITE) 394 **PACKAGE LAND CO. LTD.** (IN-HOUSE)

395 **DESGRIPPES GOBÉ & ASSOCIATES** *ANN TAYLOR*

396 **PENTAGRAM DESIGN** *Gymboree*

397 **PACKAGING CREATE, INC.** New Oji Paper Co., Ltd.

(OPPOSITE) 398 **PENTAGRAM DESIGN** Gianfranco Lotti
399 **TEAM MUI + GRAY** Aki □ 400 **DFS GROUP LTD.** DFS Merchandising Ltd.

398

399

400

401

401

402

DESIGNS FOR THE DEEP
A Philatelic Record of Submersibles

SCUBA GEAR 600 feet — PALAU 32¢	COUSTEAU DIVING SAUCER 1,350 feet — PALAU 32¢	JIM SUIT 2,000 feet — PALAU 32¢
BEAVER IV 2,000 feet — PALAU 32¢	BEN FRANKLIN 2,000 feet — PALAU 32¢	SUBMARINE (USS NAUTILUS) estimated 2,300 feet — PALAU 32¢
DEEP ROVER 3,000 feet — PALAU 32¢	BEEBE BATHYSPHERE 3,028 feet — PALAU 32¢	DEEP STAR IV 4,000 feet — PALAU 32¢
ALUMINAUT 6,250 feet — PALAU 32¢	NAUTILE 7,000 feet — PALAU 32¢	
CYANA 9,800 feet — PALAU 32¢	F.N.R.S. BATHYSCAPHE 13,287 feet — PALAU 32¢	ALVIN 13,500 feet — PALAU 32¢
MJR I 20,000 feet — PALAU 32¢	ARCHIMEDE 30,000 feet — PALAU 32¢	TRIESTE 35,800 feet — PALAU 32¢

©Palau Postal Service 1995   Lloyd Birmingham

CIVILWAR
1861 THE WAR BETWEEN THE STATES 1865

MONITOR·VIRGINIA USA 32	Robert E. Lee 32 USA	Clara Barton 32	Ulysses S. Grant 32 USA	SHILOH 32¢ USA
Jefferson Davis 32	David Farragut 32 USA	Frederick Douglass 32	Raphael Semmes 32 USA	Abraham Lincoln 32 USA
Harriet Tubman 32	Stand Watie 32 USA	Joseph E. Johnston 32	Winfield Hancock USA 32	Mary Chesnut 32 USA
CHANCELLORSVILLE USA 32	William T. Sherman 32 USA	Phoebe Pember 32	"Stonewall" Jackson 32 USA	GETTYSBURG 32¢

408 **SQUIRES & COMPANY** *Deep Ellum Arts Festival*

409 **GEER DESIGN** *Times 3 Productions*

410

411

412

413

414 **MIRES DESIGN, INC.** *BOY SCOUT TROOP #260*

(OPPOSITE PAGE) 410 **HEWARDESIGN** *JAVA THE HUT* □ 411 **FRCH DESIGN WORLDWIDE** *ACA JOE*
412 **CHARLES S. ANDERSON DESIGN CO.** *CHUMS* □ 413 **SECOND GLOBE** *(IN-HOUSE)*

415

416

415 **PENTAGRAM DESIGN** *Columbus Salame Co.* □ 416 **THE GAP, INC.** *Old Navy Clothing Co.*

CAPTIONS AND INDICES

LEGENDEN UND KÜNSTLERANGABEN

LÉGENDES ET ARTISTES

PAGE 2 ART DIRECTOR/DESIGNER: *Carsten Franke* AGENCY: *Franke Communications* ILLUSTRATOR: *Guy Billout* CLIENT: *Compass Deutschland GmbH* COUNTRY: *Germany*■ *Illustration for a brochure for Compass Deutschland GmbH in Germany.* ● *Illustration für einen Broschüre der Firma Compass in Deutschland.* ▲ *Illustration d'un brochure pour la société Compass en Allemagne.*

PAGE 4 ART DIRECTOR/DESIGNER/ILLUSTRATOR: *Siegmar Münk* AGENCY/CLIENT: *Münkillus* COUNTRY: *Germany* ■ *An illustration from a self-promotional portfolio of twelve motifs.* ● *Illustration aus einer Eigenwerbungsmappe mit 12 Motiven.* ▲ *Illustration extraites d'un portfoilo autopromotionnel constitué de 12 motifs.*

PAGE 18, #1 ART DIRECTOR: *Art Simmons* DESIGNERS: *Doug Gilliad, Don Roy* AGENCY: *HSA* PHOTOGRAPHER/ILLUSTRATOR: *Barth Tillotson* COPYWRITER: *Harry Harrison* CLIENT: *DFSR Restaurants, Inc.* PAPER: *100 lb. gloss book* COUNTRY: *USA*■ *Annual report for a mexican food chain.* ● *Jahresbericht für eine Restaurantkette, die sich auf die mexikanische Küche spezialisiert hat.* ▲ *Rapport annuel pour une chaîne de restaurants spécialisés dans la cuisine mexicaine.*

PAGE 18, #2 ART DIRECTOR/DESIGNER: *Anne Schwiebinger* COPYWRITER: *Bob Lambie* AGENCY/CLIENT: *Nike, Inc.* PRINTER: *Hennigan* COUNTRY: *USA*■ *This annual report was designed to communicate marketing direction and financial results to investors.* ● *In diesem Jahresbericht für Nike wird neben den wirtschaftlichen Resultaten auch die Marketingstrategie erläutert.* ▲ *Outre les résultats financiers, ce rapport annuel conçu pour Nike présente également la stratégie de marketing.*

PAGE 18, #3 ART DIRECTOR: *Roger Felton* DESIGNER: *David Gilligan* COPYWRITER: *Terry Fitzgerald* AGENCY: *Roger Felton Associates* CLIENT: *Centec* COUNTRY: *England*

PAGE 19, #4 ART DIRECTOR: *John Brady* DESIGNERS: *John Brady, Paula Madden* AGENCY: *John Brady Design Consultants Inc.* PHOTOGRAPHER: *Tom Gigliotti* COPYWRITER: *David Gardner* CLIENT: *Greater Pittsburgh Council* TYPEFACE: *Adobe Garamond* PAPER: *Fox River Confetti, Vintage Remarque* PRINTER: *Reed & Witting Co.* COUNTRY: *USA* ■ *To show the importance scouting programs play in the lives of youths, the agency wanted to create an inexpensive "smart" design, attract prospective donors, and feature scouting experiences in a reader-friendly format. Different paper stocks were used throughout to provide more presence and to allow for one-color printing. Stick binding patches created immediate interest to both the eyes and the hands.* ● *Hier ging es um die Bedeutung der Pfadfinderorganisation für die Jugend. Mit dem kostengünstig produzierten Bericht in handlichem Format sollten vor allem auch zukünftige Spender angesprochen werden. Um den Bericht trotz Einfarbendruck optisch interessant zu machen, wurden verschiedene Papiersorten verwendet. Ein besonderes Detail, das Hände und Augen sofort anspricht, ist die spezielle Bindung mit Ästchen.* ▲ *Pour illustrer les nombreuses activités du scoutisme et leur importance dans la vie des jeunes, l'agence a voulu créer un rapport au design accrocheur et au format pratique pouvant être produit à des conditions avantageuses et susceptible d'attirer d'éventuels donateurs. Différentes qualités de papier ont été utilisées pour rehausser le rapport imprimé en une seule couleur. Détail intéressant, la reliure aussi agréable à l'œil qu'au toucher.*

PAGE 19, #5 ART DIRECTOR: *Dana Arnett* DESIGNERS: *Curtis Schreiber, Ron Spohn* AGENCY: *VSA Partners, Inc.* PHOTOGRAPHER: *James Schnepf* COPYWRITER: *Ken Schmidt* CLIENT: *Harley-Davidson, Inc.* PAPER: *Mead Escanaba 50 lb. Gloss* TYPEFACE: *Franklin Gothic, Sabon* PRINTER: *George Rice & Sons* COUNTRY: *USA*■ *This annual report features a bullet-to-bullet style that incorporates copy, captions, and photo essays. The photography was shot internationally in Harley-Davidson markets to depict their global presence.* ● *Der Jahresbericht für Harley-Davidson bietet dank der Darstellung von Lauftext, Legenden und Photos schnellen Zugang zu den Informationen. Um die globale Präsenz der Harley-Davidson zu betonen, wurden die Aufnahmen in verschiedenen Ländern gemacht.* ▲ *Le rapport annuel d'Harley-Davidson permet de retrouver facilement les informations recherchées grâce à l'utilisation de légendes et de photos. Pour souligner la présence internationale de Harley-Davidson, les prises de vue ont été réalisées dans différents pays.*

PAGE 19, #6 ART DIRECTOR: *Howard Brown* DESIGNERS: *Howard Brown, Mike Calkins,*

Anthony Arnold AGENCY: *Urban Outfitters (in-house)* PHOTOGRAPHERS/ILLUSTRATORS: *Steve Berkowitz, Charles Peterson* COPYWRITERS: *Richard Hayne, Ken Cleeland* CLIENT: *Urban Outfitters* PAPER: *French Construction* COUNTRY: *USA*

PAGE 20, #7 ART DIRECTOR: *Heinz Wild* DESIGNERS: *Heinz Wild, Martha Eisschiel* AGENCY: *Wild & Frey* COPYWRITER: *Marianne Hassenstein* CLIENT: *Stiftung Umwelteinsatz* TYPEFACE: *Berthold Bodoni, Berthold Univers, an old Royal typewriter* PAPER: *Palettocard, Perlen Domestico, Various recycled papers* PRINTER: *Schaer Druck Thun AG* COUNTRY: *Switzerland* ■ *The client, an environmental agency, wanted a simple, recyclable annual report. A rough, unrefined approach was required, and the budget was limited. The agency used the cheapest papers available, all recycled, and the cover of the annual report also serves as an envelope. Stickers and stamps give a hand-crafted touch and lend an official air.* ● *Als Stiftung für Umweltschutz wünschte der Auftraggeber einen einfachen, kostengünstigen und umweltfreundlichen Bericht. Die Gestalter benutzten die billigsten Recycling-Papierqualitäten, und der Umschlag des Berichtes dient auch als Versandcouvert. Aufkleber und Briefmarken sorgen für ein individuelles, handgemachtes und gleichzeitig offizielles Aussehen.* ▲ *Le client, une fondation spécialisée dans la protection de l'environnement, désirait un rapport simple, écologique et peu coûteux. Les concepteurs ont opté pour les qualités de papier recyclables les moins onéreuses, et la couverture du rapport annuel sert aussi d'enveloppe. Les auto-collants et les timbres donnent une touche à la fois artisanale et officielle.*

PAGE 21, #8 CREATIVE DIRECTOR: *Kerry Leimer* COPYWRITER: *Don Varyu* PHOTOGRAPHERS: *Tyler Boley, various* AGENCY: *Leimer Cross Design Corporation* CLIENT: *Nintendo Co., Ltd.* PRINTER: *H. Macdonald Printing* COUNTRY: *USA*

PAGE 22, #9 ART DIRECTOR: *Bill Cahan* DESIGNER: *Craig Clark* AGENCY: *Cahan & Associates* ILLUSTRATOR: *Steve Vance* COPYWRITER: *Lindsay Beaman* CLIENT: *Adaptec, Inc.* TYPEFACE: *Bembo, Futura, Zapf Dingbats* PAPER: *Weyerhaeuser Cougar Opaque* PRINTER: *Alan Lithograph*■ *The client designs, manufactures and markets a comprehensive family of hardware and software solutions. Colorful, bold visuals were chosen to convey strategic messages and core competencies. The comic book style is a powerful, familiar medium with which to grab the reader's attention.* ● *Der Auftraggeber entwickelt, produziert und vermarket Hardware und Software-Lösungen. Farbenfrohe, starke visuelle Elemente wurden gewählt, um die strategischen Botschaften zu vermitteln und die wichtigsten Elemente der Leistungen der Firma zu unterstreichen. Der Comic-Heft-Stil ist ein beliebtes und wirksames Mittel, um die Aufmerksamkeit des Lesers zu wecken.* ▲ *Le client développe, produit et commercialise du matériel informatique et des progiciels. Des éléments visuels frappants aux couleurs franches ont été utilisés pour véhiculer des messages stratégiques et souligner les principaux résultats de la société. Le style bande dessinée est un moyen efficace et apprécié pour susciter l'attention du lecteur.*

PAGE 22, #10 DESIGN DIRECTOR: *Ted Stoik* ART DIRECTOR/DESIGNER: *Tim Bruce* AGENCY: *VSA Partners, Inc.* PHOTOGRAPHER: *Tony Armour* COPYWRITERS: *Lee M. Witte, Margaret C. Benson* CLIENT: *Chicago Volunteer Legal Services* PAPER: *Mohawk Vellum* TYPEFACE: *Berthold Akzidenz Grotesk* PRINTER: *Bruce Offset* COUNTRY: *USA*■ *Lawyers at Chicago Volunteer Legal Services work to protect the rights of people in the Chicago area who could not otherwise afford legal services. The annual captures the unique, "do whatever it takes" spirit of the lawyers and the clients they serve.* ● *Die Juristen der Chicago Volunteer Legal Services beraten Menschen aus dem Raume Chicago, die sich keinen Anwalt leisten könnten. Der Jahresbericht spiegelt den Geist dieser Organisation – «Tue was immer nötig ist» – und ihrer Klienten wider.* ▲ *Les juristes travaillant pour les Chicago Volunteer Legal Services défendent les droits des citoyens vivant dans la région de Chicago qui n'ont pas les moyens de se payer un avocat. Le rapport annuel reflète l'esprit de cette organisation – «fais ce que tu as à faire» – ainsi que celui de ses clients.*

PAGE 23, #11 ART DIRECTOR: *Mark Geer* DESIGNERS: *Mark Geer, Mandy Stewart* AGENCY: *Geer Design, Inc.* PHOTOGRAPHER/ILLUSTRATOR: *Chris Shinn* COPYWRITER: *Debra K. Maurer* CLIENT: *South Texas College of Law* PAPER: *Starwhite Vicksburg 88 lb., 100 lb., Strathmore Elements 80 lb.* TYPEFACE: *Officina, Helvetica Rounded, Teknik*

PRINTER: *The Beasley Company* COUNTRY: *USA* ■ *South Texas is the only private law school in Houston. When a successful dean stepped down in 1994, a concern arose that constituents would feel a leadership void. The report features 18 voluntary board members who served as the source of continuity during the transition. "Drafting a Blueprint for Excellence" introduces the board which is responsible for the plans and programs adopted by the college.* ● *South Texas ist die einzige private Hochschule in Houston, die ein Jurastudium anbietet. Nach dem Rücktritt eines erfolgreichen Dekans 1994 sprang ein Team von 18 freiwilligen Vorstandsmitgliedern für die Übergangsperiode ein, um die Kontinuität der Führung zu gewährleisten. Der Bericht stellt dieses Gremium vor, das für die Planung und das Studienprogramm verantwortlich ist.* ▲ *South Texas est la seule école privée supérieure de Houston à proposer des études de droit. A la suite de la retraite du doyen en 1994, une équipe composée de 18 volontaires, membres de la direction, prit la relève pour assurer la bonne marche de l'école durant une période transitoire. Le rapport présente ce conseil chargé de la planification et du programme d'études.*

PAGE 23, #12 ART DIRECTOR: *Rex Peteet* DESIGNERS: *Derek Welch, Rex Peteet* AGENCY: *Sibley/Peteet Design* PHOTOGRAPHERS: *Chris Hamilton, Joe Baraban, Sean McCormick* COPYWRITER/CLIENT: *United States Olympic Committee* PAPER: *Simpson Paper Co.* PRINTER: *Imperial Litho & Dryography* COUNTRY: *USA* ■ *This report seeks to convey the unrelenting commitment of athletes to achieve the opportunity to experience the Olympic moment. Through a series of photographic pairings, the individual effort and the determination of the athletes in training are contrasted with the Olympic moment–photographed in a time-exposed method. A narrative suggests what might be running through the athlete's mind.* ● *In diesem Bericht für das Olympische Komitee der USA geht es um die Bedeutung der Teilnahme an der Olympiade für die einzelnen Athleten, um ihren Einsatz und um die Vielfalt der Sportarten, die an der Olympiade und der Paralympiade vertreten sind. Die Aufnahmen zeigen einerseits die Einsamkeit, den individuellen Einsatz und die Entschlossenheit der Athleten beim Training, andererseits das Ereignis der Olympiade in Bildern, die die Spannung, Schnelligkeit und Anmut der verschiedenen Aktivitäten und Wettkämpfe zeigen. Der Text handelt von den Gedanken, die den Athleten durch den Kopf gehen mögen.* ▲ *Réalisé pour le Comité olympique des Etats-Unis, ce rapport met l'accent sur l'importance d'une participation aux Jeux Olympiques pour tout athlète. Les prises de vue montrent, d'une part, l'effort individuel et la détermination des athlètes lors de l'entraînement et, de l'autre, l'événement que constitue les Jeux Olympiques par le biais d'images traduisant la tension, la vitesse et la grâce inhérentes à chaque compétition. Le texte évoque les pensées susceptibles de traverser l'esprit des athlètes.*

PAGES 24-25, #13 ART DIRECTOR/DESIGNER: *Adelaide Acerbi* AGENCY: *Lambda SRL* EDITOR: *Fulvio Irace* PUBLISHER: *Driade* COUNTRY: *Italy* ■ *The client wanted to illustrate the coordinated graphic communication of a multi-faceted company, and to provide an analysis of production. The book depicts the industry, the debate, and the authors of an era which changed the image of industrial design, domestic product design and interior design.* ● *Hier geht es um die koordinierte graphische Kommunikation einer vielseitigen Firma sowie wie um eine Analyse der Produktion. Das Buch geht auf die Branche ein, auf die Diskussionen und die Autoren einer Ära, in der sich das Image des Designs von Industrie- und Haushaltsprodukten sowie von Inneneinrichtungen erheblich wandelte.* ▲ *Il s'agissait de faire ressortir la communication graphique coordonnée d'une société aux activités multiples et de fournir une analyse de la production. Cet ouvrage présente les aspects de ce secteur industriel ainsi que les débats et les auteurs d'une époque qui a révolutionné l'image du design de produits industriels et domestiques ainsi que la décoration intérieure.*

PAGE 26, #14 ART DIRECTOR/DESIGNER: *Shinzo Fukui* PHOTOGRAPHERS: *Yutaka Kawachi, Hiroshi Asada* ARTIST: *Robert Rauschenberg* COPYWRITER: *Tomoko Kuroda* AGENCY: *Shinzo Graphica & Associates* PUBLISHER: *Felissimo* COUNTRIES: *USA, Japan*

PAGE 27, #15 ART DIRECTOR: *Michele Wetherbee* DESIGNERS/ILLUSTRATORS: *Raul Cabra, Martin Venezky* AGENCY: *Cabra Diseño* EDITORS: *Joan Nestle, John Preston* PUBLISHER: *Harper S.F.* COUNTRY: *USA* ■ *The designers used vernacular images to convey a*

sense of familiarity with the book, while subtly playing with typical gay and lesbian stereotypes through humor.* ● *Durch Verwendung von Bildern des Alltags bemühten sich die Gestalter des Buches um ein Gefühl von Vertrautheit, wobei sie ganz subtil und humorvoll mit homosexuellen und lesbischen Stereotypen arbeiteten.* ▲ *Les concepteurs ont opté pour des images du quotidien afin de créer un effet de familiarité tout en intégrant avec subtilité et humour des stéréotypes homosexuels et lesbiens.*

PAGE 27, #16 DESIGNER: *Todd Prather* PHOTOGRAPHER: *James Elliott* CLIENT: *Student work* COUNTRY: *USA* ■ *To make this novel's jacket stand out, the designer used Indian styles, materials, and textures.* ● *Der Gestalter arbeitete mit indianischen Materialien, um dem Umschlag ein authentisches Aussehen zu verleihen.* ▲ *Afin de conférer un air d'authenticité à cette jaquette, le concepteur a travaillé avec des matériaux et des styles indiens.*

PAGE 27, #17 ART DIRECTOR/DESIGNER: *Hans-Heinrich Sures* CLIENT: *Student work* TYPEFACE: *Tribeca, Garamond 3* COUNTRY: *Germany* ■ *This cover was designed for a novel that tells the story of two Cuban musicians who immigrate to New York in the fifties. The typeface with the hand-cut headline and the forties pin-up reflect the nostalgia of old Latin music posters and record sleeves.* ● *In diesem Buch geht es um die Geschichte zweier kubanischer Musiker, die in den 50er Jahren nach New York emigrierten. Die von Hand gestaltete Titelschrift und das Pin-Up aus den 40er Jahren erinnern an alte Plakate und Schallplattenhüllen für lateinamerikanische Musik.* ▲ *Ce livre raconte l'histoire de deux musiciens cubains qui immigrèrent à New York dans les années 50. Les caractères du titre dessinés à la main et la pin-up des années 40 font penser aux vieilles affiches et aux pochettes de disque typiques de la musique latino-américaine.*

PAGE 27 #18 ART DIRECTOR: *Michael Osborne* DESIGNER: *Christopher Lehman* AGENCY: *Michael Osborne Design* ILLUSTRATOR: *José Ortega* EDITOR/PUBLISHER: *Chronicle Books* COUNTRY: *USA* ■ *To create a book design that would convey the sense of life found in the author's poetry, a dominant illustration with warm colors was combined with a clean typographic treatment on a textured paper stock.* ● *Um auf dem Umschlag das Lebensgefühl der Gedichte in diesem Buch wiederzugeben, entschied sich der Gestalter für eine dominierende Illustration in warmen Farbtönen, kombiniert mit sauberer typographischer Gestaltung und einer strukturierten Papierqualität.* ▲ *Pour rendre l'atmosphère des poèmes contenus dans cet ouvrage, le concepteur a opté pour une illustration aux tons chauds, combinée à une typographie soignée et à une qualité de papier grenu.*

PAGES 28-29, #19 ART DIRECTORS: *Woody Pirtle, John Klotnia* DESIGNERS: *John Klotnia, Brenna Garratt* AGENCY: *Pentagram Design* PUBLISHER: *Rizzoli International Publications, Inc.* COUNTRY: *USA* ■ *"The PaineWebber Art Collection" surveys the investment firm's holdings in contemporary art. Each spread is devoted to a single work. Bold but jumbled typography and bright colors convey the variety and nature of the collection, while also suggesting PaineWebber's broad corporate interests.* ● *In diesem Band geht es um die PaineWebber-Sammlung moderner Kunst. Jede Doppelseite ist einem einzigen Werk gewidmet. Die Typographie und Farben vermitteln die Vielfalt und Art der Sammlung und sind gleichzeitig ein Hinweis auf die vielfältigen Interessen dieser Investment Firma.* ▲ *Ce volume présente la collection d'art moderne PaineWebber. Chaque double page est consacrée à une seule œuvre. La typographie et les couleurs reflètent la variété et le genre de la collection et suggèrent en même temps les intérêts multiples de cette société de placement.*

PAGE 30, #20 ART DIRECTOR/DESIGNER/ILLUSTRATOR: *Hans-Heinrich Sures* CLIENT: *Student work* TYPEFACE: *Meta-Caps, Trixie* COUNTRY: *Germany* ■ *This cover was designed for a novel about a Vietnam veteran who returns to a small American town and discovers he does not fit into everyday life anymore. The designer wanted to suggest a typical American suburban home, cleanliness, and the idea that "all is quiet" and "nothing is really happening here."* ● *Umschlag für ein Buch über einen Vietnam-Veteranen, der nach seiner Rückkehr in eine amerikanische Kleinstadt feststellt, dass er hier nicht mehr hingehört. Dem Designer ging es um die Darstellung eines typisch amerikanischen Vorstadthauses und die Vorstellung, dass in dieser sauberen, ruhigen Umgebung nichts wirklich geschehen kann.* ▲ *Jaquette d'une nouvelle racontant l'histoire d'un vétéran du Viêt-nam qui rentre aux Etats-Unis et se rend compte qu'il n'a plus sa place chez lui. Le concepteur a voulu représenter un foyer typique de la banlieue des métropoles américaines et suggérer que dans cet environnement propret et tranquille, il ne se passe jamais rien.*

PAGE 30, #21 ART DIRECTOR: *Victor Weaver* DESIGNER: *Michael Schwab* AGENCY/ILLUSTRATOR: *Michael Schwab Studio* CLIENT: *Hyperion* COUNTRY: *USA* ■ *Cover illustration for "The Gettin Place."* ● *Umschlagillustration für "The Gettin Place".* ▲ *Illustration de la jaquette du livre «The Gettin Place»*

PAGE 30, #22 ART DIRECTOR/DESIGNER: *John Gall* AGENCY: *Grove/Atlantic (in-house)* ILLUSTRATOR: *Zhang Hongtu* CLIENT: *Grove/Atlantic* TYPEFACE: *Triplex* PRINTER: *Castlereach* COUNTRY: *USA* ■ *The designer wanted to create a cover for a collection of fiction by post-Tiannamen Square Chinese writers that was somewhat irreverant but not too political.* ● *Umschlag für eine Sammlung von Erzählungen chinesischer Autoren, die nach den Ereignissen auf dem «Platz des himmlischen Friedens» entstanden und kritisch, aber nicht zu politisch sind.* ▲ *Jaquette pour une collection de nouvelles d'auteurs chinois rédigées à la suite des événements de la place Tiananmen dont le contenu, sans être trop politique, traduit tout de même un esprit critique.*

PAGE 30, #23 ART DIRECTOR/DESIGNER: *John Gall* AGENCY: *Grove/Atlantic (in-house)* PHOTOGRAPHER: *Barnaby Hall* CLIENT: *Grove/Atlantic* PAPER: *Carolina Coated* TYPEFACE: *Alternate Gothic* PRINTER: *Castlereach* COUNTRY: *USA* ■ *To create a series look for the books of Henry Miller, a modular system was applied to the different types of art for the various books. The artwork concentrates on showing the sexual aspects of Miller's work. Three different color covers kept the price down.* ● *Um einen einheitlichen Auftritt der Bücher von Henry Miller zu erzielen, wurde ein System etabliert: Die Illustrationen beziehen sich alle auf die sexuellen Aspekte in Millers Büchern. Dank der Differenzierung der Umschläge durch drei verschiedene Farben wurde der Preis niedrig gehalten.* ▲ *Pour créer une présentation unitaire des livres de Henry Miller, un système modulaire a été appliqué aux différents ouvrages: les illustrations se réfèrent toutes aux aspects sexuels contenus dans son œuvre. L'utilisation de trois couleurs pour différencier les jaquettes respectives a permis de limiter les frais de production.*

PAGE 31, #24 ART DIRECTORS/DESIGNERS: *Lutz Eberle, Andreas Jung, Marcus Wichmann* AGENCY: *lahm* PHOTOGRAPHERS/ILLUSTRATORS/EDITORS: *Lutz Eberle, Andreas Jung, Marcus Wichmann* PUBLISHER: *Institut für Buchgestaltung an der Staatlichen Akademie der Bildenden Künste Stuttgart* COUNTRY: *Germany* ■ *This experimental book design was complemented with a diskette that contains a customized, password-protected font exclusively designed for the book. The password is the solution of a letter puzzle hidden throughout the text.* ● *Zu diesem experimentellen Buchdesign gehört auch eine Diskette mit einer geschützten, nur mit einem Passwort zugänglichen Schrift, die speziell für das Buch entworfen wurde. Das Passwort ist die Lösung eines Buchstaben-Puzzles, das überall im Text verborgen ist.* ▲ *La présentation expérimentale de cet livre est complétée par une disquette contenant une police protégée par un mot de passe, laquelle a été spécialement créée pour cet ouvrage. Pour trouver le mot de passe, il faut assembler en un puzzle des lettres dissimulées tout au long du texte.*

PAGES 32-33, #25 ART DIRECTOR: *Fred Woodward* PUBLISHER: *Little Brown* TYPEFACE: *Goudy Italian* PAPER: *NPI Matte Art* PRINTER: *Dai Nippon* COUNTRY: *USA*

PAGE 34, #26 ART DIRECTORS: *José Bulnes, Antoine Robaglia* AGENCY: *Bulnes & Robaglia* PUBLISHER: *Éditions Arte*

PAGE 35, #27 ART DIRECTOR/DESIGNER: *Thomas S. Schaer* AGENCY: *Thomas S. Schaer Visueller Gestalter SGV SGD* PHOTOGRAPHER: *Uli Nusko* EDITOR: *Peter Fahr* PUBLISHER: *Nemesis Verlag Pierre Farine* COUNTRY: *Switzerland* ■ *This design for two poems with political content was visualized in an unconventional way. Combined with 42 photographs, objects printed in duo-tone correlate with the texts as contextual*

or formal analogies. ● *Die Gestaltung für zwei Gedichte mit politischem Inhalt wurde auf unkonventionelle Art gelöst. Kombiniert mit 42 Photographien, funktionieren die im Duo-Ton gedruckten Objekte als textbezogene oder formale Analogien.* ▲ *Une solution inhabituelle a été choisie pour présenter ces deux poèmes politiques: combinés à 42 photographies, les objets imprimés en duotone reprennent des passages des poèmes ou établissent des analogies formelles.*

PAGE 35, #28 ART DIRECTOR/DESIGNER: *Christopher A.D.* AGENCY: *MTV Off-Air Creative* PHOTOGRAPHER/ILLUSTRATOR: *Various* PUBLISHER: *Pocket Books/Melcher Media* COUNTRY: *USA*

PAGE 35, #29 ART DIRECTOR: *Bruno Bakalovic* DESIGNER: *Nicole Wisch* AGENCY: *K/PLEX Konzepte für Kommunikation GmbH* PHOTOGRAPHER/EDITOR: *Ursula Schulz-Dornburg* PUBLISHER: *Brotmuseum Ulm* COUNTRY: *Germany*

PAGE 36, #30 ART DIRECTOR/DESIGNER: *Steve Sikora* AGENCY: *Design Guys* PHOTOGRAPHER/ILLUSTRATOR: *Vera Storman* PUBLISHER: *Consortium Book Sales* COUNTRY: *USA* ■ *The client wanted companion covers for a new and backlist book with a catalog theme of "Spring/Summer." Bright green pallets in process color were used and the same basic design was employed in duotone for the backlist.* ● *Das vorgegebene Thema war «Frühling/Sommer», und es ging um einen homogenen Auftritt für ein neues und ein älteres Buch. Die Gestalter arbeiteten mit einer leuchtend grünen Farbpalette für das neue Buch, und das gleiche Gestaltungskonzept wurde auch für das Backlist-Buch im Duoton angewendet.* ▲ *Il s'agissait de créer une présentation homogène pour deux ouvrages consacrés au thème «Printemps/Eté». Les concepteurs ont travaillé avec une palette de verts lumineux pour le nouveau livre et ont appliqué le même concept en duotone à l'ancien livre.*

PAGE 36, #31 ART DIRECTORS/DESIGNERS: *Jacques Koeweiden, Paul Postma* AGENCY: *Koeweiden Postma & Associates* PHOTOGRAPHER: *Marc Van Praag* CLIENT: *Bis Publishers* PAPER: *High-proof silk* TYPEFACE: *KP Din, Stone Serif* PRINTER: *Snoek Decaju, Gent* ■ *Each cover has a different handcrafted metal plate.* ● *Für jeden Umschlag wurde eine andere, handgemachte Metallplatte verwendet.* ▲ *Pour chaque jaquette, une nouvelle plaque de métal réalisée à la main a été utilisée.*

PAGE 36, #32 ART DIRECTOR: *Heinz Hiltbrunner* DESIGNER: *Christoph Bolz* AGENCY: *SFGB Schule fur Gestaltung Berne* COUNTRY: *Switzerland*

PAGE 36, #33 ART DIRECTOR/DESIGNER/AGENCY: *Le Petit Didier* PHOTOGRAPHER/ILLUSTRATOR: *O.H. Dancy* COPYWRITER/CLIENT: *Arsenal* PRINTER: *Offset* COUNTRY: *France*

PAGE 37, #34 ART DIRECTOR: *Gretchen Scoble* DESIGNERS: *Michael Mabry, Kristen Malan* PHOTOGRAPHER: *Daniel Proctor* EDITOR: *Bill LeBlond* AGENCY: *Michael Mabry Design* PUBLISHER: *Chronicle Books* COUNTRY: *USA* ■ *Design for a book about cooking with flavored oils.* ● *Bei diesem Kochbuch geht es um das Kochen mit aromatisierten Ölen.* ▲ *Ce livre de cuisine contient des recettes à base d'huiles aromatisées.*

PAGE 37, #35 ART DIRECTOR: *Arno Häring* DESIGNER: *Achim Kiel* PHOTOGRAPHER: *Lutz Pape* AGENCY: *Pencil Corporate Art* PUBLISHER: *Gustav Lübbe Verlag GmbH* COUNTRY: *Germany* ■ *Design for a non-fiction book by James Michener.* ● *Umschlag und Seiten eines Sachbuches von James Michener.* ▲ *Conception d'un livre de voyage.*

PAGE 37, #36 ART DIRECTOR/DESIGNER: *Yasuyo Iguchi* AGENCY: *The MIT Press Design Department* PHOTOGRAPHER: *Robert A. Melnick* EDITOR: *Matthew Abbate* ACQUIRING EDITOR: *Roger Conover* PUBLISHER: *The MIT Press* COUNTRY: *USA* ■ *Each page of this book shows a different manhole cover. The type, colors and texture found on the book jacket reflect the content.* ● *Jede Seite des Buches zeigt einen neuen Gully-Deckel. Typographie, Farben und Oberflächenbeschaffenheit des Umschlags reflektieren den Inhalt des Buches.* ▲ *Chaque page du livre montre une nouvelle bouche d'égout. La typographie, les couleurs et la texture de la jaquette se réfèrent au contenu de cet ouvrage.*

PAGE 38, #37 ART DIRECTOR: *Michael Bierut* DESIGNER: *Esther Bridavsky* AGENCY: *Pentagram Design* PHOTOGRAPHER: *Bruce Miller* CLIENT: *Peter Joseph Gallery* PRINTER:

Finlay Brothers COUNTRY: *USA* ■ *This catalogue was designed for a midtown Manhattan gallery specializing in American art furniture. All catalogues are a uniform size so together they build a coordinated library. Albert Paley's exhibition "Organic Logic" focused on the synthesis of natural forms and hard materials in his furniture. The simple, logical typography contrasts with the baroque intensity of the pictured works.* ● *Katalog für eine auf amerikanische Kunstmöbel spezialisierte Galerie im Zentrum Manhattans. Alle Kataloge haben eine einheitliche Grösse, so dass sie ein homogenes Bild ergeben. Thema von Albert Paleys Ausstellung "Organic Logic" war die Synthese von natürlichen Formen und harten Materialien. Die einfache, logische Typographie steht im Kontrast zu der barocken Intensität der gezeigten Möbel.* ▲ *Catalogue conçu pour une galerie américaine au centre de Manhattan spécialisée dans les meubles d'art. Tous les catalogues ont le même format afin de créer un effet unitaire. L'exposition d'Albert Paley intitulée «Organic Logic» s'articulait autour de la synthèse des formes naturelles et des matériaux durs utilisés pour ses créations. Simple et logique, la typographie contraste avec l'intensité baroque des meubles présentés.*

PAGE 38, #38 ART DIRECTOR: *Ruth Tulino* DESIGNER: *Walter Herrington* PHOTOGRAPHER: *Peter Hogg* ILLUSTRATOR: *Laurie Gerns* COPYWRITER: *Bernadette Soter* AGENCY: *Tulino Design, Inc.* CLIENT: *B. Via International Housewares, Inc.* COUNTRY: *USA* ■ *The brochure was designed as part of the product launch for Via International Housewares, and provides a buying guide for key retailers.* ● *Diese Broschüre ist Teil einer Produkteinführung und dient dem Einzelhandel als Bestellkatalog.* ▲ *Cette brochure conçue pour Via International Housewares fournit un guide d'achat pour les principaux détaillants.*

PAGE 39, #39 ART DIRECTOR: *Michael Gericke* DESIGNERS: *Donna Ching, Sharon Harel* AGENCY: *Pentagram Design* PHOTOGRAPHER: *Luca Vignelli* COPYWRITER: *Maeve Slavin* CLIENT: *Pallas Textiles* COUNTRY: *USA* ■ *This client produces fabrics in an unusual range of colors for interior environments. The promotions list the many names that are used to describe each basic color. Each list of color names has been "woven" typographically to create a unique textile pattern.* ● *Pallas Textiles stellt Heimtextilien in ungewöhnlichen Farben her. Hier werden die vielen verschiedenen Namen zur Bezeichnung der Grundtöne aufgeführt. Jede Liste der Farbbezeichnungen wurde typographisch «gewebt», um unterschiedliche textile Muster zu erzielen.* ▲ *Pallas Textiles propose des tissus d'ameublement aux coloris inhabituels. Les désignations des tons de base sont présentés de façon originale: chaque liste a été «tissée» typographiquement afin d'obtenir un motif textile différent.*

PAGE 39, #40 ART DIRECTORS: *Marcus Haslam, Tony Veazey* DESIGNER: *Marcus Haslam* PHOTOGRAPHER: *David Stewart* COPYWRITER: *Tony Veazey* AGENCY: *Broadbent, Cheetham, Veazey* CLIENT: *David Stewart/Shed Films* COUNTRY: *Great Britain* ■ *This brochure of still photography accompanied the short film "Cabbage" directed by David Stewart for Shed Films.* ● *Diese Broschüre mit Stilleben begleitete den Kurzfilm "Cabbage" (Kohl), in dem David Stewart für Shed Films Regie führte.* ▲ *Cette brochure de photographies accompagne le court métrage «Cabbage» (Choux) mis en scène par David Stewart pour Shed Films.*

PAGE 40, #41 ART DIRECTORS: *Scott Timms, Phillip Smith* DESIGNER: *Pam Stone* AGENCY: *Nordensson Lynn Advertising* CALLIGRAPHER: *Rob Waters* ILLUSTRATOR: *Bob Conge* COPYWRITER: *Mike Nevin* CLIENT: *Rain Bird* COUNTRY: *USA* ■ *This brochure for a leading manufacturer of irrigation products was part of a multi-faceted campaign developed for the company's commercial division and was intended to re-establish the company's products as the predominate offering in the category.* ● *Diese Broschüre für einen Hersteller von Bewässerungsprodukten gehört zu einer umfassenden Kampagne der Firma, mit der ihre führende Stellung im Markt gefestigt und das umfassende Produktangebot präsentiert werden soll.* ▲ *Conçue pour un fabricant de produits d'arrosage et d'irrigation, cette brochure faisait partie d'une vaste campagne qui devait consolider la position de leader du fabricant sur le marché et présenter sa large gamme de produits.*

PAGE 40, #42 ART DIRECTOR: *Reiner Hebe* DESIGNERS: *Anda Manea, Britta Moarefi, Joachim Reyle* ILLUSTRATOR: *Mike Loos* COPYWRITER: *Reiner Hebe* AGENCY/CLIENT: *HEBE*

Werbung & Design COUNTRY: *Germany* ■ *This brochure was created for self-promotion.* ● *Eigenwerbung einer Werbe- und Design-Agentur.* ▲ *Publicité autopromotionnelle d'une agence de publicité et de design.*

PAGE 41, #43 DESIGN DIRECTOR: *Ted Stoik* ART DIRECTOR/DESIGNER: *Tim Bruce* AGENCY: *VSA Partners, Inc.* PHOTOGRAPHER: *Stock* CLIENT: *Jack Macholl* PAPER: *Mohawk Superfine* TYPEFACE: *Janson* PRINTER: *Dupligraphics* COUNTRY: *USA* ■ *With over 14 years of experience marketing financial services, Jack Macholl was looking for a new job. The resume presents his intentions and qualifications in a bold, humorous and unassuming manner.* ● *Nach 14 Jahren Erfahrung im Marketing von Dienstleistungen im Finanzbereich suchte Jack Macholl eine neue berufliche Herausforderung. Hier werden seine Absichten und Qualifikationen auf klare, humorvolle und dabei bescheidene Art dargestellt.* ▲ *Après 14 années consacrées au marketing de services financiers, Jack Macholl cherchait un nouveau défi professionnel à relever. Ses intentions et qualités sont présentées ici sans détour, avec modestie et beaucoup d'humour.*

PAGE 42, #44 ART DIRECTOR/DESIGNER: *Marion English* AGENCY: *Slaughter-Hanson* COPYWRITER: *David Williams* CLIENT: *Amsouth Bank* COUNTRY: *USA* ■ *This brochure was designed as one of a series of handmade books dealing with the "relationship teams" theme. Since the client requested an elegant gift to send to corporate clients, it was important that the piece be unique.* ● *Eine von mehreren handgemachten Broschüren, in denen es um die Teamarbeit innerhalb einer Bank geht. Da sie an die Kunden der Bank verschickt werden sollte, war es wichtig, dass die Broschüre einzigartig wirkte.* ▲ *Cette brochure fait partie d'une série de publications réalisées à la main et consacrées à l'esprit d'équipe. Le client désirait offrir un cadeau élégant aux clients de la banque. Aussi était-il important que chaque pièce ait l'air unique.*

PAGE 42, #45 ART DIRECTOR: *Gerhard Schuschkleb* DESIGNER: *Brigitte Vegelahn* PHOTOGRAPHER: *Herwig Seemann* COPYWRITERS: *Peter Hauser, Gerhard Märtterer* DESIGNER: *Brigitte Vegelahn* AGENCY/CLIENT: *Märtterer + Schuschkleb GmbH* COUNTRY: *Germany* ■ *This self-promotional brochure was created for an advertising agency.* ● *Eigenwerbung einer Werbeagentur.* ▲ *Brochure autopromotionnelle d'une agence de publicité.*

PAGE 42, #46 ART DIRECTOR/DESIGNER: *Horacio Cobos* AGENCY: *RBMM/The Richards Group* COPYWRITER: *Mark Dunn* CLIENT: *Azrock Tile Co.* TYPEFACE: *Goudy, Futura* PRINTER: *Heritage Press* COUNTRY: *USA* ■ *This brochure introduces a new line of tile.* ● *In dieser Broschüre wird eine neue Linie von Kacheln vorgestellt.* ▲ *Cette borchure présente une nouvelle ligne de carrelages.*

PAGE 42, #47 ART DIRECTOR: *Louis Brunelle* DESIGNERS: *Louis Brunelle, Denis Saint-Pierre* PHOTOGRAPHER: *Various* COPYWRITER: *Alain Benoit* AGENCY/CLIENT: *Parallèle Communication-Design* COUNTRY: *Canada* ■ *This self-promotional brochure highlights the company's mission and covers its projects in all aspects of visual communication.* ● *In dieser Eigenwerbungsbroschüre werden die Tätigkeit der Design-Firma und ihre Projekte in allen Bereichen der visuellen Kommunikation vorgestellt.* ▲ *Cette brochure autopromotionnelle met au premier plan les activités de la société et ses projets dans tous les domaines de la communication visuelle.*

PAGE 43, #48-49 ART DIRECTORS/ILLUSTRATORS/COPYWRITERS: *Peter Grundy, Tilly Northedge* DESIGNER: *Peter Grundy* AGENCY/CLIENT: *Grundy & Northedge* COUNTRY: *England* ■ *This brochure was designed to promote the design and illustration of Peter Grundy and Tilly Northedge.* ● *Graphische Gestaltung und Illustration von Peter Grundy und Tilly Northedge, vorgestellt in einer Eigenwerbungsbroschüre.* ▲ *Cette brochure a été conçue dans le but de promouvoir le design et l'illustration de Peter Grundy et Tilly Northedge.*

PAGE 43, #50 ART DIRECTOR: *Michelle Larson* DESIGNER: *Tamra Schumacher-Dorsey* AGENCY/CLIENT: *Larson Design* COUNTRY: *USA* ■ *This "We have a multiple personality disorder" self-promotional brochure was designed to attract new clients.* ● *Diese Eigenwerbungsbroschüre eines Graphikstudios unter dem Motto «Wir haben eine*

Persönlichkeitsspaltung» wirbt um neue Kunden. ▲ Cette brochure autopromotionnelle d'une agence de graphisme avec pour devise «Nous avons des troubles multiples de la personnalité» a été conçue pour attirer de nouveaux clients.

PAGE 43, #51 ART DIRECTOR: *Jon Henderson* DESIGNERS: *Jui Ishida, Jackson Wang* ILLUSTRATOR: *Jui Ishida* AGENCY/CLIENT: *Hallmark Cards, Inc.* COUNTRY: *USA* ■ This program guide for a creative leadership conference includes conference notes, schedule and biographies. ● Programm für eine Tagung zum Thema kreative Führung. Neben Informationen und Zeitplan enthält es auch Biographien. ▲ Ce programme d'une conférence consacrée à la direction créative contient des informations, l'ordre du jour ainsi que des biographies.

PAGE 43, #52 ART DIRECTOR: *Stefan Sagmeister* DESIGNERS: *Stefan Sagmeister, Eric Zim* AGENCY: *Sagmeister Inc.* PHOTOGRAPHER: *Tom Schierlitz* COPYWRITER/CLIENT: *Stephan Schertler* PRINTER: *Robert Kushner* COUNTRY: *USA* ■ This brochure was designed for a Swiss audio company. The designers developed the concentric and elliptic logo, and then expanded that theme through the photography. The Q-tip glued onto the cover reflects its double use by audio engineers to clean the heads of the recording equipment and the consumer to clean ears in order to appreciate the sound. ● Broschüre für eine Schweizer Audio-Firma. Das konzentrische, elliptische Logo wird als Thema von der Photographie weitergeführt. Der auf den Umschlag geklebte Q-Tip ist eine Anspielung auf seine Verwendung zum Reinigen von Tonköpfen und des menschlichen Ohrs, was zu besserer Tonqualität bzw. deren Wahrnehmung führt. ▲ Brochure produite pour une société suisse spécialisée dans les équipements audio. Le logo concentrique et elliptique est repris en tant que thème dans la photographie. Le coton-tige collé sur la couverture fait allusion à son double emploi, à savoir le nettoyage des oreilles ainsi que celui des écouteurs, ce qui permet, dans les deux cas, de mieux percevoir les sons émis.

PAGE 43, #53 ART DIRECTORS/PHOTOGRAPHERS: *Peter Good, Christopher Hyde* DESIGNER/COPYWRITER: *Christopher Hyde* AGENCY: *Cummings & Good* CLIENT: *Chatham Printing Company, Inc.* COUNTRY: *USA* ■ This brochure, created for a color sheet-fed commercial printer, showcases capabilities on a newly acquired six-color press. ● In dieser Broschüre geht es um die neu erworbene Sechs-Farben-Druckmaschine einer Druckerei. ▲ Cette brochure présente les possibilitiés d'une presse à six couleurs acquise récemment par une imprimerie.

PAGES 44-45, #54, #56 ART DIRECTORS: *Paul Curtin, Keith Andersen* DESIGNER: *Keith Anderson* AGENCY: *Goodby Siverstein & Partners* PHOTOGRAPHER: *Various* COPYWRITER: *Eric Osterhaus* CLIENT: *Bell Helmets* COUNTRY: *USA*

PAGE 44, #55 ART DIRECTORS: *Paul Black, Thomas Vasquez* DESIGNER/ILLUSTRATOR: *Staci Fisher* COPYWRITER: *Jack Wooley* AGENCY: *Squires & Company* CLIENT: *Los Rios Anglers* COUNTRY: *USA* ■ This brochure is an easy-to-use reference guide on how to tie knots while fly fishing. The two-color design was produced economically and at a size that would fit in a fly fisherman's vest. ● Ein zweifarbig gedrucktes Instruktionsbüchlein für das Binden von Knoten beim Fliegenfischen, das klein genug ist, um in die Westentasche des Anglers zu passen. ▲ Petit manuel imprimé en deux couleurs sur la manière de nouer des nœuds lors de la pêche à la mouche. Grâce à son format, il se glisse aisément dans une poche de gilet.

PAGE 46, #57 ART DIRECTOR/DESIGNER: *Haruki Mori* AGENCY: *Azone + Associates* CLIENT: *Bin Ofusa* PHOTOGRAPHER: *Yoshio Kashiwaga* COPYWRITER: *Bin Ofusa* PRINTER: *Coray Corporation* ■ This book celebrates a hair designer's tenth year in business. The title "SO" means "thoughts" or "feelings towards people," reflecting the author's thoughts and gratitude. The design attempted to describe the hair designer's sincerity. ● Eine Broschüre zum zehnjährigen Jubiläum eines Coiffeurs. Der Titel SO bedeutet «Gedanken» oder «Gefühle für Menschen» und reflektiert damit die Gedanken und Dankbarkeit des Autors. In der Gestaltung der Broschüre sollte die Aufrichtigkeit des Coiffeurs zum Ausdruck kommen. ▲ Livre réalisé pour le dixième anniversaire d'un salon de coiffure. Le titre «SO» signifie «pensées» ou «sentiments envers les autres» et traduit la gratitude de l'auteur. La conception de la brochure devait transmettre la sincérité du coiffeur.

PAGE 46, #58 CREATIVE DIRECTOR: *Tony Donna* ART DIRECTOR: *Alec Vianu* AGENCY: *The Designory, inc.* PHOTOGRAPHERS: *Rick Rusing, Vic Huber* CLIENT: *Leo Burnett USA/Oldsmobile* COUNTRY: *USA*

PAGE 47, #59 ART DIRECTOR: *Michael Vanderbyl* DESIGNERS: *Michael Vanderbyl, Karin Myint* PHOTOGRAPHER: *David Peterson* COPYWRITER: *Penny Benda* AGENCY: *Vanderbyl Design* CLIENT: *Robert Talbott, Inc.* COUNTRY: *USA* ■ One of a series of brochures to promote products and image for a manufacturer of men's furnishings and neckties. ● Eine von mehreren Image-Broschüren mit Produktinformationen für einen Herrenausstatter. ▲ Une des séries de brochures pour la promotion de produits et de l'image de marque d'un fabricant de cravates et d'accessoires pour homme.

PAGE 47, #60 ART DIRECTOR: *Michael Bierut* DESIGNER: *Esther Bridavsky* AGENCY: *Pentagram Design* CLIENT: *Council of Fashion Designers of America* COUNTRY: *USA* ■ This program was designed for a leading US fashion trade association annual awards gala. It featured the pre-determined winners of various awards and served as a souvenir. ● Programm für die jährlich stattfindende Preis-Gala eines führenden Modeverbandes der USA. Es gibt Auskunft über die Gewinner der verschiedenen Preise und dient zudem als Souvenir. ▲ Ce programme a été conçu pour le gala annuel d'une des plus grandes associations professionnelles américaines de mode. Le programme de cet événement présente les gagnants d'un concours et sert de souvenir.

PAGE 48, #61 ART DIRECTOR/DESIGNER: *Michael Bierut* DESIGNER: *Emily Hayes* AGENCY: *Pentagram Design* CLIENT: *Brooklyn Academy of Music* COUNTRY: *USA* ■ This program/brochure was designed for the Brooklyn Academy of Music's Next Wave Festival, an avant garde musical event. Type is partially concealed by the stripes to suggest something "coming over the horizon," a visual metaphor for the festival's focus on emerging talents. ● Die Broschüre enthält das Programm eines Avantgarde-Musikfestivals der Musikakademie von Brooklyn. Die teilweise durch Streifen verdeckte Schrift soll andeuten, dass etwas «am Horizont auftaucht», eine visuelle Metapher für das Anliegen des Festivals, junge, aufstrebende Talente zu fördern. ▲ Programme pour le prochain festival Wave de l'Académie de Musique de Brooklyn, un spectacle musical d'avant-garde. Les caractères sont en partie cachés par des lignes pour suggérer que quelque chose «pointe à l'horizon», une métaphore visuelle sur le point central du festival portant sur les nouveaux talents.

PAGE 48, #62 ART DIRECTOR/DESIGNER/ILLUSTRATOR/CLIENT: *João Machado* COUNTRY: *Portugal* ■ This brochure showcases the illustrator's recent posters. ● In dieser Broschüre werden die neusten Plakate des Illustrators vorgestellt. ▲ Cette brochure montre les affiches les plus récentes de l'illustrateur.

PAGE 48, #63 ART DIRECTOR: *Bernice A. Thieblot* DESIGNER: *Claude Skelton* ILLUSTRATOR: *Ward Schumaker* COPYWRITER: *Linda Thorne* AGENCY: *The North Charles Street Design Organization* CLIENT: *The University of Missouri-Columbia* COUNTRY: *USA* ■ This brochure was designed to create a distinct image of the university while conveying the information necessary to generate applications from prospective undergraduates. ● Bei dieser Broschüre ging es darum, der Universität ein prägnantes Profil zu verleihen und gleichzeitig junge Leute für das Studienprogramm zu interessieren. ▲ Cette brochure a été conçue dans le but de donner une image particulière à l'université et d'attirer de nouveaux étudiants.

PAGE 48, #64 ART DIRECTOR: *Pati Núñez* DESIGNERS: *Pati Núñez, Laura Meseguer* AGENCY/CLIENT: *Estudi Pati Núñez* COUNTRY: *Spain*

PAGE 49, #65 ART DIRECTOR/DESIGNER: *Robert Louey* AGENCY: *Louey/Rubino Design Group, Inc.* PHOTOGRAPHERS/ILLUSTRATORS: *Sydney Cooper, Robert Louey, Steve Lyons* CLIENT: *Lithographix, Hopper Paper Co.* ■ The agency wanted to create a marketing promotion that would generate interest and sales for high-end production techniques and a full range of papers. ● In dieser Broschüre wird ein ganzes Sortiment von Papierqualitäten für anspruchsvolle Drucksachen vorgestellt. ▲ Cette brochure présente différentes qualités de papier destinées à des imprimés high-tech.

PAGE 50, #66 ART DIRECTOR/DESIGNER: *Dan Richards* ILLUSTRATORS: *Dan Richards, Dave Gill* COPYWRITER: *Stanley Hainsworth* AGENCY/CLIENT: *Nike, Inc.* COUNTRY: *USA* ■ *This was an invitation to a media event (held inside a penguin zoo) to introduce Nike's new Storm-F.I.T. fabric.* ● *Einladung zu einem Medien-Anlass in einem Pinguin-Zoo, um einen neuen wetterfesten Stoff von Nike vorzustellen.* ▲ *Invitation à une conférence de presse organisée dans un zoo de pingouins à l'occasion du lancement du nouveau tissu imperméable de Nike.*

PAGE 50, #67 ART DIRECTOR: *Massimo Vignelli* DESIGNERS: *Massimo Vignelli, Dani Piderman* PHOTOGRAPHERS: *Luca Vignelli (portrait), J.P. Luthy (watches)* AGENCY: *Vignelli Associates* CLIENT: *Pierre Junod Watches* COUNTRY: *Switzerland* ■ *This brochure publicized a new watch, "Halo," with interchangeable colored bezels designed by Lella and Massimo Vignelli.* ● *Hier wird die neue Uhr «Halo» vorgestellt. Sie wurde von Lella und Massimo Vignelli aus New York entworfen und hat austauschbare, farbige Fassungen.* ▲ *Cette brochure présente la nouvelle montre «Halo» à monture interchangeable, conçue par Lella et Massimo Vignelli.*

PAGE 51, #68 ART DIRECTOR: *Gerard Boissons* DESIGNER: *Philippe Saglio* PHOTOGRAPHER: *Phillipe Exbrayat* COPYWRITER: *Graphi Imprimeur* CLIENT: *Forge de Laguiole*

PAGE 52, #69 ART DIRECTOR: *Steve Liska* DESIGNER: *Kim Fry* PHOTOGRAPHER: *Steve Grubman* AGENCY: *Liska & Associates* CLIENT: *Steve Grubman Photography* COUNTRY: *USA* ■ *This brochure showcases the photographer's specialty, animal photography.* ● *Hier geht es um das Spezialgebiet des Photographen, die Tierphotographie.* ▲ *Cette brochure montre la spécialisation du photographe, à savoir la photographie animalière.*

PAGE 52, #70 ART DIRECTOR/DESIGNER: *Neil Powell* AGENCY: *Duffy Design* PHOTOGRAPHERS: *Mark La Favor, Hugh Kretschmer* COPYWRITER: *John Jarvis* CLIENT: *The Wieland Funiture Company* COUNTRY: *USA* ■ *Long known for their products targeted at the healthcare industry, the client desired to move into the architectural and design arena without disenfranchising their current clients. This capabilities brochure infused the client's manufacturing capabilities with their business philosophies.* ● *Der Auftraggeber, bekannt für seine Möbel für das Gesundheitswesen, wollte in den Bereich Architektur und Design vordringen, ohne seine bisherigen Abnehmer zu verunsichern. Bei der Broschüre ging es um eine Darstellung der Firmentätigkeit, der Herstellungskapazität und der Geschäftspolitik.* ▲ *Le client, connu pour ses meubles destinés au secteur de la santé, voulait faire une percée dans les domaines du design et de l'architecture sans inquiéter pour autant ses anciens clients. L'objectif était de présenter les activités de la société, sa capacité productrice et sa philosophie.*

PAGE 53, #71 ART DIRECTOR: *Joe Duffy* DESIGNERS: *Neil Powell, Kobe, Dan Olson* AGENCY/CLIENT: *Duffy Design* COPYWRITER: *John Jarvis* PRINTER: *Heartland Graphics* COUNTRY: *USA* ■ *This brochure features company history, philosophy, and design work through case histories. The looseleaf pages are bound into a cover so the book can be tailored for a specific prospect's request or updated with new work printed on additional pages.* ● *Die Broschüre befasst sich mit der Geschichte, Philosophie und den gestalterischen Arbeiten der Firma anhand von Fallbeispielen. Die Broschüre lässt sich dank des Heftsystems beliebig ergänzen bzw. auf besondere Bedürfnisse ausrichten.* ▲ *Cette brochure présente l'histoire de la société, sa philosophie et une sélection de ses travaux conceptuels. Conçue selon un système de feuilles mobiles, elle peut être complétée ou modifiée.*

PAGE 54, #72 ART DIRECTOR: *Bridget de Socio* PHOTOGRAPHER: *Noel Allum* COPYWRITERS: *Jacqueline Yoakum, Eldon Wong* AGENCY: *Socio X* CLIENT: *Robert Schreiber* COUNTRY: *USA* ■ *Proposal for a centennial exhibition.* ● *Vorschlag für eine Hundertjahres-Ausstellung.* ▲ *Proposition pour une exposition centenaire.*

PAGE 54, #73 ART DIRECTOR: *Torbjörn Lenskog* DESIGNERS: *Torbjörn Lenskog, Anna Svanberg Lenskog* AGENCY: *Torbjörn Lenskog AB* CLIENT: *Beckmans School of Design* COUNTRY: *Sweden* ■ *This brochure for a school of design serves as an information piece for prospective students, politicians, sponsors, and media.* ● *Diese Broschüre für eine Kunstschule dient zur Information von zukünftigen Studenten sowie von Politikern, Sponsoren und Medien.* ▲ *Cette brochure informative sur une école de design s'adresse aux étudiants potentiels, aux politiques, aux sponsors et aux médias.*

PAGE 55, #74 CREATIVE DIRECTOR: *Joe Schovitz* ART DIRECTOR/ILLUSTRATOR: *Matt Cave* DESIGNERS: *Siobhan L. Elms, Andre Seibel* PHOTOGRAPHER: *Thompson & Thompson* AGENCY: *Reed and Steven* CLIENT: *The Art Institute of Fort Lauderdale* COUNTRY: *USA* ■ *This brochure was created to excite college prospects about attending the school through a "We can take your passion and make it your career" approach. It was also designed to speak to their individual creativity in their chosen field.* ● *«Wir können aus einer Leidenschaft eine Karriere machen» ist das Motto einer Kunstschule, die mit dieser Broschüre um Schüler wirbt. Gleichzeitig werden die Begabungen in den verschiedenen Studienbereichen angesprochen.* ▲ *«De votre passion, nous ferons un métier», telle est la devise d'une école d'arts qui tente ainsi de recruter de nouveaux étudiants. Cette brochure met également l'accent sur la créativité individuelle dans les différentes disciplines à choix.*

PAGE 55, #75 ART DIRECTOR: *Kit Hinrichs* DESIGNER: *Anne Culbertson* AGENCY: *Pentagram Design* CLIENT: *University of Southern California* COUNTRY: *USA* ■ *Publication for prospective students of the University of Southern California.* ● *An zukünftige Studenten gerichtete Informationsbroschüre der University of Southern California.* ▲ *Publication informative destinée aux futurs étudiants de l'University of Southern California.*

PAGE 56, #76 ART DIRECTOR: *Zempaku Suzuki* DESIGNER: *Aritomo Ueno* PHOTOGRAPHER: *Kim Stringfellow* AGENCY: *B-BI Studio Inc.* CLIENT: *Funky Jam Corporation* COUNTRY: *USA* ■ *This calendar was produced for a fan club for Toshinobu Kubota, a Japanese pop vocalist.* ● *Kalender für einen Fan Club des japanischen Popsängers, Toshinobu Kubota* ▲ *Calendrier réalisé pour un fan club de Toshinobu Kubota, un chanteur pop japonais.*

PAGE 56, #77 CREATIVE DIRECTOR: *Serge Lutens* ART DIRECTOR/DESIGNER: *Adlai Stock* AGENCY: *Shiseido International Marketing Creative Group* PHOTOGRAPHER: *Serge Lutens* CLIENT: *Shiseido Co. Ltd.* COUNTRY: *USA*

PAGE 57, #78 ART DIRECTOR/DESIGNER: *Egon Dernbecher* AGENCY/CLIENT: *Atelier Dernbecher Werbung* PAPER: *Chromolux* TYPEFACE: *Helvetica* COUNTRY: *Germany*

PAGE 57, #79 ART DIRECTORS: *Tim Hale, Stephen Zhang* DESIGNER: *Stephen Zhang* AGENCY: *Fossil Design Studio* CLIENT: *Fossil, Inc.* PAPER: *French Paper* TYPEFACE: *Eagle, Agency, Bank Gothic, custom* PRINTER: *Steward Printing* COUNTRY: *USA* ■ *This design seeks to make the brand promotional calendar fun and functional through the typographic treatments of the holidays, moon phases and the end of the previous month and the beginning of the next month.* ● *Mit Hilfe spezieller typographischer Gestaltung der Feiertage, Mondphasen und Monatsende bzw. Monatsanfang sollte dieser Werbekalender nicht nur funktionell sein, sondern auch Spass machen.* ▲ *La typographie spéciale utilisée pour les jours fériés, les phases de lune, les débuts et fins de mois devait rendre ce catalogue publicitaire à la fois fonctionnel et amusant.*

PAGE 58, #80 ART DIRECTOR/DESIGNER/ILLUSTRATOR: *Ralf Klenner* AGENCY: *Ralf Klenner Illustration* PHOTO ASSISTANCE: *Dino Eisele* CLIENT: *Diploti Calendar* TYPEFACE: *Franklin Gothic* ■ *This calendar was created to distinguish a daughter company of KLM airlines, based in the Netherlands, from other airlines. The images are of turbines, the airline check, and a pilot.* ● *Kalender als Werbung für eine Tochtergesellschaft der niederländischen Fluggesellschaft KLM. Gezeigt sind Turbinen, eine Flugzeugwartung und ein Pilot.* ▲ *Calendrier publicitaire pour une filiale de la compagnie aérienne néerlandaise KLM. Les images montrent des turbines, la maintenance d'un avion et un pilote.*

PAGE 59, #81 ART DIRECTOR/AGENCY: *Dan Reisinger* CLIENT: *Iscar Hardmetal Tools Company Ltd.* PAPER: *Tako Superfine 300 gr.* TYPEFACE: *Helvetica, Kuenstlerscript* PRINTER: *Ideal Printing* COUNTRY: *Israel*

PAGE 60-61, #82 ART DIRECTOR/DESIGNER: *Tamotsu Yagi* AGENCY: *Tamotsu Yagi Design* COUNTRY: *USA* ■ *This installation was presented in an independent gallery within the San Francisco Museum of Modern Art. The long and narrow configuration of the gallery, two entry points to the space, and the three-dimensional nature of the many items exhibited required special attention to overall layout and fixture design. Individual exhibits, grouped according to project, were installed to unfold like a book, presenting each as if it were a chapter in the designer's career. Each exhibit item was presented in a manner consistent with its original use. For example, a book design unfolded across one wall like an accordion, opening each page for viewing.* ● *Diese Installation wurde in einer unabhängigen Galerie innerhalb des San Francisco Museum of Modern Art gezeigt. Der lange, schmale Raum mit zwei Zugängen und die vielen dreidimensionalen Ausstellungsstücke verlangten besondere Sorgfalt in der Planung der Anordung und Ausstellungshilfen. Einzelne, projektbezogene Exponate lassen sich wie ein Buch durchblättern, wobei jedes wie ein Kapitel in der Karriere des Designers dargestellt wird. In jedem Fall wurde bei der Präsentation der ursprüngliche Zweck des Exponats berücksichtig, z.B. ist ein Buch wie ein Leporello über eine Wand gezogen, so dass jede Seite angeschaut werden kann.* ▲ *Cette installation a été exposée dans une galerie indépendante du San Francisco Museum of Modern Art. La longue pièce étroite avec deux accès et les nombreux éléments d'exposition tridimensionnels ont exigé une attention particulière dans la planification de l'espace et des supports d'exposition. Certains des objets exposés peuvent être feuilletés comme un livre et constituent à chaque fois un chapitre de la vie de l'artiste. L'usage original de chaque objet a été respecté; ainsi, un livre a été déplié sur un mur comme un accordéon afin que chaque page puisse être regardée.*

PAGE 62, #83 ART DIRECTORS/DESIGNERS: *Tom Antista, Thomas Fairclough* AGENCY: *Antista Fairclough Design* CLIENT: *Ashland Petroleum* COUNTRY: *USA* ■ *This retail identity was developed for the client's brand gas stations and convenience stores. The project consisted of an entire identity change; the exterior identity was redesigned with a new color scheme, canopy design, gas island structure, and proprietary shaped trade sign.* ● *Dieses Projekt umfasste die Änderung des gesamten Erscheinungsbildes der Tankstellen und Kioske des Kunden: Ein neues Farbsystem, Gestaltung der Überdachung, Struktur des Zapfsäulenbereiches und das Markenzeichen.* ▲ *Objectif de ce projet: un changement global de l'identité des stations-service et magasins du client, à savoir un nouveau système de couleurs pour l'identité extérieure, un relookage de la toiture, une nouvelle structure autour des pompes à esssence et une nouvelle enseigne.*

PAGE 63, #84 ART DIRECTOR/DESIGNER: *Earl Gee* AGENCY: *Gee + Chung Design* CLIENT: *IBM Corporation* TYPEFACE: *Bodoni, Univers Medium Extra Condensed* COUNTRY: *USA* ■ *This form was created for the industry's first software vending machine, which enables consumers to demonstrate, place orders and take delivery directly from the kiosk. Daily satellite transmission feeds ensure that the latest version is always available. To encourage acceptance of this new method of shopping for software, the kiosk needed to be eye-catching, and state of the art, yet approachable and easy to use. The form needed to enclose IBM's existing ATM style kiosk which held a touch screen monitor, CPU and receipt printer, as well as interchangeable graphics and signage. Space station and satellite metaphors were used to create a striking, sculptural in-store presence.* ● *Hier ging es um die Schaffung einer einzigartigen Form für den ersten Verkaufsautomaten für Software, der dank Satelliten-Einspeisung immer die neuste Version enthält und dem Kunden die Möglichkeit gibt, das Programm zu testen und die Bestellung direkt einzugeben. Um diese neue Einkaufsmethode für Software populär zu machen, musste der Kiosk attraktiv und zukunftorientiert, dem Zeitgeschmack entsprechen und dabei einladend und anwenderfreundlich wirken. IBMs ATM-Kiosk mit einem Touch Screen Monitor musste in die Form integriert werden sowie CPU (Central Processing Unit) und Drucker.* ▲ *Il s'agissait de créer une forme unique pour le premier distributeur de logiciels qui contient toujours la dernière version grâce à un approvisionnement effectué par transmisson satellite. Les clients peuvent tester les logiciels, passer commande et retirer leur achat directement du distributeur. Afin de rendre cette nouvelle méthode de vente populaire, il fallait que l'installation soit attrayante, futuriste, conviviale et facile à utiliser. L'installation ATM d'IBM équipé d'un Touch*

Screen Monitor, une unité centrale de traitement et une imprimante ont été intégrées à l'installation.

PAGES 64-65, #85 ART DIRECTOR: *Mitchell Mauk* DESIGNERS: *Mitchell Mauk, Adam Brodsley* AGENCY: *Mauk Design* CLIENT: *Duncan Aviation* COUNTRY: *USA* ■ *This 30 foot by 40 foot exhibit was designed for a full-service business jet maintenance company for use at an industry convention. Because the client and its competitors utilize similar facilities and equipment, the emphasis in this exhibit was placed on the client's employees. The exhibit tower featured a photo wall of every employee. The components of the exhibit contain references to flying and aviation engineering. The ten display cases show items representing each of the company's ten divisions.* ● *Ein ca. 11x13m grosses Ausstellungsstück, das von einem Full-Service-Wartungsbetrieb für Düsenflugzeuge bei einer Industrietagung verwendet werden sollte. Da die Firma ähnliche Anlagen und Geräte wie die Konkurrenz benutzt, waren die Mitarbeiter das zentrale Thema. Es wurde eine Photowand mit Porträts der Mitarbeiter montiert, während andere Teile der Ausstattung sich auf das Fliegen und die Luftfahrttechnik beziehen. Die zehn Display-Boxen zeigen Gegenstände, die für jede der zehn Abteilungen der Firma typisch sind.* ▲ *Cet objet d'exposition de 11x13m a été conçu dans l'optique d'un congrès industriel pour une société s'occupant de la maintenance d'avions à réaction. La société utilisant des installations et des équipements similaires à ceux de la concurrence, l'accent a été mis sur le personnel. Un mur de photographies présentant les portraits des collaborateurs de la société a été monté, tandis que d'autres objets exposés ont trait au vol et à l'aérotechnique. Les dix boîtes en aluminium présentent des objets typiques inhérents à chacun des dix départements de la société.*

PAGE 66-67, #86 CREATIVE DIRECTORS: *Toshio Yamagita, Serge Lutens* ART DIRECTORS: *Aoshi Kudo, Takayasu Yamada* DESIGNER: *Takayasu Yamada* AGENCY: *Shiseido Co. Ltd.* ■ *Identity created for gift boxes and bags for a cosmetics company.* ● *Geschenkschachteln und Taschen für den Kosmetikkonzern Shiseido.* ▲ *Boîtes-cadeau et sacs Shiseido.*

PAGE 68, #87 ART DIRECTOR/DESIGNER: *Ken Ambrosini* AGENCY: *Design Partnership* CLIENT: *METRO* COUNTRY: *USA* ■ *This identity was created for a regional governmental organization addressing and legislating environmental issues. The organization embarked on a program called "Resourceful Renovation." This kiosk serves as a vehicle to educate and demonstrate earth-wise consciousness as well as utilizing recycleable materials.* ● *Erscheinungsbild für eine regionale Regierungsstelle, die sich mit Umweltgesetzen befasst und ein Programm mit dem Titel «Einfallsreiche Renovation» lancierte. Der Kiosk dient zur Informion und Förderung des Umweltbewusstseins im Hinblick auf die Wiederverwertung von Materialien.* ▲ *Identité visuelle pour une organisation gouvernementale régionale chargée de traiter des problèmes ayant trait à la protection de l'environnement. L'organisation a lancé un programme intitulé «Rénovation ingénieuse». L'installation électronique a pour but de sensibiliser les gens aux problèmes environnementaux et de les encourager à adopter un comportement écologique en recyclant, par exemple, des matériaux utilisés.*

PAGE 69, #88 ART DIRECTOR/DESIGNER: *John Ball* AGENCY: *Mires Design, Inc.* CLIENT: *California Center for the Arts* TYPEFACE: *Syntax* PRINTER: *Gordon Screen Printing* COUNTRY: *USA* ■ *These banners were created for the entrance courtyard of the California Center for the Arts. The logo was printed in four colors and typography was used in four different color combinations for an eclectic, but unified look.* ● *Diese Fahnen sind für den Vorhof des California Center for the Arts bestimmt. Das Logo wurde in vier Farben gedruckt, und die Schrift wurde in vier verschiedenen Farbkombinationen verwendet, um einen vielseitigen und doch einheitlichen Auftritt zu erzielen.* ▲ *Ces drapeaux sont destinés à la cour d'entrée du California Center of the Arts. Le logo a été imprimé en quadrichromie, et la typographie présente quatre combinaisons de couleurs pour varier la présentation tout en créant un effet unitaire.*

PAGES 70-71, #89 ART DIRECTORS/DESIGNERS: *Julie Henson, Ann Morton* AGENCY: *Thinking Caps* CLIENT: *Giant Industries* TYPEFACE: *Futura Extra Bold, Garamond Condensed Italic* COUNTRY: *USA* ■ *This design represents an updated interior and* exterior image for the client's new and existing retail locations. A bold and friendly overall thematic concept was incorporated into the interior wall and ceiling graphics, and a new color palette was developed, as were specified tile patterns for the walls and flooring. Exterior graphics and signage package were developed to coincide with the new interior and the new color palette implemented through tile patterns and paint on store and canopies. • Gestaltung der Innen- und Aussenräume von Giants neuen und existierenden Läden. Innenwände und Decken wurden im Rahmen des thematischen Konzepts mit ausdrucksvoller, freundlicher Graphik versehen, es wurde eine neue Farbpalette entwickelt sowie auch Kachelmuster für Wände und Fussböden. Die Graphik und Beschriftung für den Aussenbereich wurden auf die neue Innenraumgestaltung abgestimmt und die Farbpalette von Kacheln, Anstrich und Markisen aufgenommen. ▲ Relookage intérieur et extérieur des anciens et nouveaux magasins Giants. Dans le cadre d'un concept thématique global, les murs intérieurs et les plafonds ont été pourvus d'un graphisme expressif et accueillant, une nouvelle gamme de coloris a été développée et des motifs inédits de carrelage ont été créés pour les murs et les sols. Le graphisme et les inscriptions extérieurs ont été revus et corrigés de sorte à s'harmoniser avec le concept intérieur, soit en reprenant la même gamme de coloris.

PAGES 72-73, #90 ART DIRECTOR: *Jan Lorenc* DESIGNERS: *Jan Lorenc, Rory Myers, Gary Flesher, Charles Warren* AGENCY: *Lorenc Design* CLIENT: *Georgia-Pacific Corporation* TYPEFACE: *Pin Engleshift, Sabon* COUNTRY: *USA* ■ The objective of this project was to communicate the complexity of the client's sales and distribution network. To do this, the story was broken into six individual segments: the vision of the client and its distribution division, the sales process, the logistics and distribution process, the product collage as focus to the sales center, the distribution division and product development timeline, and the customers and customers' end-user products. • Thema war die Komplexität des Verkaufs- und Vertriebsnetzes der Georgia Pacific Corporation. Dabei ging es um sechs einzelne Segmente: Die Vision der Firma und ihrer Vertriebsabteilung; der Verkaufsprozess, Logistik und Vertriebsablauf; Produktpalette als Mittelpunkt des Verkaufszentrums; Vertriebsabteilung und zeitliche Abwicklung der Produktentwicklung; die Kunden und ihre Produkte für den Endverbraucher. ▲ L'objectif était de présenter simplement la complexité du réseau de vente et de distribution de la Georgia Pacific Corporation. Le concept s'articule autour de six segments individuels: la vision du client et celle de son service de distribution; le processus de vente et de distribution, la logistique; la ligne de produits au cœur du centre commercial; le service de distribution et le développement de produits dans le temps; les clients et les produits finaux.

PAGE 74, #91 ART DIRECTOR: *BJ Krivanek* DESIGNER: *Joel Breaux* TECHNICAL ASSISTANT: *Martha Najera* AGENCY: *BJ Krivanek Art & Design* PHOTOGRAPHER: *Jeff Kurt Petersen* FABRICATOR: *Peter Carlson Enterprises* COUNTRY: *USA* ■ This environmental design program at a large homeless shelter was comprised of two related elements: "The Orientation Rotunda" and "Electronic Statement" which were created to dignify and empower a largely invisible community. • Die Gestaltung des äusseren Umfelds eines grossen Obdachlosenheims bestand aus zwei dreidimensionalen Elementen, die geschaffen wurden, um den mehrheitlich unsichtbaren Bewohnern Würde und Selbständigkeit zu geben. ▲ Aménagement de l'espace extérieur d'un grand centre d'accueil pour sans-abri comprenant deux éléments tridimensionnels. Ces deux objets ont été créés dans le but de conférer indépendance et dignité aux pensionnaires du centre.

PAGE 75, #92 ART DIRECTOR/DESIGNER/ILLUSTRATOR: *Heward Jue* AGENCY: *Hewardesign* COPYWRITER: *Jonathan Steckler* CLIENT: *Java The Hut* TYPEFACE: *Bank Gothic* COUNTRY: *USA* ■ The challenge was to create a logo and identity system for a coffee and espresso bar with as much wit and spunk as its given name "Java The Hut." Since the name conjured up images of a creature, the designer played around with coffee beans to create a face for this creature, and it seemed to almost instantly design itself. • Hier ging es um die Schaffung eines Logos bzw. Erscheinungsbildes, das soviel Witz und Mut haben sollte wie der Name der Kaffee-Bar «Java The Hut». Weil der Name irgendwie an eine Kreatur denken lässt, experimentierte der Designer mit Kaffeebohnen, um dieser Kreatur ein Gesicht zu verleihen, das

dann fast wie von selbst entstand. ▲ Il s'agissait de créer un logo/système d'identité aussi audacieux et humoristique que le nom du café «Java The Hut», évoquant une sorte de créature. Le concepteur a travaillé avec des grains de café pour donner un visage à cette créature.

PAGE 75, #93 ART DIRECTORS: *Grenville Main, Diana Bidwill* DESIGNER: *Diana Bidwill* AGENCY: *BNA Design Limited* ILLUSTRATORS: *Diana Bidwill, John Moore* CLIENT: *Hoyts NZ Limited* TYPEFACE: *Matrix, Linoscript, Goudy* COUNTRY: *New Zealand* ■ This identity was created for a cafe and bar in a cinema complex. It utilizes 'M' from the name, and plays on the waiter icon to convey personality. The logo had variations of waiter, wine-waiter and chef. • Logo für einen Café-Barbetrieb. Das M des Names wurde mit verschiedenen Figuren kombiniert: Kellner, Sommelier oder Koch. ▲ Identité visuelle créée pour un bar-café. Le graphisme combine un "M", initiale du nom de l'établissement, et joue avec le pictogramme du serveur; il est décliné en fonction de l'activité: le serveur, le sommelier, le cuisinier.

PAGE 76, #94 ART DIRECTOR: *Michael Bierut* DESIGNERS: *Michael Bierut, Tracey Cameron* AGENCY: *Pentagram Design* PHOTOGRAPHERS: *Judy Olausen, Michael O'Neill (children's hands), Don F. Wong (museum)* CLIENT: *Minnesota Children's Museum* COUNTRY: *USA* ■ The logo, printed materials, identification, and directional sign sytems were created for a children's museum. Playing off the museum's dedication to "hands-on" activities, the agency used photogaphs of children's hands throughout the building. • Logo, Drucksachen, und Leitsystem für ein Kindermuseum. Die Aufnahmen von Kinderbänden, die im ganzen Gebäude eingesetzt wurden, sind eine Anspielung auf das Konzept des Museums: hier dürfen Kinder die Dinge mit den Händen berühren. ▲ Logo, imprimés et signalétique d'un musée pour enfants. Les photographies de mains d'enfants présentes dans tout le bâtiment rappellent le concept du musée: ici, les enfants peuvent toucher les objets avec leurs mains.

PAGE 77, #95 ART DIRECTOR: *Sally Morrow* DESIGNERS: *Sally Morrow, Donjiro Ban* PROJECT MANAGER: *Brad Berman* AGENCY: *Sandstrom Design* CLIENT: *Reebok International Ltd.* COUNTRY: *USA*

PAGE 78, #96 ART DIRECTOR/DESIGNER: *Max Robinson* AGENCY: *Max Robinson & Associates* ILLUSTRATORS: *Bruce Stewart, Lyell Down, Max Robinson* CLIENT: *Reserve Bank of Australia* PAPER: *Plastic Polymer Substrate* TYPEFACE: *Handlettering (script), Helvetica (numerals)* PRINTER: *Note printing branch–Reserve Bank of Australia* COUNTRY: *Australia* ■ The task was to make plastic bank notes acceptable to a suspicious Australian public. Ink technology gave the plastic note the 'feel' of paper. Featuring much loved-literary and artistic identities ensured the popularity of this $10 note. • Die Aufgabe bestand darin, die skeptische australische Bevölkerung von Plastikbanknoten zu überzeugen. Dank einer speziellen Druckfarbentechnik fühlt sich die Plastiknote wie Papier an. Die Porträts beliebter Persönlichkeiten aus Literatur und Kunst sorgen für die Popularität dieser 10-Dollar-Note. ▲ L'objectif était de convaincre les Australiens, plutôt sceptiques, d'utiliser des billets de banque en plastique. Grâce à une encre d'impression spéciale, ces billets donnent l'impression d'être en papier. L'effigie de personnalités appréciées du monde des arts et de la littérature rendirent ces billets de 10 dollars fort populaires.

PAGE 78, #97 ART DIRECTOR: *Bart de Groot* DESIGNER: *Hans Leydekkers* AGENCY: *Vorm Vijf Ontwerpteam bNO* CLIENT: *Proost en Brandt* PRINTER: *Drukkery Ando* ■ The client wanted a fake bank note as a gimmick; it needed to look real enough to the people who received it. The agency looked at a lot of bank notes and tried to combine technique with aesthetics while still maintaining a modern feel. • Der Auftraggeber wollte eine falsche Banknote als Gag, aber sie sollte dabei auch viel von einer richtigen Banknote haben. Das Resultat ist eine Kombination der Wesensmerkmale von traditionellen Banknoten und moderner Interpretation. ▲ Le client voulait un faux billet de banque pour faire un gag sans que ce dernier ne ressemble trop à une contrefaçon. L'agence a combiné technique et aspect esthétique tout en apportant une touche moderne.

PAGE 79, #98 ART DIRECTOR/DESIGNER/ILLUSTRATOR: *Marty Smith* AGENCY/CLIENT: *Marty Smith Technical Illustration* COUNTRY: *USA* ■ Promotional piece of a spectrometer.

● *Ein Spektrometer als Promotion für einen technischen Zeichner.* ▲ *Spectromètre promotionnel pour un dessinateur technique.*

PAGE 80, #99 ART DIRECTOR/DESIGNER: *Ronnie Peters* AGENCY: *Infogram* CLIENT: *Siemens Nixdorf* COUNTRY: *Germany* ■ *This touch-screen information kiosk was designed for German embassies and public spaces for visitors to Germany. By touching the glass screen surface, the user can navigate and retrieve information about Germany.* ● *Dieser Touch-Screen-Informationskiosk wurde für deutsche Botschaften entworfen sowie für öffentliche Räume in Deutschland, wo Touristen sie benutzen können. Durch Berühren der Glasoberfläche des Bildschirms kann der Anwender navigieren und Informationen über Deutschland abrufen.* ▲ *Destinée aux ambassades allemandes, cette installation électronique à écran sensoriel a été réalisée à l'attention des touristes. En touchant la surface de l'écran, l'utilisateur peut sélectionner les informations requises sur l'Allemagne.*

PAGE 81, #100 ART DIRECTOR: *CJ Thompson* DESIGNER: *Jeff West* AGENCY: *Gordon Bailey & Associates, Inc.* ILLUSTRATOR: *Jeff West* CLIENT: *Penneco Packaging Specialty Products* COUNTRY: *USA* ■ *This diagram demonstrates the variety of uses of plastic wastecan liners in a food service environment. An illustrated "top-off" axiometric perspective of an imaginary restaurant highlights wastecan usage sites.* ● *Das Diagramm stellt die vielseitigen Verwendungsmöglichkeiten von Plastik-Abfallsäcken für die Gastronomie dar. Die axiometrische Darstellung eines fiktiven Restaurants erlaubt die Darstellung geeigneter Plätze für den Einsatz dieser Säcke.* ▲ *Le diagramme présente les différentes possibilités d'utiliser ces sacs-poubelles en plastique destinés au secteur de la restauration. La représentation axiométrique d'un restaurant fictif montre les divers endroits où ces sacs-poubelles peuvent être placés.*

PAGE 81, #101 ART DIRECTOR/DESIGNER: *Uwe Schramm* DESIGNERS: *Josef Risling, Jackie Helgert, Torsten Krokel* AGENCY: *Schramms, Graphik-Design & Digital Media Art* CLIENT: *Messe Berlin GmbH* COUNTRY: *Germany*

PAGES 82-83, #102 ART DIRECTOR: *Bridget de Socio* DESIGNERS (spreads): *Tracy Anglo (Name that Game), John Olenyik (White Light)* DESIGNERS (covers): *(top left) Lisa Webster, (top right, bottom right) Bridget De Socio, (bottom left) John Olenyik* PHOTOGRAPHERS (spreads): *Judson Baker (Name that Game), Baron Claiborne (White Light)* PHOTOGRAPHERS (covers): *(top left) Torkil Gudnason, (top right) Stephen Sebring, (bottom left) Dah Len, (bottom right) Greg Gorman* DIGITAL TYPE: *Malcolm Turk* COPYWRITER: *Christine Muhlke* PUBLISHER: *PAPER MAGAZINE* PAPER: *Repap* TYPEFACE: *Futura, Stencil* COUNTRY: *USA* ■ *Covers: (top left) This magazine cover was designed for a "cool" summer and features the missionary of hip-bop, jazz, and rap.* ● *Magazinumschlag. Das Thema: ein 'cooler' Sommer in bezug auf Hip-Hop, Jazz und Rap.* ▲ *Couverture de magazine avec pour thème un été «cool» en référence au hip hop, au jazz et au rap.* ■ *(Top right) This cover utilizes playing cards for an issue devoted to games.* ● *Umschlag für eine Ausgabe, deren Thema Spiele sind.* ▲ *Couverture d'une publication ayant pour thème les jeux.* ■ *(Bottom left)This cover for a snowboarding issue features model Tyson and utilizes fire and ice in the logo.* ● *Diese Magazinausgabe ist dem Snowboard gewidmet. Auf dem Umschlag das Modell Tyson.* ▲ *Ce magazine, avec en couverture le modèle Tyson, est consacré au snowboard.* ■ *(Bottom right) This cover was for an autumn issue and utilizes tumbling leaves and fall foliage.* ● *Herbstlaub auf dem Umschlag der Herbstausgabe eines Magazins.* ▲ *Feuillages d'automne pour la couverture du numéro d'automne de ce magazine.*

PAGE 84, #103 ART DIRECTORS: *Mark Porter, Tibor Kalman* PHOTOGRAPHERS: *Miguel Fairbanks (Sports cover), Robert Nichols (Travel cover), Sergio Merli (Ouch/Ahia spread)* EDITOR-IN-CHIEF: *Tibor Kalman* PUBLISHER: *Benetton, COLORS* PAPER: *Alsaprint* TYPEFACE: *Franklin Gothic Condensed, Avenir* PRINTER: *Elcograph*

PAGE 85, #104 ART DIRECTOR: *Fred Woodward* PHOTOGRAPHERS: *(top left; second row, left) Mark Seliger, (top right) Matthew Rolston, (second row, right) Amy Guip, (third row, left) Mark Seliger, (third row, right; bottom row, left) Matt Mahurin, (bottom row, right) Peggy Sirota* PUBLISHER: *Wenner Media/ROLLING STONE*

PAGE 86, #105 ART DIRECTORS: *Carl Lehmann-Haupt, William Van Roden* PHOTOGRAPHER/ILLUSTRATOR: *(top left) Kristine Larsen, (top center) Doug Fitch* MAGAZINE/PUBLISHER: *METROPOLIS* COUNTRY: *USA*

PAGE 86, #106 ART DIRECTOR: *Rolf Müller* DESIGNERS: *Patricia Hepp, Christina Schels (London issue), Oliver Klimpel (Leipzig issue), Rolf Müller, Christina Schels (Moscow issue)* PHOTOGRAPHERS: *Gerhard Westrich (Leipzig issue), Vladimir Chaika, (Moscow issue)* AGENCY: *Büro Rolf Muller* CLIENT: *Heidelberger Drucksmachinen* PRINTER: *Heidelberger Drucksmachinen AG* TYPEFACE: *Univers, Walbaum, Formata* COUNTRY: *Germany* ■ *The purpose was to create an unusual icon for a city's name.* ● *Hier ging es um die Schaffung einer ungewöhnlichen Ikone für den Namen einer Stadt.* ▲ *Il s'agissait de créer une icône inhabituelle pour le nom de cette ville.*

PAGE 87, #107 ART DIRECTOR: *Peter Breul* PHOTOGRAPHERS: *(top left) Susan Lamèr, (top right) Christin Losta, (bottom left) Peter Lindbergh, (bottom right) Sarah Moon* PUBLISHER: *Frankfurter Allgemeine Magazin* COUNTRY: *Germany* ■ *Covers for FAZ MAGAZIN referring to features in their respective issues.* ● *Umschläge des FAZ MAGAZINS, die sich auf Beiträge in den jeweiligen Ausgaben beziehen.* ▲ *Couvertures du FAZ MAGAZIN qui se réfèrent à des thèmes précis abordés dans les numéros respectifs.*

PAGE 88, #108 ART DIRECTOR: *Peter Breul* PHOTOGRAPHERS/ILLUSTRATORS: *(top) Susan Lamèr, (second and fourth) Heinz Edelmann, (bottom) Christin Losta* PUBLISHER: *Frankfurter Allgemeine Magazin* COUNTRY: *Germany* ■ *Cover and spreads from FAZ MAGAZIN.* ● *Umschlag und Doppelseiten aus dem FAZ MAGAZIN.* ▲ *Couverture et doubles pages du FAZ MAGAZIN se référant aux thèmes suivants.*

PAGE 88, #109 ART DIRECTOR/DESIGNER: *Vince Frost* PHOTOGRAPHER: *Various* AGENCY: *Frost Design* CLIENT: *Big Location*

PAGE 89, #110 ART DIRECTOR: *Alan Fletcher* PUBLISHER: *DOMUS* ■ *Covers: (left) There are always two ways of looking at something.* ● *Es gibt immer zwei Arten, die Dinge zu betrachten.* ▲ *Il y a toujours deux façons de considérer les choses.* ■ *(Right) The portrait was made by carefully folding a page that appears in certain issues urging readers to take an annual subscription to the magazine. The caption is "Portrait of a DOMUS Subscriber."* ● *Das Porträt entstand durch sorgfältiges Falten einer Seite, die in bestimmten Ausgaben von DOMUS als Abonnentenwerbung erscheint. Die Legende lautet: »Porträt eines DOMUS-Lesers.«* ▲ *Ce portrait a été obtenu en pliant soigneusement une feuille, laquelle apparaît dans certains numéros de DOMUS pour inciter les gens à souscrire à un abonnement. La légende signifie: «Portrait d'un lecteur de DOMUS».*

PAGE 90, #111 ART DIRECTOR/DESIGNER: *Vince Frost* PHOTOGRAPHER: *Matthew Donaldson* EDITOR: *David Robson* AGENCY: *Frost Design* CLIENT: *Newspaper Publishing PLC* PAPER: *Newsprint* TYPEFACE: *Gill* PRINTER: *Quebecor Printing PLC, Corby* ■ *INDEPENDENT Magazine had lost its particularity and its grip on its readers. The brief was to produce something that sustained the magazine's comittment to intelligence, good writing, good photography, and visual elegance.* ● *INDEPENDENT Magazine hatte mit Image- und Leserschwund zu kämpfen. Bei der Neugestaltung ging es darum, den hohen Anspruch der Zeitschrift in bezug auf Text- und Bildbeiträge sowie ihre hervorragende Präsentation hervorzuheben.* ▲ *INDEPENDENT Magazine devait redorer son image pour reconquérir son lectorat. La nouvelle conception devait répondre aux critères exigeants du magazine, à savoir des articles intelligents et bien rédigés, de belles photographies et une présentation élégante.*

PAGE 90, #112 ART DIRECTOR: *Hans Wolf* DESIGNER: *Bas van der Paardt* PUBLISHER: *BLAD Magazine* PHOTOGRAPHERS: *(left) Boudewijn Smit, (center) Malcolm Venville, (right) Gyro/Steve Grassse* EDITOR: *Ronald Kraayeveld* COPYWRITERS: *(center) Jack Meijers, (right) Gyro/Steve Grasse* CLIENT: *VNU/Admedia bv* PRINTER: *Koninklijke Smeets Offset bv (KSO)* ■ *(center) Cover BLAD 3: 'On expedition,' Glen Baxter, British illustrator and author of comic books, likes to dress up as an army combatant. BLAD had an interview with "The Colonel." The text is a reference to the* 'weird' captions that accompany the illustrator's images: "Suddenly it occured to Baxter that he was supposed to be the cover hero." ● *Umschlag der Zeitschrift* BLAD: *«Auf Expedition». Glen Baxter, britischer Illustrator und Autor von Comics-Büchern, verkleidet sich gerne als Armeeangehöriger.* BLAD *machte ein Interview mit dem "Colonel". Der Text ist eine Anspielung auf die skurrilen Bildlegenden des Illustrators: 'Plötzlich begriff Baxter, dass man ihn zum Titelhelden machen wollte.'* ▲ *Couverture du magazine* BLAD: *«On expedition». Le Britannique Glen Baxter, illustrateur et auteur de bandes dessinées, aime à se déguiser en militaire.* BLAD *a interviewé le «Colonel». Le texte fait allusion aux légendes bizarres de l'illustrateur: «Tout à coup, Baxter comprit qu'on voulait faire de lui le héros de la couverture.»* ■ *(Right) Cover* BLAD 1: "Don't try to define us. We'll define ourselves" is a copy line from a campaign by Gyro, the Philadelphia-based agency. ● *Umschlag der Zeitschrift* BLAD: *«Versuchen Sie nicht, uns zu analysieren. Wir analysieren uns selbst.» Das ist eine Schlagzeile aus einer Kampagne von Gyro, der Agentur aus Philadelphia.* ▲ *Couverture du magazine* BLAD: *«N'essayez pas de nous définir. Nous nous définissons nous-mêmes.» Telle est la devise d'une campagne de Gyro, une agence de Philadelphie.*

PAGE 90, #113 ART DIRECTOR: *René Abbühl* PHOTOGRAPHER: *(left and right) Andy Tan, (center) Marc de Groot* CLIENT: *De Geillustreerde Pers* COUNTRY: *The Netherlands*

PAGE 91, #114 ART DIRECTOR: *René Abbühl* CLIENT: *De Geillustreerde Pers* COUNTRY: *The Netherlands*

PAGE 91, #115 ART DIRECTOR/DESIGNER: *Janet Froelich* PHOTOGRAPHER: *David Seidner ("Optic Verve"), Javier Vallhonrat ("An Upward Spiral"), David Seidner ("Headstrong")* STYLIST: *Franciscus Ankoné* PUBLISHER: *The New York Times Co.* COUNTRY: *USA* ■ *Editorial design for the* NEW YORK TIMES MAGAZINE. ● *Redaktionelle Gestaltung für einen Artikel im* NEW YORK TIMES MAGAZINE. ▲ *Conception rédactionnelle paru dans le* NEW YORK TIMES MAGAZINE.

PAGE 92, #116 ART DIRECTOR: *John Rushworth* DESIGNERS: *John Rushworth, Nick Finney* COPYWRITER: *Paul Drolshagen* AGENCY: *Pentagram Design, Ltd.* CLIENT: *Polaroid UK* COUNTRY: *England*

PAGE 92, #117 CREATIVE DIRECTOR: *Michael Grossman* ART DIRECTOR: *Paul Roelofs* PHOTO EDITOR: *Susan Goldberger* PHOTOGRAPHER: *Andre Baranowski* MAGAZINE/PUBLISHER: *GARDEN DESIGN, Meigher Communications.* COUNTRY: *USA* ■ *The concept was to create a simple, beautiful, outstanding cover.* ● *Hier ging es um die Gestaltung eines einfachen, aussergewöhnlich schönen Umschlags.* ▲ *L'objectif était de créer une couverture simple, belle et accrocheuse.*

PAGE 92, #118 DESIGNER: *Michi Toki* AGENCY: *Toki Design* PHOTOGRAPHER: *Pierre et Gilles* EDITOR IN CHIEF: *Andy Grundberg* EXECUTIVE EDITOR: *Deborah Klochko* MAGAZINE/PUBLISHER: *SEE: A JOURNAL OF VISUAL CULTURE, The Friends of Photography* COUNTRY: *USA* ■ *To preserve the integrity of the original photographic image, it was presented as a full bleed with the logo in its standard placement, eye-catching but unobtrusive. The color of the logo is balanced with the highlights of the foliage.* ● *Um die Integrität der Aufnahme zu wahren, wurde sie randabfallend gezeigt, wobei das Logo am üblichen Ort blieb, attraktiv und doch unaufdringlich. Die Farbe des Logos wurde der Aufnahme angepasst.* ▲ *Afin de respecter l'intégralité de la photographie originale, la reproduction recouvre la totalité du papier. Le logo, qui a gardé son emplacement original, attire le regard sans être frappant pour autant. La couleur du logo a été adaptée à la photographie.*

PAGE 92, #119 ART DIRECTOR: *Stephen Coates* EDITOR: *Rick Poyner* PUBLISHER: *Wordsearch Ltd* PRINTER: *Burrups Ltd.*

PAGE 93, #120 ART DIRECTOR/DESIGNER: *Dawn Kish* PHOTOGRAPHER/ILLUSTRATOR: *Jon Jensen* EDITOR: *Kathleen Gasperini* MAGAZINE/PUBLISHER: *W.I.G. Magazine* COUNTRY: *USA* ■ *This cover seeks to impart an image of change, and to let women escape and metamorphosize as they wish. Also, a bald woman on a cover of a publication called* WIG *is fun and a bit ironic. The art director shaved her own head and set the photo up. Then she and the photographer worked with texture and color to*

bring in the observer and keep him or her there. ● *Ein kahl geschorene Frau auf dem Umschlag des Magazins* WIG *(Perücke), was nicht einer gewissen Ironie entbehrt. Hier ging es um Veränderung für die Frauen, die Möglichkeiten des Entkommens, der Metamorphose. Ein Umschlag, der den Betrachter oder die Betrachterin neugierig machen sollte.* ▲ *A la fois ironique et humoristique, cette couverture présentant une femme au crâne rasé sur la couverture du magazine* WIG *(perruque) doit inciter les femmes à changer, à se métamorphoser selon leurs envies. L'objectif était de susciter la curiosité des lecteurs potentiels.*

PAGE 94, #121 ART DIRECTOR: *Thomas G. Fowler* DESIGNERS: *Karl Maruyama, Thomas G. Fowler* AGENCY: *Tom Fowler, Inc.* CLIENT: *Pfizer* PAPER: *Fox River Confetti* TYPEFACE: *Adobe Garamond* PRINTER: *H.T. Woods, Inc.* COUNTRY: *USA* ■ *This invitation to a holiday party presents the party goer with a memorable keepsake reminiscent of the theme and location of the event.* ● *Einladung zu einer Party, die auf den Ort und den Anlass hinweisen und dem Empfänger als Souvenir dienen sollte.* ▲ *Carton d'invitation sur lequel figurent le lieu et le thème de la manifestation, et destiné à être conservé en souvenir d'une fête mémorable.*

PAGE 94, #122 ART DIRECTOR/ILLUSTRATOR: *Sascha Weihs* TYPEFACE: *Futura* PRINTER: *Siebdruckerei Zchetner* ■ *This wedding announcement, made from natural materials, was created for good friends who love nature.* ● *Diese Hochzeitsanzeige aus natürlichen Materialien wurde für ein Paar entworfen, das sehr naturverbunden und zudem mit dem Gestalter befreundet ist.* ▲ *Le concepteur a créé ce faire-part de mariage réalisé avec des matériaux naturels pour un couple d'amis «écolo».*

PAGE 95, #123 ART DIRECTOR/DESIGNER: *Lee Perrault* AGENCY: *Via Design Inc.* PHOTOGRAPHER: *Brian Wilder* ILLUSTRATOR: *David M. Carroll* COPYWRITERS: *Lee Perrault, Richard W. Moore* CLIENT: *The Audobon Society of New Hampshire* TYPEFACE: *Wade, Roughouse* PAPER: *Domtar Naturals (primary), French Dur-o-tone Butcher off white, Curtis "Brightwater" (secondary)* PRINTER: *Printers Square* COUNTRY: *USA* ■ *The client wanted a gift to thank corporate and private donors. The agency created this limited edition, individually constructed book and container, designed to be kept by the recipient because of its meaningful contents and presentation.* ● *Eine Naturschutzorganisation wollte sich bei ihren Spendern mit einem Geschenk bedanken. Es entstand ein in limitierter Auflage produziertes und individuell gestaltetes Buch mit Kassette. Inhalt und Präsentation sollten den Empfänger überzeugen, das Geschenk aufzuheben.* ▲ *Cadeau fait par une société de protection de la nature, pour remercier ses donnateurs. L'agence créa une édition limitée comprenant un livre et sa boîte de rangement. Contenu et présentation devaient donner envie aux destinataires de conserver l'ouvrage.*

PAGE 96, #124 ART DIRECTOR/ILLUSTRATOR: *Werner H. Schmidt* AGENCY: *Daily Art* CLIENT: *Deutsche Leasing AG* PAPER: *Microwellle, Chromolux* TYPEFACE: *Perpetua, Univers* PRINTER: *Fritzsche-Siebdruck, Maintal* COUNTRY: *Germany*

PAGE 96, #125 ART DIRECTOR/DESIGNER: *Sam Kuo* AGENCY/CLIENT: *Kuo Design Office* PAPER: *Strathmore* TYPEFACE: *Futura Book* COUNTRY: *USA* ■ *This self-promotional piece served as social commentary.* ● *Diese Eigenwerbung ist ein Kommentar zur heutigen Gesellschaft.* ▲ *Cette publicité autopromotionnelle est un commentaire sur notre société.*

PAGE 96, #126 ART DIRECTORS: *Brad Hochberg, Debi Hochberg* DESIGNERS: *Brad Hochberg, Dana Hochberg* COPYWRITER: *Brad Hochberg* CLIENT: *Debi and Brad Hochberg* MATERIALS: *Wood, sheet metal* COUNTRY: *USA* ■ *Materials with a rough texture and look were used to create a birth announcement that distinctly said "boy."* ● *Materialien mit rauher Oberfläche wurden für diese Geburtsanzeige benutzt, die ganz eindeutig besagt, dass es sich um einen Jungen handelt.* ▲ *Des matériaux à la texture rêche ont été utilisés pour ce faire-part de naissance qui indique clairement qu'il s'agit d'un garçon.*

PAGE 97, #127 ART DIRECTOR/DESIGNER: *Rick Vaughn* PHOTOGRAPHER: *David Nufer* PRODUCT PHOTOGRAPHER: *Michael Barley* AGENCY/CLIENT: *Vaughn Wedeen Creative* PRINTER: *Albuquerque Printing* PAPER: *Simpson Starwhite Vicksburg* COUNTRY: *USA* ■ *This annual Christmas promotion was created to thank the people who helped the* *design firm throughout the year.* ● *Diese jährliche Weihnachtsgabe geht als Dank an die Kunden einer Design-Firma.* ▲ *Promotion de Noël annuelle créée pour une agence de design qui voulait ainsi remercier les clients et les personnes qui l'ont aidée tout au long de l'année.*

PAGE 98, #128 ART DIRECTOR: *Nan Finkenaur* DESIGNER: *Carmine Vecchio* AGENCY: *Milton Bradley Co.* PHOTOGRAPHER: *Hot Shots* ILLUSTRATOR: *Erik Ela* COUNTRY: *USA*

PAGE 99, #129 ILLUSTRATOR/CLIENT: *Cathleen Toelke* COUNTRY: *USA* ■ *Non-representational color is used to evoke the mood in this pastel. This personal work is one of a series of faces that explores different emotional moods.* ● *Diese persönliche Arbeit in Pastelltönen gehört zu einer Serie, die sich mit verschiedenen emotionalen Stimmungen befasst.* ▲ *Ce travail personnel réalisé dans des tons pastel s'insère dans une série qui traite des différentes émotions et humeurs.*

PAGE 100, #130 ART DIRECTOR/DESIGNER/ILLUSTRATOR: *Seymour Chwast* AGENCY: *Pushpin Group Inc.* CLIENT: *Berman Printing, Mohawk Paper Mills* TYPEFACE: *Gothic Wide, Gothic Bold, DeVinne* COUNTRY: *USA* ■ *Illustration for a promotional calendar.* ● *Illustration für einen Werbe-Kalender.* ▲ *Illustration pour un calendrier publicitaire.*

PAGE 101, #131 ART DIRECTOR: *Peter Breul* ILLUSTRATOR: *Peter Krämer* CLIENT: *Frankfurter Allgemeine Zeitung GmbH* COUNTRY: *Germany* ■ *This digital illustration was part of a special issue on watches and jewelry. It was based on a constructed drawing of the watch.* ● *Diese digitale Illustration stammt aus einer Ausgabe des FAZ MAGAZINS, in der es um Uhren und Schmuck geht. Grundlage war eine Zeichnung der Uhr.* ▲ *Cette illustration a paru dans un numéro de FAZ MAGAZIN consacré à l'horlogerie et à la bijouterie. L'illustration numérique reprend le dessin d'une montre.*

PAGE 102, #132 SENIOR GRAPHIC DESIGNER/ILLUSTRATOR: *Andrea McCann* SENIOR EXHIBIT DESIGNER: *Robert Bacigal* AGENCY: *Monterey Bay Aquarium in-house Exhibit Design Department* CLIENT: *Monterey Bay Aquarium* COUNTRY: *USA* ■ *This illustration of a common dolphin (Delphinus delphis) was featured in "Ocean Travelers," an exhibit of seasonal and permanent animal residents of Monterey Bay in California.* ● *Diese Darstellung eines Delphins (Delphinus delphis) entstand für «Ocean Travelers», eine Ausstellung über die saisonale und permanente Meeresbevölkerung der Monterey Bay von Kalifornien.* ▲ *Illustration d'un dauphin (delphinus delphis) pour «Ocean Travelers», une exposition sur la faune aquatique saisonnière et et permanente de Monterey Bay en Californie.*

PAGE 102, #133 DESIGNER/ILLUSTRATOR: *Luba Lukova* AGENCY: *Luba Lukova Studio* CLIENT: *The Living Theatre* COUNTRY: *USA* ■ *This illustration is part of a cycle of poster sketches for the Living Theatre Play "Anarchia" by Hanon Reznikov.* ● *Die Illustration gehört zu einem Zyklus von Plakatskizzen für das vom Living Theatre aufgeführte Stück 'Anarchia' von Hanon Reznikov.* ▲ *Cette illustration fait partie d'une série de saynètes présentées sur des affiches et extraites de la pièce «Anarchia» de Hanon Reznikov jouée par le Living Theatre.*

PAGE 102, #134 DESIGNER/ILLUSTRATOR: *Gary Blakeley* AGENCY/CLIENT: *Aitken & Blakeley* TYPEFACE: *Franklin Gothic Heavy* COUNTRY: *Canada* ■ *This illustration was created for a promotional piece to showcase the agency's design and illustration. The illustration of the Leica IIF was rendered with minute detail, using Adobe Illustrator and Dimensions.* ● *Illustration als Eigenwerbung eines Design- und Illustrations-Studios. Die Leica IIF wurde bis ins kleinste Detail mit Hilfe von Adobe Illustrator Software originalgetreu wiedergegeben.* ▲ *Illustration autopromotionnelle d'une agence spécialisée dans le design et l'illustration. Grâce à l'utilisation du logiciel Adobe Illustrator, la reproduction de l'appareil photo*

PAGE 103, #135 ART DIRECTOR/DESIGNER: *Kelly Doe* ILLUSTRATOR: *Frank Viva* CLIENT: THE WASHINGTON POST TYPEFACE: *Futura Extra Bold* COUNTRY: *Germany* ■ *For this illustration, THE WASHINGTON POST was looking for a variety of clothing styles representing some of the recognizables trends from the 20th century. They hired a stylist in Boston to scour the vintage clothing stores in the area. The selection*

of clothing was then photographed on models. The photos were used as the foundation for the photomontage. ● *Das Thema dieser Illustration für THE WASHINGTON POST waren Modetrends im 20. Jahrhundert. Eine Stylistin durchkämmte in Boston verschiedene, einschlägige Kleidergeschäfte und Brockenstuben. Danach wurden die Kleider an Modellen photographiert, und diese Aufnahmen dienten dann als Grundlage für die Photomontage.* ▲ *Les tendances de la mode des années 20 ont servi de thème à cette illustration pour THE WASHINGTON POST. Une styliste de Boston a été engagée pour passer au peigne fin les boutiques et friperies de la région. Les vêtements qu'elle a sélectionnés ont été photographiés sur des mannequins. Les images en résultant ont ensuite été utilisées pour un photomontage.*

PAGE 104, #136 ART DIRECTOR/DESIGNER: *Daniel Koh* AGENCY: *Addison Design Company* ILLUSTRATOR: *John Springs* CLIENT: *Samsung* TYPEFACE: *Meta* COUNTRY: *Korea* ■ *This illustration was created for a Samsung "Salute to Inventors" calendar.* ● *Illustration aus einem Samsung-Kalender, der Erfindern gewidmet ist.* ▲ *Illustration extraite d'un calendrier Samsung consacré aux inventeurs.*

PAGE 105, #137 ART DIRECTOR/DESIGNER: *Michael Gunselman* AGENCY: *Michael Gunselman, Inc.* ILLUSTRATOR: *Guy Billout* CLIENT: *New Jesery Resources Corp.* COUNTRY: *USA* ■ *Illustrations for an annual report for a New Jersey energy holding company.* ● *Illustrationen für einen Jahresbericht einer Holding-Gesellschaft im Energiebereich.* ▲ *Illustrations pour le rapport annuel d'une holding active dans le secteur de l'énergie.*

PAGE 105, #138 ART DIRECTOR/DESIGNER: *Carsten Franke* AGENCY: *Franke Communications* ILLUSTRATOR: *Guy Billout* CLIENT: *Compass Deutschland GmbH* COUNTRY: *Germany* ■ *Illustrations for a brochure for Compass Deutschland GmbH in Germany.* ● *Illustration für einen Broschüre der Firma Compass in Deutschland.* ▲ *Illustration d'un brochure pour la société Compass en Allemagne.*

PAGE 106, #139 ART DIRECTOR/DESIGNER/ILLUSTRATOR: *Wieslaw Smetek* PUBLISHER: *Eburon-Delft* ■ *Pastiche of Rembrandt: "Anato Mie Des Dr. Tulp."* ● *Eine Persiflage auf Rembrandt: «Anatomie des Dr. Tulp.»* ▲ *Pastiche de Rembrandt: «Anatomie du Dr Tulp.»*

PAGE 106, #140 ART DIRECTORS: *Iku Akiyama, Shogo Kawahara* DESIGNER: *Shogo Kawahara* AGENCY: *Clip Inc.* ILLUSTRATOR: *Iku Akiyama* CLIENT: *Tokyo Digital Phone Co., Ltd.* COUNTRY: *Japan* ■ *These illustrations appeared in a gift calendar for a portable phone company. The illustrator tried to create a happy image in an urban and cheerful atmosphere.* ● *Diese Illustrationen stammen aus einem Kalender für einen Hersteller von Handies, der sich ein freundliches Bild in einer urbanen, fröhlichen Atmosphäre gewünscht hatte.* ▲ *Ces illustrations proviennent d'un calendrier pour un fabricant de téléphones sans fil. L'illustrateur a essayé de créer une atmosphère empreinte de joie dans un environnement urbain.*

PAGE 107, #141 ILLUSTRATOR/CLIENT: *Peder Stougård* COUNTRY: *Denmark* ■ *These illustrations were created to evoke emotion. The illustrator takes the essence of his experiences and tries to convert them into a figurative language of his own.* ● *«Ohne Phantasie gibt es keine Erfahrungen, und Phantasie ist es, die das Leben lebenswert macht», sagt der dänische Künstler Peder Stougård, der seinen Bildern keine Titel gibt, um den Betrachter nicht festzulegen.* ▲ *«Seule l'imagination est génératrice d'expériences et donne du piment à la vie.» C'est ainsi que l'artiste danois Peder Stougård conçoit la vie. Celui-ci ne donne pas de titres à ses productions afin de ne pas en influencer l'interprétation.*

PAGE 107, #142 ART DIRECTOR/DESIGNER/ILLUSTRATOR: *Siegmar Münk* AGENCY/CLIENT: *Münkillus* COUNTRY: *Germany* ■ *Capricorn and Libra two illustrations from a self-promotional portfolio of twelve motifs.* ● *Steinbock und Waage – zwei Illustrationen aus einer Eigenwerbungsmappe mit 12 Motiven.* ▲ *Capricorne et balance, deux illustrations extraites d'un portfoilo autopromotionnel constitué de 12 motifs.*

PAGE 108, #143 ILLUSTRATOR/CLIENT: *Fabio Isaya* ■ *"Havana"* ● *«Havana»* ▲ *«Havana»*

PAGE 108, #144 ART DIRECTOR: *Steven Heller* ILLUSTRATOR: *Mirko Ilic´* CLIENT: *THE NEW YORK TIMES* COUNTRY: *USA* ■ *This illustration was created for a book review of four different books about the bombing of Hiroshima and Nagasaki. The illustrator wanted to use predictable icons (the mushroom cloud, Japanese flag) in a new way.* ● *Illustration für die Besprechung von vier Büchern über den Abwurf der Atombombe auf Hiroshima und Nagasaki. Es ging um eine neue Darstellung bekannter Bilder (Atompilz und japanische Flagge).* ▲ *Illustration conçue dans le cadre d'une critique de quatre ouvrages consacrés au bombardement d'Hiroshima et de Nagasaki. L'illustrateur a utilisé des images évocatrices (champignon atomique et drapeau japonais).*

PAGE 108, #145 DESIGNER: *Irene Gallo* ILLUSTRATOR: *Frances Middendorf* TYPEFACE: *Garamond* COUNTRY: *USA* ■ *The illustrator wanted to draw attention to the plight of Haitian refugees who were being turned away from American shores. Idyllic colors draw in the viewer of this overcrowded raft of refugees. Among the numbers is a death mark of a voodoo priestess; in the distance is a figure of St. Christopher, the saint who is believed to protect the overseas traveler.* ● *Thema dieser Illustration sind die Flüchtlinge aus Haiti, die von den Amerikanern nicht an Land gelassen wurden. Idyllische Farben lenken den Blick des Betrachters auf das überladene Floss der Flüchtlinge. Unter den Nummern erkennt man das Todeszeichen einer Voodoo-Priesterin; in der Ferne die Gestalt des St. Christopherus, dem Schutzheiligen der Reisenden.* ▲ *Thème de cette illustration, des réfugiés d'Haïti refoulés près des côtes américaincs. Les couleurs idylliques dirigent le regard de l'observateur sur l'embarcation surchargée. Parmi les nombres, on reconnaît le signe de mort d'une prêtresse voodoo, au loin, St. Christopher, le patron des voyageurs.*

PAGE 108, #146 ILLUSTRATOR: *Dennis Corrigan* CLIENT: *Corrigan Gallery of Humorous and Romantic Art* COUNTRY: *USA* ■ *"The Night Shift" depicts future victims of industrial pollution who, somehow, manage to think their condition is quite groovy.* ● *«Die Nachtschicht» zeigt die Opfer der Industriegesellschaft, die es fertigbringen zu glauben, dass es ihnen ganz gut geht.* ▲ *«L'équipe de nuit» montre les victimes de la société industrielle qui persistent à croire que tout est au mieux dans le meilleur des mondes.*

PAGE 108, #147 ART DIRECTOR/DESIGNER/ILLUSTRATOR: *Wieslaw Smetek* CLIENT: *Zuk Records* ■ *Charcoal pencil illustration of W.A. Mozart with horn from a portrait of Mozart by Barbara Krafft. The illustration was used for a CD and poster for the album "Eine Kleine Horn-Musik."* ● *Kohlezeichnung von Mozart mit Horn nach einem Porträt von Barbara Krafft. Die Illustration für die CD «Eine kleine Horn-Musik» und ein Plakat verwendet.* ▲ *Illustration au fusain de Mozart avec cor selon un portrait de Barbara Krafft. Ce dessin a été utilisé pour une affiche et un CD intitulé «Petite musique de cor».*

PAGE 108, #148 ART DIRECTOR/DESIGNER/ILLUSTRATOR: *Wieslaw Smetek* CLIENT: *Zuk Records* ■ *Charcoal pencil portrait of Solohorn Zbigniew Zuk for the album "Horn Obsession."* ● *Kohledarstellung des Horn-Solisten Zbigniew Zuk für das Album «Horn Obsesssion».* ▲ *Portrait au fusain de Zbigniew Zuk pour l'album «Obsession du cor».*

PAGE 109, #149 ILLUSTRATOR: *Dennis Corrigan* CLIENT: *Corrigan Gallery of Humorous and Romantic Art* COUNTRY: *USA* ■ *"Going Home" spent three years of its life as a little landscape painting that needed something. The solution involved transforming the shape of a stylized hill into a sleek, dark red car with drowsy occupants.* ● *«Going Home» war ursprünglich ein kleines Landschaftsbild, dem etwas fehlte Die Lösung war die Verwandlung des angedeuteten Hügels in ein schnittiges, dunkelrotes Auto mit schläfrigen Insassen.* ▲ *«Going home» était à l'origine une petite peinture d'un paysage à laquelle il manquait quelque chose. La solution a consisté à transformer la colline en une voiture racée de couleur rouge foncé dont les occupants semblent assoupis.*

PAGE 109, #150 ART DIRECTOR: *Astrid Borowski* EDITORIAL DIRECTOR: *Jörg Albrecht* ILLUSTRATOR: *Ludvik Glazer* CLIENT: *ZEIT MAGAZIN* TYPEFACE: *Die Zeit, Wochenzeitung* COUNTRY: *Germany* ■ *Double-spread illustration for three articles on the subject of*

time in *ZEIT MAGAZIN*. ● *Doppelseitige Illustration zu drei Beiträgen über das Thema "Zeit" im ZEIT MAGAZIN.* ▲ *Illustration double page pour trois sujets consacrés au thème du temps dans le magazine ZEIT.*

PAGE 110, #151 ART DIRECTORS: *Pamela Kuehl, Gretchen Dow Simpson* DESIGNER/ILLUSTRATOR: *Gretchen Dow Simpson* AGENCY: *KSL Designers* CLIENT: *Winross* TYPEFACE: *Gill Sans, Bodoni* COUNTRY: *USA* ■ *This illustration was created for producers of promotional truck models. The "roadways of America" theme was used to inspire nostalgia and quality of product to American corporations.* ● *Illustration für eine Firma, die Modelle von Firmenwagen herstellt. Das Thema "Strassen von Amerika" sollte Erinnerungen an gute alte Zeiten wachrufen und amerikanische Firmen von der Qualität des Angebots überzeugen.* ▲ *Illustration pour une société qui produit des modèles de véhicules d'entreprise. Empreint de nostalgie, le thème «roadways of America» doit convaincre les clients de la qualité de l'offre.*

PAGE 110, #152 AGENCY: *Dyga Design* COUNTRY: *Poland* ■ *"Green Doggy"* ● *«Green Doggy»* ▲ *«Green Doggy»*

PAGE 111, #153 ART DIRECTOR: *Carla Hall* DESIGNERS: *Lisa Mooney, Jim Keller* AGENCY: *Carla Hall Design Group* ILLUSTRATOR: *Jeff Koegel* CLIENT: *CS First Boston* COUNTRY: *USA* ■ *The illustrator wanted to portray a thoughtful and informed approach to financial decision making in this brochure used by brokers, investment bankers, and analysts.* ● *Illustration für eine Broschüre, die von Börsenmaklern, Investment Bankern und Analysten benutzt wird. Es ging um eine seriöse Darstellung des finanzwirtschaftlichen Themas* ▲ *Illustration d'une brochure destinée aux courtiers, aux investisseurs et aux analystes financiers.*

PAGE 111, #154 ART DIRECTOR/DESIGNER: *Karen Knorr* AGENCY: *Wechsler & Partners, Inc.* ILLUSTRATOR: *Nicholas Wilton* CLIENT: *Donaldson, Lufkin & Jenrette* COUNTRY: *USA* ■ *This illustration for a bylined article personalized abstract concepts and dramatized intangible benefits of an investment service (research, advice, intelligence).* ● *Eine der Illustrationen für ergänzende Beiträge der Geschäftsführer, in denen die abstrakten Konzepte erläutert und die Vorteile eines Investment Service (Untersuchung, Rat, Intelligenz) dargestellt werden.* ▲ *Une des illustrations accompagnant des textes rédigés par les gestionnaires d'une société, lesquels ont pour objectif de clarifier des concepts abstraits et de présenter les avantages d'un service d'investissements (recherche, conseil, intelligence).*

PAGE 111, #155 ART DIRECTOR: *Ron Toelke* ILLUSTRATOR: *Cathleen Toelke* COPYWRITER: *Bob Chase* CLIENT: *One Great Hour of Sharing* COUNTRY: *USA* ■ *A fund raising poster was needed for an international charity that helps empower impoverished communities. A multi-cultural cooperative effort is shown to help the people rise above their needs. A somber but hopeful foreground figure is contrasted in front of a bright, positive scene of people helping each other.* ● *Illustration für ein Plakat, das einer internationalen Wohlfahrtsorganisation als Spendenaufruf dient. Spezielles Anliegen der Organisation ist die Unterstützung verarmter Gemeinden und Wohngebiete. Das Thema ist gegenseitige Hilfe.* ▲ *Affiche conçue pour une association caritative dans le but de collecter des fonds pour les communautés les plus défavorisées. Thème de l'affiche: l'entraide.*

PAGE 112, #156 ART DIRECTOR: *Andrew Cawrse* AGENCY: *Cawrse & Effect* CLIENT: *"Consider it Dunn"* TYPEFACE: *Optima* PRINTER: *Pinsbury Press* COUNTRY: *Australia* ■ *The client needed stationery that was memorable and explained its gift service. Using a self-revealing present re-expressed the joy and surprise of receiving a gift. The play on the client's family name explains the service.* ● *Briefschaft für einen Geschenk-Service. Es ging um einen einprägsamen Auftritt und Darstellung der Dienstleistung: «Consider it (done) Dunn» bedeutet soviel wie «Betrachten Sie es als erledigt».* ▲ *Le client, une société spécialisée dans les cadeaux voulait une présentation de papier marquante qui explique ses prestations. Le jeu de mots avec le nom de famille du client «Consider it (done) Dunn» signifie «Considérez que l'affaire est réglée».*

PAGE 112, #157 ART DIRECTORS: *Mary Scott, Paul Farris* DESIGNERS: *Paul Farris, Winnie Li* AGENCY/CLIENT: *Maddocks & Company* PAPER: *Cranes Crest* TYPEFACE: *Meta* PRINTER:

Burdge, Inc. COUNTRY: *USA* ■ *The agency wanted to create an identity system that avoided the use of a traditional symbol/logotype and used an energetic arrangement of typography, blind embossing, and lithography.* ● *Statt eines Symbols/Logos arbeiteten die Gestalter hier mit der Typographie, Prägedruck und Lithographie.* ▲ *L'agence a voulu créer un système d'identité axé sur la typographie, le gaufrage et la lithographie.*

PAGE 112, #158 ART DIRECTOR: *Jennifer Morla* DESIGNERS: *Jennifer Morla, Craig Bailey* AGENCY: *Morla Design* PHOTO IMAGING: *Mark Eastman* CLIENT: *San Francisco Production Group* PAPER: *Starwhite Vicksburg Tiara vellum 80 lb. text, 110 lb. cover* TYPEFACE: *Bodoni Book, Boy Plain, Franklin Gothic extra condensed, Univers 65 Bold Extended* PRINTER: *Bacchus Press* COUNTRY: *USA* ■ *This identity is for a San Francisco-based video production facility that specializes in video animation, sound and film. The company is known by its acronym SFPG. The animated logo is paired with various portraits to playfully illustrate their work.* ● *SFPG ist ein Akronym für eine Videoproduktionsfirma in San Francisco, die sich auf Video-Animation, Ton und Film spezialisiert hat. Das 'animierte' Logo wird durch verschiedene Porträts ergänzt, um die Tätigkeit spielerisch darzustellen.* ▲ *Identité visuelle créée pour une société de production vidéo de San Francisco, la SFPG, spécialisée dans l'animation vidéo, le son et le film. Le logo « animé » est associé à différents portraits qui illustrent les activités de l'entreprise de manière ludique.*

PAGE 112, #159 CREATIVE DIRECTORS: *Kent Hunter, Aubrey Balkind* DESIGNERS: *Brett Gerstenblatt, Kin Yuen* AGENCY: *Frankfurt Balkind Partners* CLIENT/PRINTER: *Pantone, Inc.* COUNTRY: *USA*

PAGE 113, #160 ART DIRECTOR: *Michael Cronan* DESIGNERS/ILLUSTRATORS: *Michael Cronan, Anthony Yell* COPYWRITER: *Douglas Cruickshank* AGENCY: *Cronan Design* CLIENT: *NEWMEDIA MAGAZINE* PAPER: *Starwhite Vicksburg* TYPEFACE: *Rotis Semi-serif* PRINTER: *Honeywell & Todd* COUNTRY: *USA*

PAGE 113, #161 DESIGNER: *Jo Davison* AGENCY/CLIENT: *The Edison Group* PAPER: *Champion Pageantry, Curtis Tuscan Antique* TYPEFACE: *Sabon, Frutiger* PRINTER: *Meyers Printing* COUNTRY: *USA* ■ *The client wanted a stationery system which expressed that although the firm is very cohesive, it is made up of unique individuals. A large letter "E" was used on all pieces to signify the company, but the business cards utilized the individual employee's initial.* ● *Mit diesem Briefpapier sollte zum Ausdruck kommen, dass die Firma trotz ihrer Geschlossenheit aus einzigartigen Persönlichkeiten besteht. Das grosse «E» wurde überall verwendet, um die Firma darzustellen, aber auf den Visitenkarten wurde die Initiale des Names des betreffenden Mitarbeiters eingesetzt.* ▲ *Ce papier à lettres devait montrer que même si une grande cohésion règne entre les collaborateurs de la société, ceux-ci sont des individus à part entière avec toutes leurs spécificités. Le grand «E» a été utilisé partout pour représenter la société, tandis que les initiales des différents collaborateurs figurent sur les cartes de visite.*

PAGE 114, #162 DESIGNERS: *Chris Cortilet, Jeff Schweigert* AGENCY: *Yamamoto Moss* CLIENT: *J.W. Fry Photography* PRINTER: *The John Roberts Company* COUNTRY: *USA* ■ *This letterhead was created to target creative professionals and to build name recognition for the client. The frying pan visually portrays the photographer's ability to "make things sizzle."* ● *Briefkopf als neuer Auftritt eines Photographen, der damit besonders die Werbebranche ansprechen will. Die Bratpfanne ist als Hinweis darauf zu verstehen, dass er die 'Dinge zum Brutzeln' bringen kann.* ▲ *Nouvelle en-tête réalisée dans le cadre d'un relookage du système d'identité d'un photographe s'adressant en particulier aux professionnels de la publicité. La poêle à frirefait allusion aux capacités du photographe, c.-à-d. qu'il arrive à faire «crépiter» les choses.*

PAGE 114, #163 ART DIRECTORS/DESIGNERS: *Jacques Koeweiden, Paul Postma* AGENCY: *Koeweiden Postma Associates* CLIENT: *Jaap Stablie* PAPER: *Japanese paper with silver structure* TYPEFACE: *Photoshop-manipulated Push Tong Type* PRINTER: *Drukker Randstad* COUNTRY: *The Netherlands*

PAGE 114, #164 ART DIRECTOR: *Jack Anderson* DESIGNERS: *Jack Anderson, David Bates* AGENCY: *Hornall Anderson Design Works, Inc.* ILLUSTRATOR: *David Bates* CALLIGRAPHER: *George Tanagi* CLIENT: *Capons* PAPER: *Classic laid Writing, laser-compatible Peppered Bronze* TYPEFACE: *Custom, Goudy* COUNTRY: *USA* ■ *The objective was to design a new identity for a chain of rotisserie chicken take-out restaurants. The design was to focus on the style of cooking as a motif. A spinning tornado design as the chicken's body depicts a quick 'take out' mentality as opposed to a dine-in restaurant. The zig-zag edge of the letterhead communicates the idea of take-out bags. Warm full-bleed colors on the back of the letterhead illustrate upscale take out.* ● *Ein neues Erscheinungsbild für eine Kette von Take-Out-Hähnchen-Restaurants. Ein Hähnchen in Form eines Tornados steht für Schnelligkeit des Take-Out-Systems im Gegensatz zu den üblichen Restaurants. Die gezackte Kante des Briefpapiers ist eine Anspielung auf die Tüten, in denen die Hähnchen verpackt werden. Warme Farben auf der Rückseite des Briefpapiers sollen das gehobene Niveau der Kette verdeutlichen.* ▲ *Il s'agissait de créer une nouvelle identité pour une chaîne de restaurants proposant du poulet rôti à emporter. Le graphisme devait traduire la spécificité de ces restaurants: ainsi, le poulet est-il représenté sous la forme d'une tornade, symbolisant la rapidité du service par rapport aux restaurants classiques. La découpe du papier en-tête reprend celle des sachets d'emballage. Au verso, les couleurs chaudes à fond perdu donnent un côté « chic », correspondant au positionnement haut de gamme de cette chaîne.*

PAGE 115, #165 ART DIRECTOR: *Peter Good* DESIGNER: *Christopher Hyde* AGENCY: *Cummings & Good* CLIENT: *Chatham Printing* PAPER: *Strathmore Writing* TYPEFACE: *Gill Sans* PRINTER: *Chatham Printing* COUNTRY: *USA* ■ *The client, a small printery, wanted a simple contemporary signature to be used on all print materials. A digitized letterform 'C' and varying colors on the stationery elements were used to suggest the printing process.* ● *Der digitalisierte Buchstabe C wurde in verschiedenen Farben auf allen Drucksachen der kleinen Druckerei verwendet und ist eine Anspielung auf den Druckprozess.* ▲ *Le client, un petit imprimeur, souhaitait une signature actuelle, pouvant être utilisée sur l'ensemble de ses imprimés. Pour suggérer l'activité de l'entreprise, la lettre "C" a été digitalisée et déclinée en diverses couleurs.*

PAGE 115, #166 DESIGNER/ILLUSTRATOR: *Iwen Chen* PAPER: *Reflection Ginger, Reflection White* PRINTER: *HP, Laser 4MP* TYPEFACE: *BerbardMad and Gill Sans* COUNTRY: *USA* ■ *This resume was created to express the designer's personality, design ability and cultural background. The meanings of her Chinese name are explained on each spread. On the last spread, the characters are presented on the left, accompanied by a resume on the right. The self-promotion is handstitched in the form of a traditional Chinese booklet.* ● *Diese Eigenwerbung einer chinesischen Graphikerin ist handgenäht und hat das Format eines traditionellen chinesischen Büchleins. Die Bedeutungen ihres chinesischen Namens werden auf jeder Doppelseite erklärt, auf der letzten Seite befinden sich links die Schriftzeichen, ergänzt durch ein Resumé auf der rechten Seite.* ▲ *Publicité autopromotionnelle d'une graphiste évoquant la culture et l'habileté inhérentes aux Chinois. Les significations de son nom chinois sont expliquées sur chaque double page. Sur la dernière page, les caractères sont présentés à gauche et complétés par un résumé sur la droite.*

PAGE 115, #167 ART DIRECTOR/DESIGNER: *Spencer Walters* AGENCY: *S.D. Zyne* CLIENT: *Computer Repair* PAPER: *Strathmore Elements, Dots* TYPEFACE: *Gill Sans Light* PRINTER: *The Phoenix Printery* COUNTRY: *USA* ■ *To create a unique, aesthetically pleasing, functional identity system for an over-saturated field in technology, the designer used normal everyday objects in a new and visually compelling way to both entice the viewer and inform. The idea that the logo is basically a band aid allows it to be used as such, thus sealing the letterhead and wrapping around the business card.* ● *Um ein einzigartiges, attraktives und funktionales Erscheinungsbild in einer Branche zu schaffen, die von der Technologie geprägt ist, verwendete der Gestalter alltägliche Gegenstände auf ganz ungewöhnliche Art, um das Interesse des Betrachters zu wecken und ihn zu informieren. Die Idee, dass das Logo im Grunde ein Heftpflaster ist, führte dazu, es auch als solches zu verwenden.* ▲ *Pour créer une identité visuelle originale, séduisante et fonctionnelle dans une branche saturée de technologie, le designer a choisi de jouer de manière insolite avec des* *objets courants pour retenir l'attention de l'observateur d'une part et l'informer de l'autre. L'idée que le logo n'est en fait qu'un sparadrap l'a incité à s'en servir comme tel, en tant que système de fermeture de l'en-tête.*

PAGE 115, #168 ART DIRECTOR/DESIGNER/PHOTOGRAPHER: *Michael Vanderbyl* AGENCY: *Vanderbyl Design* CLIENT/PRINTER: *Campbell Group* ■ *In designing a stationery system for a printing company, a series of photographic images, instead of a logo, were used to represent the craft of printing* ● *Um das Druckgewerbe darzustellen, wurden für dieses Briefpapier Photos statt einem Logo eingesetzt.* ▲ *Afin de présenter le métier d'imprimeur, une série de photographies a été retenue pour ces imprimés en lieu et place d'un logo.*

PAGE 116, #169 ART DIRECTOR: *Joseph Rattan* DESIGNER/ILLUSTRATOR: *Greg Morgan* AGENCY: *Joseph Rattan Design* CLIENT: *Group Gallagher* COUNTRY: *USA* ■ *Logo for a public relations and marketing company.* ● *Logo für eine Public Relations und Marketing-Firma.* ▲ *Logo d'une société de RP et de marketing.*

PAGE 116, #170 ART DIRECTOR: *Jack Anderson* DESIGNERS: *Jack Anderson, Brian O'Neill* AGENCY: *Hornall Anderson Design Works, Inc.* CLIENT: *Gang of Seven* TYPEFACE: *Custom* COUNTRY: *USA* ■ *To design a logo that for a bicycle racing team, the agency incorporated the symbol of a ram with wings to depict speed and reflect the name of the race, which was called "Ram-Rod."* ● *Logo für ein Rennrad-Team, das einerseits Geschwindigkeit symbolisiert, andererseits auf den Namen des Rennens 'Ram-Rod' (Ram =Widder) anspielt.* ▲ *Ce logo au bélier ailé a été créé pour une équipe de coureurs cyclistes. Il symbolise la vitesse et fait référence au nom de la course: Ram-Rod – le mot «ram» signifiant «bélier».*

PAGE 116, #171 ART DIRECTOR/DESIGNER: *Sally Morrow* AGENCY: *Sandstrom Design* ILLUSTRATORS: *Sally Morrow, Janée Warren* CLIENT: *Portland Brewing* COUNTRY: *USA* ■ *The designer wanted to develop a "friendly" and humorous icon to represent a brewing company. German trade symbols suggest the Germanic character of the brewery.* ● *Eine freundliche, humorvolle Ikone für eine Brauerei, die auf die deutsche Bierbrautradition anspielt.* ▲ *Icône sympathique et humoristique pour une brasserie, qui évoque la tradition de brassage de la bière allemande.*

PAGE 116, #172 ART DIRECTOR/DESIGNER/ILLUSTRATOR: *Ken Koester* AGENCY: *Brainstorm Inc.* CLIENT: *Q.-Ink* COUNTRY: *USA* ■ *To develop this identity for a photographers' representative, the agency created a simple, direct mark to which designers, art directors and people in the industry can relate.* ● *Ein einfaches, einpräsames Logo für eine Photographen-Agentur.* ▲ *Logo simple et accrocheur d'une agence de photographes.*

PAGE 116, #173 ART DIRECTORS: *Byron Jacobs, Bethany Bunnell, Joe Kurzer* DESIGNER: *Byron Jacobs* AGENCY: *PPA Design Ltd.* CLIENT: *STAR Radio* COUNTRY: *Hong Kong* ■ *The agency created an umbrella identity for this client, a radio station which focuses on popular music hits from 1970-1990.* ● *Ein vielseitig anwendbares Logo für eine Radio-Station, die vor allem Hits von 1970-1990 spielt.* ▲ *Graphisme pouvant être aisément décliné, créé pour une station de radio diffusant essentiellement des tubes des années 70 à 90.*

PAGE 116, #174 ART DIRECTOR/DESIGNER: *Elizabeth Jowaisas* AGENCY: *Jowaisas Design* CLIENT: *Cazenovia Rowing Club* COUNTRY: *USA* ■ *To create a logo for a local rowing club to be used primarily on t-shirts, the designer chose a traditional look to reflect rowing tradition and the conservative climate of the community. The star is a distinguishing element of the club and appears on its oars. Colors were selected by the club members.* ● *Dieses Logo für einen lokalen Ruderclub sollte vor allem auf T-Shirts verwendet werden. Der traditionelle Look entspricht der langen Tradition dieser Sportart und dem konservativen Klima der Gemeinde. Der Stern ist ein Zeichen des Clubs und erscheint auch auf den Riemen. Die Farben wurden von den Clubmitgliedern ausgesucht.* ▲ *Créé pour un club d'aviron régional, ce logo devait avant tout servir de motif à des tee-shirts. Il fallait communiquer l'image d'un sport empreint d'une longue tradition et l'attitude plutôt conservatrice de la commune. L'étoile, symbole du club, se retrouve sur les rames. Les membres du club ont eux-mêmes choisi les couleurs.*

PAGE 116, #175 ART DIRECTOR: *Joseph Rattan* ILLUSTRATOR: *Greg Morgan* AGENCY: *Joseph Rattan Design* CLIENT: *Prime Retail* COUNTRY: *USA* ■ *Logo created for the location of a retail outlet shopping center in Florida.* ● *Logo für ein Grosshandels-Shopping Center in Florida.* ▲ *Logo d'un centre commercial en Floride.*

PAGE 116, #176 ART DIRECTOR: *Chris McCullick* ART DIRECTOR: *Greg Hoffman* DESIGNER: *Chris McCullick* AGENCY/CLIENT: *Nike, Inc.* COUNTRY: *USA* ■ *This logo was designed for a grassroots marketing group that uses Hummers to travel to various sporting events around the country.* ● *Logo für eine regionale Nike-Marketing-Gruppe, die Geländefahrzeuge bei ihren Reisen an die verschiedenen Sportveranstaltungen im Lande benutzt.* ▲ *Logo pour un groupe de marketing de Nike. Ses représentants utilisent des véhicules tout-terrain pour se rendre aux diverses manifestations sportives du pays.*

PAGE 116, #177 DESIGNER: *Rex Peteet* AGENCY: *Sibley/Peteet Design* CLIENT: *Scotland Yards Fabric* COUNTRY: *USA* ■ *The designer used the Scotland Yard name for the identity of this designer fabric store. The logo plays off the implied heritage of the country and the store's pet Scottish Terrier mascot, Murphy.* ● *Logo für einen Designer-Soffladen mit dem Namen "Scotland Yards Fabrics". Das Maskottchen des Ladens, der schottische Terrier Murphy, und das traditionelle Image Grossbritanniens inspirierten zu dieser Lösung.* ▲ *Le designer a utilisé le nom « Scotland Yards Fabrics » pour l'identité d'un magasin de créations textiles. Le logo joue sur l'idée des traditions séculaires britanniques et l'image du scott terrier Murphy, mascotte du magasin.*

PAGE 117, #178 ART DIRECTOR/DESIGNER: *Horacio Cobos* AGENCY: *RBMM/The Richards Group* ILLUSTRATOR: *Wayne Johnson* CLIENT: *Amerifest Dallas* COUNTRY: *USA*

PAGE 117, #179 ART DIRECTOR/DESIGNER/ILLUSTRATOR: *Horacio Cobos* AGENCY: *RBMM/The Richards Group* CLIENT: *Architect Luis Mejio* COUNTRY: *USA*

PAGE 117, #180 ART DIRECTOR: *Mark Sackett* DESIGNERS: *Mark Sackett, Wayne Sakamoto* AGENCY: *Sackett Design Associates* CLIENT: *DFS Group Limited* ■ *This brand mark was used to identify various lines of products sold at tourist destinations in Taiwan.* ● *Dieses Markenzeichen wurde für verschiedene Produkte verwendet, die an Touristen in Taiwan verkauft werden.* ▲ *Cette identité a été utilisée pour divers produits vendus à des touristes séjournant à Taïwan.*

PAGE 117, #181 ART DIRECTOR/DESIGNER/ILLUSTRATOR: *Horacio Cobos* AGENCY: *RBMM/The Richards Group* CLIENT: *Multiple Sclerosis Society* COUNTRY: *USA*

PAGE 117, #182 ART DIRECTOR: *Kit Hinrichs* DESIGNER: *Jackie Foshaug* AGENCY: *Pentagram Design* CLIENT: *Columbus Salame* COUNTRY: *USA*

PAGE 117, #183 ART DIRECTOR/DESIGNER: *Justus Oehler* AGENCY: *Pentagram Design* CLIENT: *Museum für Post & Kommunikation* ■ *The German Postmuseum decided to shed its cozy, but slightly dull image in favor of a more exciting one. The agency was commissioned to create a new name and identity to signify the museum's new status as a collective foundation.* ● *Das Deutsche Postmuseum hatte beschlossen, sein 'gemütliches', aber etwas langweiliges Image zugunsten eines aufregenderen Erscheingunsbildes aufzugeben. Ein neuer Name und Auftritt wurde geschaffen, um den neuen Status als Stiftung hervorzugeben.* ▲ *Le musée de la poste allemande avait décidé d'abandonner son image «douillette», plutôt ennuyeuse, au profit d'une identité plus marquante. L'agence a dû créer un nouveau nom et une nouvelle identité pour indiquer le changement de statut de ce musée, devenu une fondation.*

PAGE 117, #184 AGENCY: *Planet Design Company* CLIENT: *Angelic Brewing Co.* COUNTRY: *USA* ■ *To set the brewing company apart from the competition, the designer combined the images of angels and beer. While "Angelic" suggests pristine images, the beer suggests an element of naughtiness.* ● *Der Name der Brauerei und der Wünsch, sich von der Konkurrenz zu unterscheiden, führte zu dieser Kombination von Engeln und Bier, sozusagen von Makellosigkeit und einer gewissen Unartigkeit.* ▲ *Le nom de la brasserie et la volonté de se démarquer* de la concurrence ont conduit à cette combinaison entre ange et bière qui évoque à la fois pureté, innocence et une certaine forme d'indocilité.

PAGE 117, #185 ART DIRECTOR: *Kit Hinrichs* DESIGNER: *Jackie Foshaug* AGENCY: *Pentagram Design* CLIENT: *The Gymboree Corporation* COUNTRY: *USA*

PAGE 117, #186 ART DIRECTOR/DESIGNER: *Tom Antista* AGENCY: *Antista Fairclough Design* CLIENT: *National Physician's Network* COUNTRY: *USA* ■ *The client wanted a powerful logo to represent its networking service. To reflect the key elements of the name, a waving flag was entwined with the universal medical symbol of the red cross.* ● *Logo für ein medizinisches Service-Netz. Als Symbol für den Namen wurde die amerikanische Flagge mit dem Symbol des Roten Kreuzes kombiniert.* ▲ *Logo pour un réseau de services médicaux. Le drapeau américain et le symbole de la Croix-Rouge reflètent les principaux éléments du nom.*

PAGE 117, #187 ART DIRECTOR/DESIGNER/ILLUSTRATOR: *Horacio Cobos* AGENCY: *RBMM/The Richards Group* CLIENT: *All Wrapped Up* COUNTRY: *USA*

PAGE 117, #188 ART DIRECTOR/DESIGNER: *Jeff Weithman* ILLUSTRATOR: *David Gill* AGENCY/CLIENT: *Nike, Inc.* COUNTRY: *USA* ■ *To create an identity for a line of infant products, the corporate brand logo was infused with a "looney toons" feel.* ● *Markenzeichen für eine Linie von Nike-Kinderschuhen.* ▲ *Logo pour une ligne de chaussures Nike pour enfants.*

PAGE 117, #189 ART DIRECTOR: *José Serrano* DESIGNERS: *Mike Brower, José Serrano* PHOTOGRAPHER: *Carl VanderSchuit* ILLUSTRATOR: *Tracy Sabin* AGENCY: *Mires Design, Inc.* CLIENT: *Voit Sports, Inc.* COUNTRY: *USA*

PAGE 117, #190 ART DIRECTOR/DESIGNER: *Craig Frazier* AGENCY: *Frazier Design* CLIENT: *Xaos Tools, Inc.* COUNTRY: *USA* ■ *Logo created for a computer software company.* ● *Logo für eine Computer Software-Firma.* ▲ *Logo d'une société proposant des logiciels.*

PAGE 117, #191 ART DIRECTOR/DESIGNER/AGENCY: *Byron Jacobs* CLIENT: *Bruce and Sue Mullins* COUNTRY: *Hong Kong* ■ *Aspects of an island off the coast of Australia known for the dolphins which inhabit its coastline are visually represented in the identity for this yacht which was named for the island.* ● *Eine Insel vor der Küste Australiens, die wegen ihrer Delphine bekannt ist, lieferte die Idee für das Logo einer Yacht, die den Namen der Insel trägt.* ▲ *Le graphisme de ce yacht s'inspire d'une île située au large des côtes australiennes et réputée pour ses dauphins.*

PAGE 117, #192 ART DIRECTOR/DESIGNER: *Evgeny Taborisskiy* AGENCY: *Ima-Press Publishers* CLIENT: *Bio Mix*

PAGE 118, #193 ART DIRECTOR/DESIGNER: *Michael Vanderbyl* AGENCY: *Vanderbyl Design* CLIENT: *Abra Cadabra* COUNTRY: *USA* ■ *This symbol for a racing yacht can be used on spinnakers, crew uniforms, jackets and foul weather gear.* ● *Dieses Symbol für eine Regatta-Yacht wurde auf den Spinnakern, den Mannschaftsuniformen, Jacken und der Sturmausrüstung angebracht.* ▲ *Ce symbole pour un yacht de course peut être utilisé sur des spinnakers, les uniformes de l'équipage, leur veste et leurs vêtements imperméables.*

PAGE 119, #194 ART DIRECTOR/DESIGNER: *Louise Fili* ILLUSTRATOR: *Anthony Russo* AGENCY: *Louise Fili Ltd.* CLIENT: *Crawford Doyle Booksellers* PAPER: *Rives* TYPEFACE: *Nikolas Cochin* PRINTER: *Soho Letterpress* COUNTRY: *USA* ■ *This business card for a bookstore uses the tactile quality of the letterpress to emphasize the personal, non-superstore qualities of this Madison Avenue bookstore.* ● *Diese Visitenkarte für einen Buchladen an der Madison Avenue, New York, wurde im Buchdruck hergestellt, um die persönliche, intime Atmosphäre des Ladens zum Ausdruck zu bringen.* ▲ *Carte de visite réalisée pour une librairie de Madison Avenue à New York. La qualité tactile de la typographie évoque l'atmosphère personnalisée du magasin par opposition aux « supermarchés » du livre.*

PAGE 119, #195 DESIGNER: *Les Kerr* AGENCY: *The Knape Group* CLIENT: *The Station Store* COUNTRY: *USA* ■ *The agency wanted to create a symbol that implied that high-qual-*

ity television programming can be as conveniently accessible as products at the neigherborhood grocery store. ● *Die Botschaft dieses Logos: TV-Programmierung kann so leicht zugänglich sein wie die Produkte im Laden um die Ecke.* ▲ *L'agence désirait créer un symbole suggérant que la programmation télévisée haut de gamme est aussi accessible que les produits de l'épicier du coin.*

PAGE 119, #196 ART DIRECTOR/DESIGNER/ILLUSTRATOR: *Peter Good* AGENCY: *Peter Good Graphic Design* CLIENT: *Custom Covers* COUNTRY: *USA* ■ *This logo was created for a company which specializes in the design of custom canvas coverings.* ● *Logo für eine Firma, die sich auf die Herstellung von massgeschneiderten Leinwand-Überzügen spezialisiert hat.* ▲ *Logo d'une société spécialisée dans la création de revêtements en toile sur mesure.*

PAGE 119, #197 ART DIRECTORS: *Chuck Johnson, Art Garcia* DESIGNER: *Art Garcia* ILLUSTRATORS: *Neill Whitlock, Art Garcia* AGENCY: *Brainstorm Inc.* CLIENT: *Dallas Society of Visual Communications (DSVC)* COUNTRY: *USA* ■ *This identity was created for the "Speaker Profile" section of a publication for the Dallas Society of Visual Communications.* ● *Logo für die "Speaker Profile"-Kolumne einer Publikation der Dallas Society of Visual Communications, in der Referenten vorgestellt. werden.* ▲ *Graphisme créé pour la rubrique «Speaker Profile» d'une publication de la Dallas Society of Visual Communications.*

PAGE 119, #198 ART DIRECTOR: *Dennis Crowe* DESIGNER: *John Pappas* AGENCY: *Zimmermann Crowe Design* CLIENT: *Marin Academy* COUNTRY: *USA* ■ *This design was created for a private high school. The Redwood tree symbolizes growth and individualism.* ● *Logo für eine private höhere Schule. Der Baum symbolisiert Wachstum und Individualität.* ▲ *Graphisme créé pour une école privée. Le séquoia symbolise la croissance et l'individualisme.*

PAGE 119, #199 ART DIRECTOR: *Joseph Rattan* DESIGNER/ILLUSTRATOR: *Diana McKnight* AGENCY: *Joseph Rattan Design* CLIENT: *Marketing Vision* COUNTRY: *USA* ■ *This logo was created for a strategic marketing and product development corporation.* ● *Logo für eine Firma, die sich mit Marketing und Produktentwicklung befasst.* ▲ *Logo d'une société spécialisée dans le marketing et le développement de produits.*

PAGE 119, #200 AGENCY: *Planet Design Company* CLIENT: *Mirror Mountain Motorcycles* COUNTRY: *USA* ■ *This logo was created for a custom motorcycle design company.* ● *Logo für eine Firma, die individuell dekorierte Motorräder anbietet.* ▲ *Logo créé pour personnaliser des motos (customs).*

PAGE 119, #201 DESIGNER: *Robert Rosol* CLIENT: *Student project (Nike)* COUNTRY: *USA*

PAGE 119, #202 ART DIRECTOR/DESIGNER/ILLUSTRATOR: *Mike Campbell* AGENCY: *Campbell Fisher Ditko Design, Inc.* CLIENT: *Digiscope* COUNTRY: *USA* ■ *This identity was created for a special effects company. The agency utilized a simple brush stroke that capitalizes on the concept "all the tricks of the trade."* ● *Firmenzeichen für eine Firma, die Spezialeffekte produziert. Der einfache Pinselstrich steht für das Konzept: «Alle Tricks der Branche.»* ▲ *Identité visuelle pour une société spécialisée dans les effets spéciaux. Le logo, un simple trait de pinceau, évoque le concept: «toutes les ficelles du métier».*

PAGE 119, #203 ART DIRECTORS: *Joe Duffy, Neil Powell* DESIGNER/ILLUSTRATOR: *Neil Powell* AGENCY: *Duffy Design* CLIENT: *Wieland Furniture* COUNTRY: *USA* ■ *This identity for a furniture company seeks to integrate the three-dimensional quality of the company's product-while repositioning the company within the marketplace.* ● *Dieses Logo für einen Möbelhersteller spielt mit der dreidimensionalen Qualität des Produktes. Es sollte der Firma zu einem neuen Image im Markt verhelfen.* ▲ *Identité visuelle d'un fabricant de meubles jouant avec l'aspect tridimensionnel du produit et visant à repositionner l'entreprise sur le marché.*

PAGE 119, #204 ART DIRECTOR/DESIGNER: *Mike Hicks* AGENCY: *Hixo Inc.* CLIENT: *Inkspots* COUNTRY: *USA* ■ *The client, a production company, wanted to create a division that dealt only with television ads. The agency created a graphic indicative of the name, which integrated an element of the parent company's* logo in the new division's identity. ● Logo für die TV-Spot-Produktionstochter einer Filmproduktionsfirma. Das neue Logo enthält ein Element des Logos der Muttergesellschaft. ▲ Le client, une société de production, souhaitait créer un département spécialisé dans les publicités télévisées. L'agence élabora un graphisme qui intègre un élément du logo de la société-mère et indique le nom du département.

PAGE 119, #205 CREATIVE DIRECTOR: Primo Angeli ART DIRECTORS: Carlo Pagoda, Primo Angeli DESIGNERS: Marcelo De Freitas, Primo Angeli CLIENT: San Francisco Film Society COUNTRY: USA ■ This identity was created for a film society and its international festival. The pictogram, to suggest the ideas of "international" and "San Francisco," utilizes a universal, non-verbal symbol portraying a director in motion in the center of the filmmaking process. ● Logo für ein internationales Filmfestival in San Francisco. Das Piktogramm, das für die Internationalität und den Ort des Festivals steht, zeigt einen Regisseur bei der Arbeit. ▲ Identité visuelle créée pour un festival cinématographique international à San Francisco. Le pictogramme représentant un metteur en scène en plein travail évoque l'internationalité et le lieu du festival.

PAGE 119, #206 ART DIRECTOR: Michael Bierut DESIGNERS: Michael Bierut, Dorit Lev AGENCY: Pentagram Design CLIENT: Gotham Equities COUNTRY: USA ■ The agency wanted to design a logo for a young real estate firm that evoked earlier, more "heroic" times. ● Logo für eine junge Immobilienfirma, das auf frühere, «heroischere» Zeiten anspielt. ▲ Logo pour une agence immobilière qui évoque les temps passés, plus héroïques.

PAGE 119, #207 ART DIRECTOR: Joseph Rattan DESIGNER/ILLUSTRATOR: Diana McKnight AGENCY: Joseph Rattan Design CLIENT: Prime Retail COUNTRY: USA ■ Logo created for a factory outlet shopping center in Florida. ● Logo für ein Shopping Center in Florida, das für den Grosshandel bestimmt ist. Logo d'un centre commercial en Floride.

PAGE 119, #208 ART DIRECTOR/DESIGNER: José Serrano AGENCY: Mires Design, Inc. ILLUSTRATOR: Tracy Sabin CLIENT: Industry Pictures TYPEFACE: FF Gothic COUNTRY: USA ■ To communicate the idea of comraderie in the industry and the client's company, the agency incorporated the three principles of the company and created a 1930s and 40s feel. ● Logo im Stil der 30/40er Jahre für eine Filmproduktionsfirma. Das Thema war die Kameradschaftlichkeit in der Branche. Dargestellt sind die drei Prinzipien der Firma. ▲ La communication est axée sur le thème de la camaraderie dans l'industrie cinématographique et la compagnie du client; l'agence a intégré les trois «grandes valeurs» de l'entreprise, en utilisant un style années 30 et 40.

PAGE 119, #209 ART DIRECTOR: Supon Phornirunlit DESIGNER/ILLUSTRATOR: Rodney Davidson AGENCY: Dogstar Design CLIENT: Supon Design Group COUNTRY: USA ■ The agency needed a book jacket icon for a book on logos and trademarks. The icon incorporated an eye, hand and figure, representing visual recognition (eye), trade (hand), and distinctive personality (figure). ● Gesucht war ein Zeichen für ein Buch über Logos und Markenzeichen. Das Auge steht für visuelles Erkennen, die Hand für die Wirtschaft, die Figur für Persönlichkeit. ▲ Jaquette d'un livre consacré aux logos et aux marques déposées. L'œil symbolise l'identification visuelle, la main, les relations commerciales et le personnage, la personnalité.

PAGE 119, #210 ART DIRECTOR/DESIGNER: Michael Vanderbyl AGENCY: Vanderbyl Design CLIENT: Coyote Books COUNTRY: USA ■ This logo was created for a bookstore which is open after hours because of its location in a theater district. ● Logo für einen Buchladen, der für die Besucher der nahegelegenen Theater auch am späten Abend geöffnet ist. ▲ Logo d'une librairie ouverte tard le soir dans un quartier de théâtres à San Francisco, où les amateurs peuvent se rendre après le spectacle.

PAGE 119, #211 ART DIRECTOR: Joseph Rattan DESIGNER/ILLUSTRATOR: Greg Morgan AGENCY: Joseph Rattan Design CLIENT: The Grammarian Group COUNTRY: USA ■ This mark was created for a literary organization. ● Logo für eine sprachwissenschaftliche Vereinigung. ▲ Logo créé pour un cercle littéraire.

PAGE 119, #212 ART DIRECTOR/DESIGNER/ILLUSTRATOR: Maggie Macnab AGENCY: Macnab Design Visual Communication CLIENT: Body Wisdom COUNTRY: USA ■ The designer wanted to graphically define a day spa/body products business as directly and interestingly as possible. ● Logo für ein Schönheitszentrum und Körperpflegeprodukte. ▲ La démarche du graphiste a été de présenter des produits de soin pour le corps de la façon la plus directe et la plus intéressante.

PAGE 119, #213 ART DIRECTORS/DESIGNERS: John Homs, Robin Schroeder ILLUSTRATOR: Scott Wright CALLIGRAPHER: Michael Clark AGENCY/CLIENT: VanAlt Group Incorporated COUNTRY: USA ■ Logo created for a design and marketing communications company. ● Logo für eine Design- und Marketing-Firma. ▲ Logo d'une société de design et de marketing.

PAGE 119, #214 ART DIRECTOR/DESIGNER/ILLUSTRATOR: Greg Valdez AGENCY: Pennebaker Design CLIENT: VISTA Corp. COUNTRY: USA ■ The client needed a mark for a new electronic filing system that files and retrieves graphic and text documents. ● Gefragt war ein Zeichen für ein neues elektronisches Ablagesystem für Graphik- und Textdokumente. ▲ Le client cherchait une marque pour un nouveau système de classement électronique pour textes et graphiques.

PAGE 119, #215 ART DIRECTOR/DESIGNER: Scott Johnson AGENCY: Scott Johnson Design CLIENT: Barnabas International COUNTRY: USA ■ This logo was created for a marathon. ● Logo für einen Marathon. ▲ Logo créé à l'occasion d'un marathon.

PAGE 119, #216 ART DIRECTOR/DESIGNER: Michael Vanderbyl AGENCY: Vanderbyl Design CLIENT: Aegis COUNTRY: USA ■ This logo for a real estate company represents the meaning of "Aegis"—"shield" or "protector." ● Das Logo für die Immobilienfirma Aegis interpretiert den Namen, der Schild bzw. Schutz bedeutet ▲ Logo d'une société immobilière jouant sur le nom « Aegis » qui signifie « bouclier » ou « protection ».

PAGE 119, #217 ART DIRECTOR/DESIGNER: Morteza Momayez AGENCY: Momayez Studio CLIENT: Foroutan Carpet Co. COUNTRY: Iran

PAGE 119, #218 DESIGNER: Michael Schwab ILLUSTRATOR/AGENCY: Michael Schwab Studio CLIENT: Larry Mahan Boot Company COUNTRY: USA

PAGE 120, #219 ART DIRECTOR: Bridget de Socio DESIGNERS: Malcolm Turk, Bridget de Socio DIGITAL ARTIST: Malcolm Turk AGENCY: Malcolm Turk Studios CLIENT: PAPER MAGAZINE COUNTRY: USA ■ These magazine logos were created to coincide with the themes of the issues. ● Diese Zeitschriftenlogos beziehen sich auf bestimmte Themen in den Ausgaben. ▲ Ces logos de magazine se réfèrent à des thèmes précis présentés dans différents numéros.

PAGE 121, #220 ART DIRECTOR: John McConnell DESIGNERS: John McConnell, Alan Dye AGENCY: Pentagram Design Ltd. CLIENT: Granada Hospitality Ltd. COUNTRY: England ■ This logo was created for a new coffee bar concept for motorway service stations. The symbol represents a drink on the move. ● Logo für ein neues Kaffee-Bar-Konzept, das für Tankstellen konzipiert wurde. Das Symbol zeigt ein Getränk in Bewegung. ▲ Logo réalisé dans le cadre d'un nouveau concept, à savoir un bar-café destiné aux stations à essence des autoroutes. Le symbole représente une boisson en mouvement.

PAGE 121, #221 ART DIRECTOR/DESIGNER/ILLUSTRATOR: Mark Geer AGENCY: Geer Design, Inc. CLIENT: Times 3 Productions COUNTRY: USA ■ Corporate identity for a film production company. ● Firmenzeichen für eine Filmproduktionsfirma. ▲ Identitié visuelle d'une société de productions cinématographiques.

PAGE 121, #222 ART DIRECTOR: John Muller DESIGNER: David Shultz AGENCY: Muller + Company CLIENT: J. Gilberts COUNTRY: USA ■ Logo created for a restaurant. ● Logo für ein Restaurant. ▲ Logo d'un restaurant.

PAGE 121, #223 ART DIRECTORS: Grenville Main, Diana Bidwill DESIGNER: Diana Bidwill AGENCY: BNA Design Limited ILLUSTRATORS: Diana Bidwill, John Moore CLIENT: Hoyts NZ Limited TYPEFACE: Matrix, Linoscript, Goudy COUNTRY: New

Zealand ■ *This identity was created for a cafe and bar. It utilizes 'M' from the name, and plays on the waiter icon to convey personality. The logo had variations of waiter, wine-waiter and chef.* ● *Logo für einen Café-Barbetrieb. Das M des Names wurde mit verschiedenen Figuren kombiniert: Kellner, Sommelier oder Koch.* ▲ *Identité visuelle créée pour un bar-café. Le graphisme combine un "M", initiale du nom de l'établissement, et joue avec le pictogramme du serveur; il est décliné en fonction de l'activité: le serveur, le sommelier, le cuisinier.*

PAGE 122, #224 ART DIRECTOR: *Malcolm Grear* AGENCY: *Malcolm Grear Designers* CLIENT: *Atlanta Committee for the Olympic Games* COUNTRY: *USA*

PAGE 123, #225 ART DIRECTOR/DESIGNER: *Scott Mires* ILLUSTRATOR: *Dan Thoner* AGENCY: *Mires Design, Inc.* CLIENT: *Intel Corp.* TYPEFACE: *Times New Roman Condensed* COUNTRY: *USA* ■ *This icon was created to promote a new "intelligent" embedded microprocessor technology. The strategy was to incorporate the idea that there is nothing as intelligent as the human brain. . . yet.* ● *Logo für eine neue, intelligente Micro-Prozessor-Technologie. Die integrierte Botschaft ist jedoch, dass nichts so intelligent ist wie das menschliche Gehirn.* ▲ *Logo créé pour une nouvelle technologie de microprocesseurs intelligente. La stratégie consistait à communiquer l'idée que rien ne peut surpasser le cerveau humain... pour l'instant.*

PAGE 123, #226 ART DIRECTOR/DESIGNER: *Sami Hokkanen* AGENCY: *Giraffe Werbeagentur* CLIENT: *Andreas Labes* COUNTRY: *Germany*

PAGE 123, #227 ART DIRECTORS: *Eric Rickabaugh, Mark Krumel* DESIGNER: *Eric Rickabaugh* AGENCY: *Rickabaugh Graphics* CLIENT: *The Walker Group* COUNTRY: *USA* ■ *This symbol (part of a group of three symbols) was designed to represent a division of a company which distributes parts for electrical contractors. Each division was symbolized by an animal. Infloor conduit is represented by a bull symbolizing strength, flexible conduit by a snake symbolizing flexibility, and distribution (this logo) by an eagle symbolizing speed. A lightning bolt was used in each symbol to represent the unifying element of electricity.* ● *Das Symbol, das Teil einer Gruppe von drei Symbolen ist, steht für eine Abteilung der Firma, die Elektriker beliefert. Jede Abteilung wird durch ein Tier symbolisiert, wobei die unter Putz verlegten Leitungen durch einen Stier (=Stärke) im Logo haben, die flexiblen Kabel eine Schlange (=Beweglichkeit) und die Vertriebsabteilung einen Adler (= Geschwindigkeit). Der in allen drei Logos auftauchende Blitz symbolisiert Elektrizität.* ▲ *Elément graphique d'une famille de trois symboles, créé pour une entreprise d'équipement électrique. Chaque département de l'entreprise est symbolisé par un animal. Le taureau symbolise la résistance des câbles enterrés, le serpent la flexibilité des câbles souples et l'aigle la rapidité de la distribution. L'éclair récurrent dans chaque logo symbolise l'électricité, élément unificateur.*

PAGE 123, #228 ART DIRECTOR: *Alan Chan* DESIGNERS: *Alan Chan, Cetric Leung* AGENCY: *Alan Chan Design Company* CLIENT: *Hong Kong Seibu Enterprise Ltd.*

PAGE 123, #229 ART DIRECTOR/DESIGNER: *Michael Vanderbyl* AGENCY: *Vanderbyl Design* CLIENT: *Windquest (DeVos family)* COUNTRY: *USA* ■ *This symbol for a racing yacht can be used on spinnakers, crew uniforms, jackets and foul weather gear.* ● *Dieses Symbol für eine Regatta-Yacht wurde auf den Spinnakern, den Mannschaftsuniformen, Jacken und der Sturmausrüstung angebracht.* ▲ *Ce symbole pour un yacht de course peut être utilisé sur des spinnakers, les uniformes de l'équipage, leur veste et leurs vêtements imperméables.*

PAGE 123, #230 DESIGNERS: *Daniel Weil, John McConnell, Jon Greenfield* DESIGN ASSISTANTS: *Alan Dye, Tom Lloyd, Stuart Oldridge* AGENCY: *Pentagram Design Ltd.* CLIENT: *Granada Hospitality* COUNTRY: *England* ■ *This identity was created for a new coffee bar concept for motorway service stations. The design draws on continental influences and the traditions of first class travel in its heyday.* ● *Logo für ein neues Kaffee-Bar-Konzept, das für Tankstellen konzipiert wurde. Hier wird auf Einflüsse des alten Kontinentaleuropas und die anspruchsvolle Reisetradition früherer Zeiten angespielt.* ▲ *Logo réalisé dans le cadre d'un nouveau concept, à savoir un bar-café destiné aux stations à essence des autoroutes. Il fait allusion aux influences du Vieux Continent et aux traditionnels voyages de première classe de jadis.*

PAGE 123, #231 ART DIRECTOR: *Charles S. Anderson* DESIGNERS: *Charles S. Anderson, Todd Piper-Hauswirth* ILLUSTRATOR: *Charles S. Anderson* AGENCY: *Charles S. Anderson Design Company* CLIENT: *HOW Magazine* COUNTRY: *USA* ■ *Identity for an international design magazine.* ● *Logo für ein internationales Design-Magazin.* ▲ *Identité visuelle d'un magazine de design international.*

PAGE 123, #232 ART DIRECTOR: *Rex Peteet* DESIGNER: *Derek Welch* AGENCY: *Sibley/Peteet Design* CLIENT: *Central and South West* COUNTRY: *USA* ■ *This identity was created for an electrical utility holding company's annual summer picnic which had a western theme. The rodeo cowboy rides and tames a lighting bolt which replaces the expected bucking bronco.* ● *Ein Westernthema für das Logo, das speziell für das jährliche Sommerpicknick einer Elektrofirma entworfen wurde. Im Hinblick auf die Branche wurde anstelle des zu zähmenden Wildpferdes ein Blitz verwendet.* ▲ *Logo créé pour le pique-nique annuel d'une compagnie d'électricité, qui avait lieu cette année-là sur le thème du western. Le cow-boy chevauche un éclair en lieu et place d'un étalon fougueux.*

PAGE 123, #233 ART DIRECTOR/DESIGNER: *Sami Hokkanen* AGENCY: *Giraffe GMBH* CLIENT: *ORB/Rockradio B* TYPEFACE: *Einborn, Über zeichnet* COUNTRY: *Germany* ■ *This logo was developed for a new music radio station. The use of an unconventional typeface helped to obtain a strong identity. The "B" stands for Brandenburg, the region in which the the station can be heard.* ● *Durch den Einsatz einer unkonventionellen Typographie wurde ein starker visueller Auftritt für einen neuen Regionalradio-Musiksender geschaffen. Das «B» steht für Brandenburg.* ▲ *Grâce à une typographie inhabituelle, une forte identité a été créée pour cette nouvelle station de radio régionale diffusant de la musique. Le «B» signifie Brandenburg.*

PAGE 123, #234 ART DIRECTOR/DESIGNER: *Christoph Bolz* AGENCY: *SFGB Schule für Gestaltung Berne* TYPEFACE: *Frutiger* COUNTRY: *Switzerland* ■ *This logo was graduate student work for a fictitious international film festival showcasing road movies.* ● *Studentenarbeit für ein fiktives internationales Filmfestival.* ▲ *Projet d'un étudiant réalisé pour un festival cinématographique international fictif.*

PAGE 123, #235 ART DIRECTOR/DESIGNER/ILLUSTRATOR: *Kyosti Varis* COUNTRY: *Finland*

PAGE 124, #236 ART DIRECTORS: *Eric Rickabaugh, Mark Krumel* DESIGNER: *Michael Smith* AGENCY: *Rickabaugh Graphics* CLIENT: *Grant Medical Center* COUNTRY: *USA* ■ *For a medical center annual report, the agency chose the human figure to represent the hospital staff. The figure supports various symbols which represent the hospital's concerns: finance, health, spirit, growth and caring.* ● *Als Symbol für den Jahresbericht eines Krankenhauses wurde eine menschliche Gestalt gewählt, die das Spitalpersonal symbolisiert. Diese Gestalt stützt verschiedene andere Symbole, die für diverse Bereiche des Spitals stehen: Finanzen, Gesundheit, Atmosphäre, Wachstum und Fürsorge.* ▲ *Rapport annuel d'un centre médical. L'être humain symbolise le personnel de l'hôpital. Il porte différents éléments graphiques, symboles des préoccupations de l'hôpital: finances, santé, courage, croissance et compassion.*

PAGE 124, #237 ART DIRECTOR: *Michael Cronan* DESIGNERS: *Michael Cronan, Anthony Yell* AGENCY: *Cronan Design* ILLUSTRATOR: *Michael Cronan* CLIENT: *Engineering Animation, Inc.* TYPEFACE: *Bodoni, Meta* COUNTRY: *USA*

PAGE 124, #238 ART DIRECTORS: *Tika Buchanan, Julia Precht* DESIGNER/ILLUSTRATOR: *Tika Buchanan* AGENCY: *Maddocks and Company* CLIENT: *The American Craft Museum* COUNTRY: *USA* ■ *This identity was designed for a fundraiser/show. Banquet photographs from the thirties and forties were combined with contemporary tableware shots to provide a combination of old world reflection and current style.* ● *Auftritt für ein Benefiz-Bankett. Aufnahmen aus den dreissiger und vierziger Jahren wurden mit zeitgenössischen Photos von Tafelgedecken kombiniert.* ▲ *Identité créée à l'occasion d'un banquet de collecte de fonds. La combinaison de photographies des années trente et quarante avec des prises de vue actuelles de linge de table fait ressortir la différence de style.*

PAGE 124, #239 CREATIVE DIRECTOR/ART DIRECTOR: *Michael Jager* DESIGNERS: *Michael Jager, Callie Johnson, Vicki McCafferty* ILLUSTRATOR: *Dan Krovatin* AGENCY: *Jager Di*

Paola Kemp Design CLIENT: *Harvest Market* PRINTER: *Design Printing* COUNTRY: *USA* ■ *This identity was created for a gourmet food market in Vermont. The agency wanted to represent passion for food with a friendly humanizing attitude.* ● *Erscheinungsbild für einen Delikatessen-Markt in Vermont. Durch einen freundlichen Auftritt sollte die Freude an Nahrungsmitteln dargestellt werden.* ▲ *L'agence s'est attachée à représenter les plaisirs de la bonne chère tout en conférant une touche sympathique et humaine à cette identité visuelle réalisée pour un marché de délicatesses dans le Vermont.*

PAGE 125, #240 ART DIRECTOR/DESIGNER: *Craig Frazier* AGENCY: *Frazier Design* CLIENT: *Magico* COUNTRY: *USA* ■ *Trademark for a digital animation and production company.* ● *Markenzeichen für eine Firma, die sich mit digitaler Animation und Produktion befasst.* ▲ *Marque de fabrique d'une société spécialisée dans l'infographie et la production de films.*

PAGE 125, #241 ART DIRECTORS: *Matt Cave, Russell Parker* DESIGNER/DIGITAL MANIPULATION: *Matt Cave* AGENCY: *Reed and Steven* CLIENT: *Bluxo Records* PRINTER: *Aim Riverside Press* COUNTRY: *USA* ■ *The agency sought to create an identifiable icon for a new record label that would be easily recognized and adaptable for the label's diverse artists and products. A billiard ball was chosen for its easy recognition and adaptability. Its simple shape and graphics allow it to be utilized almost anywhere and lends the label a 'cool' atittude many already associate with billiards.* ● *Der Billardball wurde als Ikone für ein neues Plattenlabel gewählt, weil er dank der einfachen Form einprägsam und vielseitig anwendbar ist. Hinzu kommt, dass Billard.bei vielen Leuten als 'cool' gilt.* ▲ *Label d'une nouvelle maison de disques. La boule de billard a été retenue pour la simplicité de sa forme, facilement identifiable, qui permet une grande souplesse dans l'adaptation du logo à différents artistes et produits. Le billard est en outre associé à un style de vie décontracté.*

PAGE 125, #242 ART DIRECTORS: *Jason Bacon, Greg Hoffman* DESIGNER/ILLUSTRATOR: *Jason Bacon* AGENCY/CLIENT: *Nike, Inc.* COUNTRY: *USA* ■ *This identity was created for a company-sponsored rowing event.* ● *Zeichen für eine von Nike gesponserte Ruderregatta.* ▲ *Graphisme créé pour une compétition d'aviron sponsorisée par Nike.*

PAGE 125, #243 ART DIRECTOR: *Mark Sackett* DESIGNERS: *Mark Sackett, Wayne Sakamoto* AGENCY: *Sackett Design Associates* ILLUSTRATOR: *Calvin Patlon* CLIENT: *Firefighters in the Schools* COUNTRY: *USA* ■ *This identity was created for a non-profit organization that teaches fire safety in grade schools.* ● *Logo für eine Non-Profit-Organisation, deren Mitglieder an Schulen Vorträge über Brandverhinderung halten.* ▲ *Logo pour une organisation non gouvernementale dont les membres visitent des écoles et donnent des conférences sur la prévention du feu.*

PAGE 125, #244 ART DIRECTORS: *Dana Arnett, Melissa Waters* DESIGNERS: *Curtis Schreiber, Ken Fox, Adam Smith* AGENCY: *VSA Partners, Inc.* CLIENT: *Harley-Davidson, Inc.* PAPER: *Vintage Remarque Gloss 80 lb.* TYPEFACE: *Hand drawn, Futura* COUNTRY: *USA* ■ *This logo was created for a licensing program. To establish a brand within a brand, the well-known bar and shield logo was incorporated into a larger, more visual shape that was distinctive but easy to distuinguish from the corporate logo.* ● *Logo für eine Marke innerhalb einer Marke: Das bekannte Harley-Davidson-Logo wurde in eine grössere Form verarbeitet, die den Firmencharakter wahrte, aber trotzdem leicht zu unterscheiden ist.* ▲ *Logo créé dans le but d'asseoir une marque à l'intérieur d'une autre marque. Le célèbre logo Harley-Davidson a été intégré dans une forme plus grande, plus «visuelle», distincte et qui se différencie aisément du logo institutionnel.*

PAGE 126, #245 ART DIRECTORS: *Janine Rubinfier, Bob Francis* AGENCY: *Rubin Postaer and Associates* CLIENT: *California Pizza Kitchen* PAPER: *Taslin with Laminate* COUNTRY: *USA* ■ *A changeable and inexpensively produced menu and insert were needed for this restaurant. The design had to be visually exciting, uniquely "Californian" and usefully presented and organized. Four different menu jackets were created—each with different high-quality four-color images on the outside for fun and visual impact—along with two-color replaceable menu inserts. The menu art was ultimately applied to the staff uniforms and ties.* ● *Speisekarte für*

ein kalifornisches Restaurant. Für ein attraktives Äusseres der vier verschiedenen Umschläge sorgen die mehrfarbigen Bilder, während die austauschbaren Einlagen im Zweifarbendruck produziert wurden. Die Graphik der Speisekarte wurde auch für die Personaluniformen und die Krawatten verwendet.* ▲ *Menu avec encart d'un restaurant californien, conçu pour être facile à modifier et produit à moindre coût. Le graphisme devait être visuellement accrocheur, typiquement californien, mais également clair dans sa présentation. Quatre jaquettes ont été créées – soit quatre couvertures en quadrichromie, aux visuels forts et «fun», et quatre encarts en bichromie pour les menus. Le même graphisme a été décliné pour les uniformes et les cravates du personnel.*

PAGE 126, #246 ART DIRECTOR: *Lori B. Wilson* DESIGNER: *Sharon Le June* ILLUSTRATOR: *Susan Miller* AGENCY: *David Carter Design & Associates* CLIENT: *Hyatt Regency, Osaka* COUNTRY: *Japan*

PAGE 127, #247 ART DIRECTOR: *Gene Seidman* DESIGNER: *Ana Rogers* AGENCY: *Rogers Seidman Design Team* CLIENT: *Campagna Restaurant* COUNTRY: *USA* ■ *The inspiration stemmed from seeing Cinzano posters painted on the sides of barns dotting the Tuscan landscape. The design objective was to synthesize the essence of Tuscan cuisine with a New York edge.* ● *Inspiriert wurde diese Broschüre durch auf Wände gemalte Cinzano-Werbung in der Toskana. Das Ziel war, das Wesentliche der toskanischen Küche mit einem Touch vom New Yorker Lebensgefühl zu verbinden.* ▲ *Cette brochure s'inspire de publicités Cinzano peintes sur des façades en Toscanie. L'objectif était de faire transparaître l'essence de la cuisine toscane en y apportant une touche new-yorkaise.*

PAGE 127, #248 DESIGNER: *Jill Giles* AGENCY: *Giles Design* PHOTOGRAPHERS: *Amos Chan, Robert Mizono, David Leach, Robert Peak* CALLIGRAPHER: *Jack A. Molloy* CLIENT: *St. Lukes Foundation* PAPER: *Karma Natural* TYPEFACE: *Novarese, Novarese Bold* PRINTER: *Padgett Printing* COUNTRY: *USA* ■ *The client needed an inexpensive menu program that could also serve as a souvenir. The program carries elements of poster and invitation design (metallic inks, calligraphy, an antique 'regal' quality) and was printed in three colors on donated paper.* ● *Gefragt war eine kostengünstige Speisekarte, die auch als Souvenir dienen sollte. Es wurden Elemente des Plakates und der Einladung zu dem speziellen Anlass verwendet, z.B. Metallic-Farben, Kalligraphie und das 'königliche' Thema.* ▲ *Le but était de concevoir un menu peu coûteux à réaliser, pouvant être emporté comme souvenir. Des éléments de l'affiche et du carton d'invitation ont été repris, tels que les encres métallisées, la calligraphie, le côté ancien et précieux. L'impression a été réalisée en trois couleurs; le papier est le produit d'une donation.*

PAGE 127, #249 ART DIRECTOR: *Bob Dennard* DESIGNERS: *Bob Dennard, James Lacey, Chris Wood* PHOTOGRAPHY: *Brown Brothers Stock Photography* ILLUSTRATORS: *James Lacey, Chris Wood, Warren Hill* AGENCY: *Dennard Creative Inc.* CLIENT: *Bennigan's Restaurants* COUNTRY: *USA* ■ *This lunch menu was created for prototype test units throughout the United States.* ● *Mittags-Menukarte für Pilot-Speiselokale überall in den USA.* ▲ *Menu de restaurants-pilote répandus dans tous les Etats-Unis.*

PAGE 128, #250 ART DIRECTOR/DESIGNER: *José Serrano* AGENCY: *Mires Design, Inc.* PHOTOGRAPHER: *Chris Wimpey* CLIENT: *Deborah Liv Johnson* TYPEFACE: *Latin* PRINTER: *Rush Press* COUNTRY: *USA* ■ *This CD design was created to introduce a new recording artist. The agency wanted to give the packaging a look that reflected the type of music and country influence.* ● *CD einer neuen Künstlerin. Die Verpackung sollte die Art der Musik und den Country-Einfluss reflektieren.* ▲ *Le graphisme de ce CD présente une nouvelle artiste et évoque son style musical, marqué par des influences country.*

PAGE 128, #251 ART DIRECTORS: *Eric Spillman, Richard Bates* DESIGNERS: *Eric Spillman, Eric Altenburger* AGENCY: *Art Industria* PHOTOGRAPHER: *Unknown (US Naval Institute Archives)* RECORD CO.: *Atlantic Records* ARTIST/ALBUM: *Led Zeppelin/The Complete Studio Recordings* TYPEFACE: *Din Schriften, Engschrift* MANUFACTURER: *AGI* COUNTRY: *USA* ■ *The client asked for a device to contain ten discs comprising all Led Zeppelin studio recordings and reproducing all the original LP artwork. The agency designed six book-like carriers: five books to hold two CDs each with the* *sixth book containing an essay, photographs and track listings. The image of a dirigible under construction suggests the assembly of many parts and reflects the fact that it is a complete set of studio recordings. The kaleidoscopic effect of the mirrored imagery and the use of the velvet are a reflection of the music genre.* ● *Gefragt waren Behälter, in denen zehn CDs mit Studioaufnahmen von Led Zeppelin Platz finden würden. Ausserdem sollten die Originalhüllen der LPs reproduziert werden. Das Ergebnis sind sechs buchähnliche Hüllen, von denen fünf jeweils 2 CDs enthalten, während die sechste einen Photo-Essay und die Liste der Stücke enthält.* ▲ *Le client désirait un système de rangement pouvant contenir l'ensemble des dix CD des enregistrements studio de Led Zeppelin et présentant leurs 33 tours originaux. L'agence créa six éléments ressemblant à des livres: les cinq premiers contiennent deux CD chacun et le sixième renferme un livret avec des photos et les titres des morceaux. L'image d'un dirigeable en construction évoque l'assemblage de différents éléments et suggère qu'il s'agit d'une compilation complète des enregistrements en studio. Quant à l'effet kaléidoscopique des images réfléchies et au velours du fond, ils situent le genre musical.*

PAGE 129, #252 ART DIRECTORS: *Robin Lynch, Laurie Goldman* DESIGNER: *Laurie Goldman* ILLUSTRATOR: *John Van Hamersveld* RECORD CO.: *Blue Thumb Records (GRP Recording Company)* ARTIST/ALBUM: *Various Artists/All Day Thumbsucker Revisited (The History of Blue Thumb Records)* TYPEFACE: *Interstate Family* MANUFACTURER: *AGI* COUNTRY: *USA* ■ *The agency wanted to create a package which pays homage to a record company known for its eclectic roster and counter-culture marketing approach. The package was designed around an original piece of art from the record company. Inside the CD booklet, the Pop Art illustration was reinterpreted to reflect the design and typographic attitudes of the 90s, maintaining the pop colors and comic book style of the original art.* ● *Hier ging es um ein Package für eine Plattenfirma, die für ihr aussergewöhnlich vielseitiges Programm und ihren Subkultur-Auftritt bekannt ist. Zentrales Thema bildete ein Originalkunstwerk im Besitz Plattenfirma. In der CD-Broschüre wird eine neue Interpretation dieser Pop-Art-Illustration verwendet: Design und Typographie entsprechen dem Stil der neunziger Jahre, aber Farben und Comics-Stil des Originals bleiben gewahrt.* ▲ *L'agence désirait créer un packaging qui rende hommage à une maison de disques réputée pour son éclectisme et son approche marketing marginale. Le packaging est conçu autour d'une œuvre d'art originale appartenant à la maison de disques. A l'intérieur du livret du CD, l'illustration pop art a été réinterprétée dans le style graphique et typographique des années 90, mais les couleurs «pop» et l'esprit BD ont été conservés.*

PAGE 129, #253 DESIGNER: *Allen Weinberg* DESIGN ASSISTANT: *Paul Martin* AGENCY: *Sony Music (in-house)* PHOTOGRAPHY: *Stock* RECORD CO.: *Sony Music* ARTIST/ALBUM: *Aerosmith/Box of Fire* COUNTRY: *USA* ■ *This package design for 12 CDs had to stand out from the other box sets in a store. A "Trompe l'œil" box was created, with a burnt match as the handle.* ● *Eine spezielle Box für 12 CDs: Trompe-l'œil mit einem abgebrannten Streichholz als Griff.* ▲ *Ce coffret de 12 CD devait attirer l'attention sur les points de vente. Le designer réalisa un coffret en trompe l'œil, où une allumette consumée fait office de poignée.*

PAGE 130, #254 ART DIRECTORS: *Chris Jones, Tommy Steele, Jeffery Fey, Blind Melon* DESIGNER: *Jeffery Fey* PHOTOGRAPHER: *Danny Clinch* AGENCY: *Capitol Records (in-house)* CLIENT: *Capitol Records, Inc.* ARTIST/ALBUM: *Blind Melon/Soup* TYPEFACE: *Kaufman, Copperplate, Times, Bureau Grotesques* PRINTER: *AGI* COUNTRY: *USA* ■ *The record company wanted to create a unique presentation for the follow-up record of a group whose first record sold more than a million copies. Playing on the theme of the record's title song, "Soup," the package incorporates elements of a menu including "diner typography" and photography.* ● *Hier ging es um die Präsentation der zweiten CD einer Gruppe, deren erste CD mit Verkäufen von über einer Million Stück ein Riesenerfolg gewesen war. Der Titel-Song "Soup" lieferte das Thema für die Gestaltung, die tpyische Elemente (Typographie und Photographie) einer Speisekarte enthält.* ▲ *Il s'agissait de présenter le deuxième CD d'un groupe dont le premier disque s'était vendu à plus d'un million d'exemplaires. Le graphisme joue sur le thème de la chanson-titre intitulée « Soup », typographie et visuel évoquant la carte d'un restaurant.*

PAGE 130, #255 ART DIRECTORS: *Thomas Sassenbach, Christina Krutz* DESIGNER/AGENCY: *Christina Krutz* CLIENT: *BMG Ariola Media GmBH* COUNTRY: *Germany*

PAGE 131, #256 ART DIRECTOR: *Stefan Sagmeister* DESIGNERS: *Stefan Sagmeister, Veronica Oh* AGENCY: *Sagmeister Inc.* PHOTOGRAPHER: *Tom Schierlitz* RECORD CO.: *Energy Records* ARTIST/ALBUM: *H.P. Zinker/Mountains of Madness* PAPER: *100 lb. Gloss* PRINTER: *Disc Graphics* COUNTRY: *USA* ■ *This cover was designed for a music CD with lyrics that deal with angst and schizophrenia in big city life. When the designer first arrived in New York, an elderly, distinguished looking man passed him on the sidewalk and began shouting obscenities. The incident came to mind as the designer created the cover design. A calm image and a frantic image of an old man were printed in green and red respectively and placed in a red tinted plastic case. The green turns black, the red image becomes invisible, and the old man becomes frantic when the booklet is pulled out of the case.* ● *Hülle für eine Musik-CD, deren Text von Angst und Schizophrenie des Grossstadtlebens handelt. Die Figur des alten Mannes geht auf ein Erlebnis des Designers zurück: Als er zum ersten Mal in New York eintraf, begegnete er einem vornehm aussehenden älteren Herrn, der plötzlich Obzönitäten herausschrie. Für die CD-Hülle produzierte er zwei Bilder: das eines ruhigen und das eines wahnsinnigen alten Mannes, in Rot bzw. in Grün gedruckt. In der rotgefärbten Plastikhülle wird das rote Bild unsichtbar, während das grüne schwarz wirkt.* ▲ *Boîtier d'un CD, dont les textes parlent de la peur et de la schizophrénie qu'engendre la vie dans les grandes villes modernes. Le personnage du vieil homme fait référence à un événement qui marqua le graphiste: arrivé de fraîche date à New York, il rencontra un vieux monsieur fort bien mis qui l'abreuva soudain des pires obscénités. Il créa deux images, l'une d'un vieil homme serein, l'autre d'un vieillard fou, l'une imprimée en vert, l'autre en rouge. Dans le boîtier en plastique rouge, l'image imprimée en rouge disparaît tandis que celle imprimée en vert se détache en noir.*

PAGE 131, #257 ART DIRECTOR: *Minato Ishikawa* DESIGNER: *Kayoko Akiyama* AGENCY: *Minato Ishikawa Associates Inc.* PHOTOGRAPHER: *Takahiro Shikama* RECORD CO.: *Edoya Records Ltd.* ARTIST/ALBUM: *Pink Cloud/the period* MANUFACTURER: *Japan Sleeve Company Ltd.* COUNTRY: *Japan* ■ *"Pink Cloud" is one of the long lasting rock groups in Japan. The group separated after fifteen years of working together. "the period" is their last album.* ● *Pink Cloud ist eine japanische Rock-Gruppe, die sich nach 15 Jahren trennte. "the period" ist ihr letztes gemeinsames Album.* ▲ *Pink Cloud est le nom d'un groupe de rock japonais dont les musiciens se séparèrent au terme d'une collaboration de quinze ans – un record au Japon! « the period » est le titre de leur dernier album.*

PAGE 131, #258 CREATIVE DIRECTOR: *Michael Jager* ART DIRECTOR/DESIGNER/DIGITAL ILLUSTRATION: *Kirk James* PHOTOGRAPHERS: *Cynthia Levine, Kirk James, Alex Williams, Hubert Schriebl* CLIENT: *Q-Prime* ARTIST/ALBUM: *Def Leppard/Vault* COUNTRY: *USA* ■ *This CD packaging was created for an anthology of Def Leppard's first fifteen years. The agency wanted to reflect the band's history, but also demonstrate the direction of the band's new music. The cover image and slipcase works as a metaphor for the band's past and as the notion of the jewel box as a precious container.* ● *CD-Hülle für eine Anthologie der ersten 15 Jahre der Band Def Leppard. Hier ging es um die Darstellung der Geschichte der Band und um ihre neue Musik.* ▲ *Packaging de CD pour une anthologie des 15 premières années du groupe Def Leppard. L'agence a voulu présenter l'histoire du groupe tout en montrant l'évolution de leur musique.*

PAGE 131, #259 ART DIRECTOR/DESIGNER: *Deborah Norcross* PHOTOGRAPHER: *Cati Gonzales (cover), Deborah Norcross (interior)* RECORD CO.: *Luaka Bop, Inc., Warner Bros Records* ARTIST/ALBUM: *Cornershop/Woman's Gotta Have It* COUNTRY: *USA* ■ *To reflect the band's attitude and create a sexy, sociable, street-funky image suggesting a cornershop, the designer imitated a 60s pantyhose package.* ● *Um den Stil der Band zu reflektieren und ein sexy, funky und gleichzeitig geselliges Images eines Ladens an der Ecke zu suggerieren, diente eine Strumpfhosenverpackung aus den sechziger Jahren als Vorbild für diese CD-Hülle.* ▲ *Boîtier de CD. Pour refléter le style musical du groupe et suggérer l'image funk, sexy et conviviale d'un petit magasin de disques de quartier, le designer s'est inspiré d'un packaging de collants créé dans les années 60.*

PAGE 132, #260 ART DIRECTORS: *Jeffery Fey, Tommy Steele* DESIGNER: *Jeffery Fey* AGENCY: *Capitol Records (in-house)* ILLUSTRATION: *Hatch Show Prints (logo, cover art)* CLIENT: *Capitol Records, Inc.* ARTIST/ALBUM: *Bonepony/Stomp Revival* PAPER: *Finch Opaque, Bright White Vellum* TYPEFACE: *Times, Copperplates, Century Schoolbook, Engravers* PRINTER: *Queens Group* COUNTRY: *USA* ■ To create a unique package for a group's first record, the designers found wood-cut typography and line cuts of tent-show revival meetings and re-created the feeling of vintage poster art. ● *Um eine einzigartige Hülle für die erste CD der Gruppe zu schaffen, griff der Gestalter auf Holzschnittbuchstaben und Texte zurück, die sich auf alte Zelt-Shows beziehen, so dass ein Auftritt im Stil alter Plakate gelang.* ▲ *Afin de créer un boîtier original pour le premier CD d'un groupe, les graphistes ont utilisé des caractères de gravure sur bois et au trait qui font référence à l'époque des spectacles sous chapiteau, recréant ainsi le style des affiches de collection.*

PAGE 132, #261 ART DIRECTOR/DESIGNER: *Deborah Norcross* PHOTOGRAPHER/ILLUSTRATOR: *Chris Beirne* RECORD CO.: *Reprise Records* ARTIST/ALBUM: *Filter/Short Bus* TYPEFACE: *Futura, Folio* COUNTRY: *USA* ■ The band did not want to look like Nine Inch Nails. The solution was to have the cover/logo look like an intravenous bottle, merely informative. ● *Um nicht wie die Band 'Nine Inch Nails' auszusehen, entschied man sich für eine Hülle/ein Logo mit einer intravenösen Flasche.* ▲ *Le groupe voulait éviter toute confusion avec les Nine Inch Nails. La solution retenue présente une perfusion intraveineuse, intégrée au logo/à la jaquette.*

PAGE 133, #262 ART DIRECTOR/DESIGNER: *Mark Burdett* AGENCY: *Sony Music (in-house)* PHOTOGRAPHER/ILLUSTRATOR: *Frank Ockenfels* RECORD CO.: *Sony Music* ARTIST/ALBUM: *'Keb' Mo'/Keb' Mo'* TYPEFACE: *Confidential* COUNTRY: *USA*

PAGE 133, #263 ART DIRECTOR: *Sandy Lee* DESIGNERS: *Sandy Lee, Tom Hunt, Nate Durrant* AGENCY: *Momentum Design* ARTIST/ALBUM: *John Morriarty Trio/So Many Stars* TYPEFACE: *Adobe Garamond, Bank Gothic* COUNTRY: *USA* ■ The agency used typography inspired by timelapsed photographs of the night sky to reflect the title of the CD, "So Many Stars." The silver finish of the CD sparkles in the light against the background. ● *Zeitrafferphotos des Nachthimmels inspirierten zu dieser Typographie für eine CD mit dem Titel "So Many Stars". Die silbrige CD leuchtet im Licht gegen den Hintergrund.* ▲ *La typographie de ce boîtier de CD s'inspire d'une série de photographies image par image du ciel prises de nuit, en référence au titre du disque: So Many Stars. Le CD, argenté, brille et se détache sur le fond.*

PAGE 133, #264 ART DIRECTORS/DESIGNERS: *D. Mark Kingsley, Karen Greenberg* AGENCY: *Greenberg Kingsley, Inc.* PHOTOGRAPHER: *Mark Malabrigo* CLIENT: *Discovery Records* ARTIST: *Screaming Headless Torsos* TYPEFACE: *Orator, Janson* PRINTER: *AGI* COUNTRY: *USA*

PAGE 133, #265 ART DIRECTORS: *Bridget de Socio, Judy Troilo* DESIGNERS: *Bridget de Socio, Mayra Morrison* PHOTOGRAPHERS: *Frank Ockenfels, Stephanie Pfriender* KEY/KEYHOLE PLATE: *Don Pywell* AGENCY: *Socio X* RECORD CO.: *Island Records* ARTIST/ALBUM: *Melissa Etheridge/Your Little Secret* PAPER: *Mead Signature* TYPEFACE: *American Typewriter, Trixie, custom* COUNTRY: *USA* ■ This CD packaging for "Your Little Secret" utilized a keyhole with single photos which could randomly slide behind the hole to give hints to the "secret." ● *CD-Hülle für "Your Little Secret". Ganz dem Titel entspreched, lassen sich als Anpielungen auf das «Geheimnis».verschiedene Photos hinter das Schlüsselloch schieben.* ▲ *Packaging de CD pour «Your Little Secret». Diverses photographies peuvent être placées derrière le trou de serrure et donnent des indices sur le «secret».*

PAGE 133, #266 ART DIRECTOR/DESIGNER/PHOTOGRAPHER: *Mark Linkous* AGENCY: *Capitol Records (in-house)* RECORD CO.: *Capitol Records, Inc.* ARTIST: *Sparklehorse* TYPEFACE: *Trixie* COUNTRY: *USA* ■ For his first record, the artist created his own package using his own photographs. ● *Der Künstler gestaltete die Hülle für seine erste CD selbst und verwendete auch eigene Photos.* ▲ *L'artiste a créé lui-même le boîtier de son premier CD. Il est également l'auteur des photographies utilisées.*

PAGE 133, #267 ART DIRECTOR/DESIGNER: *Peter Felder* DESIGNER: *René Dalpra* PHOTOGRAPHER: *Herbert Rauch* AGENCY: *Felder Grafik Design* CLIENT: *Big Band Club Dornbirn* COUNTRY: *Austria*

PAGE 133, #268 ART DIRECTOR/DESIGNER: *Sara Rotman* PHOTOGRAPHER: *Michael McLaughlin* ILLUSTRATOR: *Steve Wacksman* AGENCY: *Sony Music Entertainment Creative Services* RECORD CO.: *550 Music/Epic Records* ARTIST/ALBUM: *Eve's Plum/Cherry Alive* COUNTRY: *USA*

PAGE 133, #269 ART DIRECTORS: *Michael Buttgereit, Wolfram Heidenreich* PHOTOGRAPHER: *Hubertus Schüler* AGENCY/CLIENT: *Buttgereit & Heidenreich, Kommunikationsdesign*

PAGE 133, #270 ART DIRECTOR/DESIGNER: *Alec Bathgate* RECORD CO.: *Flying Nun Records* ARTIST/ALBUM: *Various/Abbasalutely* COUNTRIES: *England, New Zealand*

PAGE 133, #271 ART DIRECTOR: *Tommy Steele* DESIGNER: *Jeffery Fey* AGENCY: *Capitol Records (in-house)* PHOTOGRAPHER: *Ethan A. Russell* RECORD CO.: *Capitol Records, Inc.* ARTIST/ALBUM: *John Hiatt/Walk On* TYPEFACE: *Copperplate, Ironmonger, Times, Blackoak* PRINTER: *AGI* COUNTRY: *USA* ■ This package for an established artist's first record with the record company utilized unexpected photography and traditional typography, and presented them together in a modern way. ● *Die Kombination ungewöhnlicher Photographie und traditioneller Typographie sorgte für eine aussergewöhnliche CD-Hülle. Es ist die erste CD eines etablierten Künstlers, die er unter dem Capital Records Label herausbringt.* ▲ *Boîtier de CD original résultant de l'association de photographies insolites et d'une typographie classique, créé pour le premier disque d'un artiste célèbre.*

PAGE 133, #272 ART DIRECTOR/DESIGNER: *Sara Rotman* AGENCY: *Sony Music Entertainment Creative Services* PHOTOGRAPHERS/ILLUSTRATORS: *Jason Stang, Sara Rotman* RECORD CO.: *Columbia Records* ARTIST/ALBUM: *Corrosion of Conformity/7 Days* COUNTRY: *USA*

PAGE 133, #273 ART DIRECTOR: *Mirko Ilić* AGENCY: *Mirko Ilić Corp.* PHOTOGRAPHER: *Stock (front cover), Rajko Bizjak (interior)* RECORD CO.: *Helidon* ARTIST/ALBUM: *Buldozer/Noc´* MANUFACTURER: *Delotiskarna* TYPEFACE: *Helvetica* COUNTRY: *Slovenia* ■ The band commisssioned a package and logo for their album "Noc¯" which means "night." The cover uses stock images which reminded the designer of Slovenia. Since the album would be sold in areas of the former Yugoslavia, the logo combines two accents, and the word is repeated in a circle to create an ominous and dark look to reflect the sentiments of the songs. ■ *Der Titel der CD bedeutet «Nacht». Die für die Hülle ausgesuchten Archivphotos erinnerten den Gestalter an Slovenien. Da die CD in Gebieten des ehemaligen Jugoslawien verkauft werden soll, besteht das Logo aus einer Kombination von zwei Akzenten. Durch die Wiederbolung des Wortes in einem Kreis wird eine düstere. Stimmung erzeugt, die den Songs entspricht.* ▲ *Les photographies d'archives choisies pour le boîtier rappelaient la Slovénie au graphiste. Le disque étant essentiellement destiné à être vendu en l'ex-Yougoslavie, le logo combine deux accents serbocroates. La répétition du mot « Noc´ » – titre du disque signifiant « la nuit » – dans un cercle crée une atmosphère sombre, pesante, en accord avec la musique et les textes des chansons.*

PAGE 134, #274 ART DIRECTOR/DESIGNER: *Beth Parker* PRODUCT PHOTOGRAPHER: *Andrew Swaine* AGENCY: *Phillips Design Group* CLIENT: *Atlantic Technology* PRINTER: *Rand Whitney* TYPEFACE: *Syntax* PAPER: *E-flut, Federal SBS* COUNTRY: *USA* ■ This line of packaging for computer accessories was designed to lighten up the products' images and to help them stand out in the chaotic environment of the typical computer superstore. ● *Verpackungsgestaltung für Computer-Zubehör. Hier ging es darum, dem Image des Produktes mehr Leichtigkeit und eine unverwechselbare Präsenz im chaotischen Umfeld des typischen Computer-Ladens zu geben.* ▲ *Ligne d'emballages pour des accessoires pour ordinateur. L'objectif était d'améliorer l'image des produits et leur permettre de se démarquer dans l'environnement chaotique des magasins informatiques.*

PAGE 134, #275 ART DIRECTOR/DESIGNER: *Anthony Luk* ILLUSTRATOR: *Steven Lyons* AGENCY: *Profile Design* CLIENT: *Ascend Communications, Inc.* PRINTER: *Citation Press* TYPEFACE: *Industria, Bank Gothic* PAPER: *22PT Springhill Paper* COUNTRY: *USA* ■ This packaging was created for a firm which develops, manufactures, and markets *wide-area-network accessible products that support a large spectrum of end-user applications.* ● *Programmpaket einer Firma, die Produkte entwickelt, herstellt und vermarktet, die im Netzwerk zugänglich sind und ein grosses Spektrum von Anwender-Applikationen unterstützen.* ▲ *Packaging créé pour une société qui développe, fabrique et commercialise des produits accessibles sur un réseau très entendu, supportant une large gamme d'applications utilisateur.*

PAGE 135, #276 ART DIRECTOR: *Laurie DeMartino Anderson* DESIGNERS: *Laurie DeMartino Anderson, Mary Jo Ames* AGENCY: *Studio d Design* PHOTOGRAPHER: *Steve Belkowitz* CLIENT: *Concierge Software Company* COUNTRY: *USA* ■ *The purpose was to package a new product for a new company. The dance steps were incorporated to represent the product name, as well as illustrate the linking capabilities of the software.* ● *Hier um es um die Verpackung eines neuen Produktes einer neuen Firma. Die Tanzschritte stehen für den Produktnamen und illustrieren gleichzeitig die Verknüpfungsfähigkeit der Software.* ▲ *Packaging conçu pour un nouveau produit d'une nouvelle société. Les pas de danse représentent le nom du produit et font également allusion aux possibilités du logiciel.*

PAGE 136, #277 ART DIRECTOR/DESIGNER: *Ronnie Peters* AGENCY: *Infogram* PROGRAMMER: *Ronnie Peters* COUNTRY: *USA* ■ *This prototype is for an interactive touch screen public telephone application. The talking and visual multilingual system includes interactive white and yellow pages, instructions for calling, video integration, and emergency services* ● *Prototyp eines Touch-Screen-Gerätes für den öffentlichen Telephoneservice. Zum sprechenden und visuellen mehrsprachigen System gehören Telephonbuch und Branchenverzeichnisse, Instruktionen für das Telephonieren, Videovorrichtung und Notdienst.* ▲ *Prototype d'une application téléphonique interactive publique à écran sensoriel. Un annuaire, des pages jaunes, des instructions pour téléphoner, une installation vidéo et un service de secours font partie de ce système parlant et visuel qui propose plusieurs langues à choix.*

PAGE 136, #278 ART DIRECTOR/DESIGNER: *Ronnie Peters* PROGRAMMER: *Rick Groleau* AGENCY/CLIENT: *WGBH* COUNTRY: *USA* ■ *This web site accompanies a ten-part television series produced with the BBC. It includes a visual reference to the television series and to rock and roll memorabilia, equipment, etc.* ● *Diese Web Site gehört zu einer von BBC produzierten, zehnteiligen Fernsehserie. Sie umfast einen bildlichen Verweis zu der TV-Serie und Hinweise auf Rock and Roll Memorabilia, Instrumente etc.* ▲ *Cette page Web accompagne une série télévisée produite par BBC. Elle présente une référence visuelle à la série TV, des objets-souvenir ayant trait au rock and roll, etc.*

PAGE 137, #279 ART DIRECTOR: *Hock Wah Yeo* DESIGNERS: *Hock Wah Yeo, Kelly Low* PRODUCT PHOTOGRAPHER: *Big Time Productions* AGENCY: *The Design Office of Wong & Yeo* CLIENT: *Digital Pictures* PRINTER: *Everett Graphics* COUNTRY: *USA* ■ *This packaging was created for a fast-action Kung Fu computer game.* ● *Diese Verpackung enthält ein Kung-Fu-Computerspiel, in dem es um schnelle Reaktionen geht.* ▲ *Packaging d'un jeu informatique Kung Fu où la rapidité des réactions du joueur est mise à rude épreuve.*

PAGE 137, #280 ART DIRECTOR: *Doug Akagi* DESIGNER: *Carrie Worthen* ILLUSTRATOR: *John Hersey* AGENCY: *Akagi Remington* CLIENT: *Opcode Music Systems* COUNTRY: *USA* ■ *This music software package was designed to stand out on a shelf and to explain all the features of the product.* ● *Bei dieser Verpackung für Musik-Software ging es um Produktinformation und die Wirkung im Verkaufsgestell.* ▲ *Packaging d'un logiciel de musique conçu pour se démarquer en linéaire tout en expliquant les spécificités du produit.*

PAGE 137, #281 ART DIRECTOR: *Hock Wah Yeo* DESIGNERS: *Hock Wah Yeo, Kelly Low* PRODUCT PHOTOGRAPHER: *Big Time Productions* AGENCY: *The Design Office of Wong & Yeo* CLIENT: *Digital Pictures* PRINTER: *Everett Graphics* COUNTRY: *USA* ■ *This packaging was created for a mystery adventure computer game.* ● *Packungsgestaltung für ein Abenteuer-Computerspiel.* ▲ *Packaging d'un jeu informatique d'aventures.*

PAGE 137, #282 CREATIVE DIRECTORS: *Felipé Bascope, Jon Gothold* ART DIRECTORS: *Jeff Labbé, Eric Springer* DESIGNERS: *Jeff Labbé, Garrison Smet* PHOTOGRAPHER: *Kimball*

Hall ILLUSTRATOR: *Loudvik Akopyan* AGENCY: *dGWB Advertising* CLIENT: *Qualcomm Inc.* TYPEFACE: *Bauhaus, Eurostyle, Bernhard, Courier* COUNTRY: *USA* ■ *The objective was to launch the brand and develop non-traditional packaging for a cellular phone technology and product manufacturer.* ● *Eine unkonventionelle Verpackung und Lancierung einer neuen Marke für einen Hersteller von Handies.* ▲ *Packaging original créé pour le lancement d'une nouvelle marque de téléphones cellulaires.*

PAGE 138, #283 ART DIRECTOR: *Mary Scott* DESIGNERS: *Paul Farris, Mark Verlander, David Chapple* PHOTOGRAPHER: *Donald Miller* ILLUSTRATOR: *Mark Verlander* AGENCY: *Maddocks and Co.* CLIENT: *Sony Computer Entertainment* TYPEFACE: *Template Gothic, Template Gothic Bold, OCRB Symbol, Helvetica* COUNTRY: *Japan* ■ *This game system packaging was created for the consumer electronics market targeting males ages 12—25.* ● *Diese Verpackung für Computerspiele richtet sich an ein männliches Zielpublikum im Alter von 12 bis 25 Jahren.* ▲ *L'emballage de ces jeux informatiques cible la tranche des 12–25 ans d'un public essentiellement masculin.*

PAGE 139, #284 ART DIRECTOR: *David Jensen* DESIGNERS: *David Jensen, Mark Bird, Jennifer Hayes* PHOTOGRAPHER: *Tom Hollar* AGENCY: *Jensen Design Associates* CLIENT: *Canon Computer Systems, Inc.* PRINTER: *Calsonic Miura Graphics* COUNTRY: *USA* ■ *This package was distributed to the media by Canon Computer Systems. It is designed to contain all relevant product and company information.* ● *Dieses Programmpaket mit Informationen über die Firma und ihre Produkte wurde von Canon an die Medien versandt.* ▲ *Destiné aux médias, ce kit contient toutes les informations utiles sur la société Canon et ses produits.*

PAGE 139, #285 ART DIRECTOR: *Craig Frazier* DESIGNERS: *Craig Frazier, René Rosso* ILLUSTRATOR: *Craig Frazier* AGENCY: *Frazier Design* CLIENT: *Xaos Tools Inc.* PRINTER: *Hatcher Trade Press* COUNTRY: *USA* ■ *This packaging for graphics and animation effects software targets the creative user.* ● *Diese Verpackung für eine Software für graphische und Animations-Effekte wendet sich an Gestalter.* ▲ *Packaging d'un logiciel graphique et d'animation pour designers créatifs.*

PAGE 140, #286 ART DIRECTOR: *Neal Zimmermann* DESIGNERS: *Neal Zimmermann, Claudy Mejia* PHOTOGRAPHER: *Carl VanderSchuit* AGENCY: *Zimmermann Crowe Design* CLIENT: *Electronic Arts* COUNTRY: *USA*

PAGE 140, #287 DESIGNER: *John Havel* AGENCY: *CFD Design* ILLUSTRATOR/PROGRAMMER: *Istvan Pely* PUBLISHER: *Piranha Interactive* COUNTRY: *USA* ■ *Packaging for a computer game which allows the player to travel through space and unravel the mystery of the ill-fated vessel. The visuals were impressive so the agency chose to use actual screen grabs from the program in the packaging, thus enabling the buyer to see what the game was like and saving the client illustration costs.* ● *Verpackung für ein Computer-Spiel, bei dem der Spieler durch den Weltraum reisen und das Geheimnis des in Not geratenen Raumfahrzeugs lüften kann. Zur Illustration der Verpackung wurden direkte Auszüge aus dem Spiel verwendet, was einerseits der Information des Käufers diente und andererseits Kosten einsparte.* ▲ *Packaging d'un jeu électronique qui permet à l'utilisateur de voyager à travers l'espace et de percer le secret du vaisseau spatial qui est en danger. Des extraits du jeu ont été utilisés pour le packaging afin d'informer les consommateurs et de réduire le prix de revient du produit.*

PAGE 141, #288 DESIGNER: *Tom Hough* ILLUSTRATORS: *Tom Hough, Steve Lyons* AGENCY: *Sibley/Peteet Design* CLIENT: *Nortel* PRINTER: *Wace* COUNTRY: *USA* ■ *This package for Nortel, a telecommunications equipment company, is designed to hold approximately one year's worth of three publications put out by the company.* ● *Verpackung für Nortel, Hersteller von Geräten für die Telekommunikation. Sie bietet Platz für einen Jahrgang von drei Publikationen, die von der Firma herausgegeben werden.* ▲ *Packaging créé pour la société de télécommunications Nortel, et pouvant contenir la totalité des trois publications diffusées en une année par cette société.*

PAGE 142, #289 ART DIRECTOR/DESIGNER: *Steve Sandstrom* AGENCY: *Sandstrom Design* CLIENT: *Tazo Tea Company* TYPEFACE: *Nickolas Cochin, Nuptial, Garamond No. 3*

COUNTRY: USA■ *This packaging was designed for a producer of select hot and loose teas, tea and fruit juice bottled beverages and concentrates.● Packungsgestaltung für einen Händler ausgewählter Teesorten, der auch Tee- und Fruchtgetränke in Flaschen sowie Konzentrate anbietet.▲ Cet emballage a été conçu pour un producteur de thés de premier choix qui propose également des thés et des jus de fruits en bouteille et des concentrés.*

PAGE 143, #290 ART DIRECTOR/DESIGNER: *Hansjörg Bolt* ILLUSTRATOR: *Heike Grein* AGENCY: *Bolt, Koch & Co.* CLIENT: *Volg Konsumwaren AG* COUNTRY: *Switzerland ● Brand development and package design for the in-house labels of a food chain.■ Markenentwicklung und Verpackungsgestaltung für die Eigenmarken einer Schweizer Lebensmittelkette.▲ Développement de marque et design du packaging des produits d'une chaîne de magasins d'alimentation suisse.*

PAGE 143, #291 ART DIRECTOR/DESIGNER: *Yasuo Tanaka* AGENCY: *Package Land Co, Ltd.* CLIENT: *Arab Coffee Co, Ltd.* COUNTRY: *Japan ■ Corporate logo mark and coffee package design. ● Marken- und Verpackungsgestaltung für einen Kaffee. ▲ Conception du logo d'entreprise et de l'emballage d'un café.*

PAGE 143, #292 ART DIRECTOR/DESIGNER: *Steve Sandstrom* AGENCY: *Sandstrom Design* CLIENT: *Tazo Tea Company* TYPEFACE: *Nickolas Cochin, Nuptial, Garamond No. 3* COUNTRY: *USA ■ This packaging was designed for a producer of select hot and loose teas, tea and fruit juice bottled beverages and concentrates.● Packungsgestaltung für einen Händler ausgewählter Teesorten, der auch Tee- und Fruchtgetränke in Flaschen sowie Konzentrate anbietet.▲ Cet emballage a été conçu pour un producteur de thés de premier choix qui propose également des thés et des jus de fruits en bouteille et des concentrés.*

PAGE 143, #293 ART DIRECTOR/DESIGNER: *Hansjörg Bolt* ILLUSTRATOR: *Heike Grein* AGENCY: *Bolt, Koch & Co.* CLIENT: *Volg Konsumwaren AG* COUNTRY: *Switzerland ● Brand development and package design for the in-house labels of a food chain.■ Markenentwicklung und Verpackungsgestaltung für die Eigenmarken einer Schweizer Lebensmittelkette.▲ Développement de marque et design du packaging des produits d'une chaîne de magasins d'alimentation suisse.*

PAGE 143, #294 ART DIRECTOR: *Alan Lidji* DESIGNERS: *Alan Lidji, Janet Cowling* PHOTOGRAPHERS: *Lynn Sugarman, Jim Olvera* ILLUSTRATOR: *Alan Lidji* AGENCY: *Lidji Design Office* CLIENT: *Aromance Home Fragrances* PRINTER: *Pelikan Press* TYPEFACE: *Minion* COUNTRY: *USA■ This high-end home fragrance packaging was designed for the low-end impulse buyer. ● Diese Verpackung für ein Raumparfum sollte den preisbewussten, spontanen Käufer ansprechen. ▲ Emballage d'un parfum d'intérieur destiné à favoriser les achats spontanés.*

PAGE 144, #295 ART DIRECTOR: *Barrie Tucker* DESIGNERS/ILLUSTRATORS: *Barrie Tucker, Jody Tucker* PRODUCT PHOTOGRAPHER: *Simon Vaughn* AGENCY: *Tucker Design* CLIENT: *Saddlers Creek Winery* PRINTER: *Label Leaders South Australia* TYPEFACE: *Arcadia, Uncial Script* PAPER: *Jac Wlk 202–self-adhesive* COUNTRY: *Australia ■ This packaging was created for a premium red wine from the Hunter Valley. ● Packungsgestaltung für einen erstklassigen australischen Wein aus dem Hunter Valley. ▲ Cet emballage a été conçu pour un vin rouge australien de la Hunter Valley.*

PAGE 145, #296 ART DIRECTOR/DESIGNER/ILLUSTRATOR: *Neil Powell* PHOTOGRAPHER: *Karen Capucilli* AGENCY: *Duffy Design* CLIENT: *The Coca-Cola Company* COUNTRY: *USA■ This brand identity and package system for a line of 100% juices and juice blends is intended to communicate attributes of an honest, straight-forward product.● Packungsfamilie für reine Säfte und Saftgetränke. Hier ging es um die Darstellung eines ehrlichen, soliden Produktes.▲ Famille d'emballages pour des jus de fruits 100% naturels et des cocktails de jus de fruits. Simplicité et honnêteté, tels étaient les deux critères qui devaient transparaître à travers l'image de ces produits.*

PAGE 145, #297 ART DIRECTOR: *Akio Okumura* DESIGNER: *Mitsuo Ueno* DESIGNER: *Emi Kajihara* AGENCY: *Packaging Create* AGENCY: *Dentsu Inc. Kansai* CLIENT: *Gekkeikan* TYPEFACE: *Univers, custom* COUNTRY: *Japan ■ This packaging was created for a*

Japanese sake. ● Packungsgestaltung für einen japanischen Sake. ▲ Emballage conçu pour un saké japonais.

PAGE 146, #298 ART DIRECTOR/DESIGNER/ILLUSTRATOR: *Alejandro Mayans* AGENCY: *Acento Advertising* CLIENT: *Cacique Inc.* TYPEFACE: *Westwood* COUNTRY: *USA ■ The agency wanted to establish a unique western look for a cheese that is used mainly in Texas-Mexican cuisine. ● Ein spezieller Auftritt im Western-Look für einen Käse, der vor allem in der texanisch-mexikanischen Küche verwendet wird.▲ L'agence joua sur le style western pour positionner un fromage essentiellement utilisé dans la cuisine tex-mex.*

PAGE 147, #299 ART DIRECTORS: *Masaya Yamaguchi, Jun Sato* DESIGNER: *Jun Sato* PRODUCT PHOTOGRAPHER: *Naoto Kato* AGENCY: *Gallery Interform* CLIENT: *Art Against AIDS Project* PRINTER: *Kotobuki Seiban Insatsu Co., Ltd* TYPEFACE: *Times Regular, Gill Sans Bold, Rotis San serif bold* PAPER: *Recycled Board Paper* COUNTRY: *Japan ■ Art Against AIDS Japan is an event in which artists all over the world offer their work to raise funds for the American Foundation for AIDS Research. This package consists of postcards featuring the participating artists' work. The package is designed to be economical, portable, and "environment friendly." The elastic band represents the confinement of AIDS. ● Art Against AIDS ist eine Aktion von Künstlern aus aller Welt, die Werke zur Verfügung stellen, deren Erlös einer amerikanischen Stiftung für AIDS-Forschung zugute kommt. Diese Verpackung enthält Postkarten, auf denen die zum Verkauf angebotenen Kunstwerke abgebildet sind. Sie sollte sparsam, handlich und umweltfreundlich sein. Das Gummiband symbolisiert das Eingesperrtsein der AIDS-Kranken. ▲ A l'origine d'Art Against AIDS Japan, des artistes du monde entier qui font don de leurs œuvres afin de réunir des fonds destinés à l'American Foundation for AIDS Research. Cet emballage contient des cartes postales illustrant les travaux des artistes. L'emballage est conçu pour être économique, portable et respectueux de l'environnement. L'élastique symbolise l'«emprisonnement» que vivent les personnes touchées par le sida.*

PAGE 147, #300 ART DIRECTOR/DESIGNER/ILLUSTRATOR: *Peter King Robbins* PRODUCT PHOTOGRAPHER: *Jeremy Samuelson* AGENCY/CLIENT: *BRD Design* PRINTER: *Foundation Press* FOUNDRY: *Ascast* TYPEFACE: *Arbitrary* PAPER: *French Aged Newsprint* COUNTRY: *USA ■ This self-promotion/holiday gift was created for a graphic design studio. ● Weihnachtsgeschenk als Eigenwerbung eines Graphik-Design-Studios. ▲ Ce cadeau de Noël, également utilisé à des fins promotionnelles, a été créé pour une agence de design graphique.*

PAGE 147, #301 ART DIRECTOR: *Alan Colvin* DESIGNER: *Kar Wu* ILLUSTRATOR: *Michael Schwab* AGENCY: *Nike, Inc.* CLIENT: *Nike/Kids Foot Locker* PRINTER: *Irwin Hodson Printing Co.* COUNTRY: *USA ■ This gift box for kids was created to be used for the client's sports products. ● Diese Geschenkbox für Kinder wurde für Nikes Sportprodukte entworfen.▲ Cette boîte-cadeau pour enfants est destinée aux clients qui achètent des articles de sport Nike.*

PAGE 147, #302 ART DIRECTORS: *Seymour Chwast, Samuel Antupit* DESIGNER: *Seymour Chwast* PRODUCTION MANAGEMENT/PACKAGING: *The Actualizers* AGENCY: *The Pushpin Group* CLIENT: *Harry N. Abrams* PRINTER: *Diversified Graphics, Inc.* TYPEFACE: *Handlettering, News Gothic* PAPER: *James River Paper Corporation* COUNTRY: *USA ■ This package sports ready-to-assemble paper animals, from Apollo the dog to Lana Banana the monkey. ● Diese Verpackung enthält Papiertiere zum Zusammensetzen.▲ Cet emballage contient des animaux en papier à assembler.*

PAGE 148, #303 ART DIRECTOR: *Adrian Pulfer* DESIGNERS: *Adrian Pulfer, Mary Jane Callister* PHOTOGRAPHER: *Matt Mahurin* AGENCY: *Adrian Pulfer Design* CLIENT: *Raje* PRINTER: *Packaging Corp. of America* TYPEFACE: *Helvetica Compressed, Sabon* COUNTRY: *USA*

PAGE 149, #304 ART DIRECTOR: *Gertraud Hilbert* AGENCY: *Werbeatelier Fick Werbeagentur GmbH* CLIENT: *Rosenthal AG* COUNTRY: *Germany ■ The package design and the complete visual image of the glass series "diVino," a sub-brand of Rosenthal targeted at the younger consumer, is based on the shape of the* rhombus and its half form, the triangle. Shown are gift packages containing two each of three different types of glasses. ● Basis dieser Trinkglas-Serie «diVino», eine Rosenthal-Spezialinie für jüngere Zielgruppen, ist die Rautenform und ihre halbe Grundform, das Dreieck. Hier die Geschenkverpackungen mit je 2 Stück von drei verschiedenen Gläsern. ▲ Le concept graphique de l'emballage et l'image visuelle de la série de verres «diVino», une sous-marque de Rosenthal ciblant les jeunes consommateurs, se basent sur les formes d'un rhombe et sa demi-forme, le triangle. Ici, des pochettes-cadeau contenant chacune deux des trois types de verres fabriqués.

PAGE 149, #305 ART DIRECTORS: Fritz Haase, Harald Schweers DESIGNERS: Andreas Wilhelm, Claudia Buchmann-Tunsch AGENCY: Atelier Haase & Knels CLIENT: Stanwell Vertriebs GmbH PRINTER: Bohlmeier & Co. COUNTRY: Germany ■ Package design for the launch of a range of cigarillos. ● Verpackungsgestaltung für die Neueinführung von Zigarillos. ▲ Design d'emballage pour le lancement de cigarillos.

PAGE 149, #306 ART DIRECTOR: Jeff Weithman DESIGNERS: Jeff Weithman, Chris McCullick AGENCY/CLIENT: Nike, Inc. PRINTER: Seattle Packaging Corporation TYPEFACE: Futura PAPER: Corrugated Cardboard - E flute COUNTRY: USA ■ This corporate packaging was designed to be environmentally sound. It uses 100% recycled paper and no glue to construct the box. This campaign launches the "swoosh only" identity and new age logo into retail. ● Diese umweltfreundliche Box wurde aus 100% wiederverwertetem Papier ohne Klebstoff hergestellt. Mit dieser Kampagne wird das nur aus einem Haken bestehende Nike-Logo im Einzelhandel eingeführt. ▲ Respectueux de l'environnement, cet emballage a été réalisé sans colle, avec du papier entièrement recyclé. Cette campagne devait introduire le logo new age dans les commerces de détail.

PAGE 150, #307 ART DIRECTOR: Akio Okumura DESIGNER: Katsuji Minami AGENCY: Packaging Create Inc. CLIENT: New Oji Paper Co., Ltd. TYPEFACE: Original COUNTRY: Japan

PAGE 150, #308 ART DIRECTORS: Charles S. Anderson, Todd Piper-Hauswirth DESIGNER: Todd Piper-Hauswirth PHOTOGRAPHER: Darrell Eager AGENCY: Charles S. Anderson Design Company CLIENT: Sierra Designs COUNTRY: USA

PAGE 150, #309 ART DIRECTOR: Doo H. Kim DESIGNERS: Dongil Lee, Seunghee Lee AGENCY: DooKim Design CLIENT: Utoo Zone, Samsung Corporation COUNTRY: Korea ■ This design concept is based on the stylized form of a woman wearing a hat with feathers. The elegance of the imagery was upgraded by using gold and silver on the cap in order to attract young women in their twenties and thirties who pursue intellectual, sophisticated, and modern styles. ● Das Gestaltungskonzept basiert auf der stilisierten Form einer Frau, die einen mit Federn geschmückten Hut trägt. Die Eleganz des Auftritts wird durch die Silber- und Goldtöne des Huts unterstützt. Zielgruppe sind gebildete, moderne Frauen zwischen 20 und 40 Jahren. ▲ Concept reposant sur une forme stylisée d'une femme portant un chapeau à plumes. Les touches dorées et argentées du chapeau renforcent cette impression d'élégance. Groupe cible: femmes sophistiquées, cultivées et modernes, entre 20 et 40 ans.

PAGE 150, #310 ART DIRECTOR: Akio Okumura DESIGNER: Katsuji Minami AGENCY: Packaging Create, Inc., SIA Co., Ltd CLIENT: Cow Brand Soap, Kyoshinsha Co., Ltd. COUNTRY: Japan

PAGE 151, #311 ART DIRECTOR: Jack Anderson DESIGNERS: Jack Anderson, David Bates PRODUCT PHOTOGRAPHER: Tom McMackin AGENCY: Hornall Anderson Design Works, Inc. CLIENT: Smith Sport Optics PRINTER: Union Bay Label TYPEFACE: Gill Sans Extended PAPER: Durotone, Speckletone, chipboard COUNTRY: USA ■ This packaging was created for a line of sunglasses. ● Packungsgestaltung für eine Linie von Sonnenbrillen. ▲ Emballage créé pour une ligne de lunettes de soleil.

PAGE 152, #312 ART DIRECTOR/DESIGNER: Stan Church ILLUSTRATOR: Joe Cuticone AGENCY: Wallace Church Associates, Inc. CLIENT: Shaw Nautical PAPER: French Speckletone TYPEFACE: Custom PRINTER: Weston Engraving COUNTRY: USA

PAGE 152, #313 ART DIRECTOR: Stefan Oevermann DESIGNER: Carolin Peiseler ILLUSTRATORS: Claudia Less, Stefan Oevermann AGENCY: Pharma Performance GmbH CLIENT: Mundipharma GmbH PRINTER: Pharma Performance TYPEFACE: Futura Bold COUNTRY: Germany ■ For this "Power Man" campaign, an original Power-Pack containing Trumundin®-gimmicks was created. The slogan referring to the client as "pain specialist" draws attention to their broad dosage range of painkiller products. ● Packungsgestaltung im Rahmen einer speziellen Kampagne für ein Schmerzmittel. Es ging darum, den Hersteller als «Scherzspezialisten» darzustellen und auf sein breites Schmerzmittelsortiment hinzuweisen. ▲ Emballage utilisé dans le cadre d'une campagne publicitaire pour un remède contre la douleur. Il est fait allusion au fabricant, «Le spécialiste de la douleur», et à sa vaste gamme de produits.

PAGE 153, #314 ART DIRECTOR/DESIGNER: Minoru Tabuchi PHOTOGRAPHER: Akinori Hasegawa AGENCY: Daiko Advertising, Inc. CLIENT: Fujitsu Tokushima Systems Engineering Ltd. COUNTRY: Japan

PAGE 154, #315 DESIGNER: Alan Colvin AGENCY: Duffy Design CLIENT: Jim Beam COUNTRY: USA ■ This project was commissioned to celebrate the 200th anniversary of Jim Beam. The decanter was designed for a special bourbon and is contained in a gift box that uses elements from the product's history and the decanter design. ● Zum 200jährigen Bestehen von Jim Beam entworfene Geschenkbox für einen besonderen Bourbon. Für die Box wurden Elemente von Jim Beams Geschichte und der Flaschengestaltung verwendet. ▲ Emballage-cadeau contenant un bourbon spécial conçu à l'occasion du 200ème anniversaire de Jim Bean. L'emballage présente des éléments de l'histoire du produit et de son design.

PAGE 154, #316 ART DIRECTOR/ILLUSTRATOR: Rain Pikand DESIGNER: Andrus Lember PRODUCT PHOTOGRAPHER: Jaak Kadak AGENCY: Division CLIENT: Saku Brewery, Ltd. PRINTER: Lauttasaaren Paino TYPEFACE: Handlettering, M Grotesk, Engravers Gothic COUNTRY: Finland ■ This packaging was created for an Estonian brewery which produces specialty beers for events or seasons. Saku Porter was produced for the Christmas season. ● Packungsgestaltung für eine estländische Brauerei, die Bier für spezielle Anlässe, Jahreszeiten und Feiertage herstellt. Saku Porter war für die Weihnachtszeit bestimmt. ▲ Emballage conçu pour une brasserie en Estonie qui produit des bières pour des occasions spéciales, des fêtes, des festivals ou selon les saisons. La bière Saku Porter a été créée pour les fêtes de fin d'année.

PAGE 155, #317 ART DIRECTORS: Steve Mitchell, Bill Thorburn DESIGNER: Chad Hagen COPYWRITER: Matt Elhardt AGENCY: Thorburn Design CLIENT: Millenium TYPEFACE: Trade Gothic COUNTRY: Germany ■ The packaging contains a liquor product with the identity of an industrial oil. ● Ein Kräuterlikör, verpackt wie ein industrielles Öl. ▲ Liqueur aux herbes avec un emballage rappelant celui d'une huile pour voiture.

PAGE 155, #318 ART DIRECTOR: Jack Anderson DESIGNERS: Jack Anderson, Larry Anderson, Bruce Branson-Meyer PRODUCT PHOTOGRAPHER: Tom McMackin ILLUSTRATOR: Mark Summers AGENCY: Hornall Anderson Design Works, Inc. CLIENT: William & Scott Company PRINTER: Zumbiel (6-pack), Inland Printing (labels), Zapata (caps) TYPEFACE: Copperplate, Reckleman, handlettering COUNTRY: USA ■ The packaging design encompasses six-pack carrier cartons, bottles, and labels for Rhino Chasers beer. ● Tragkartons, Flaschen und Etiketten für ein Bier der Marke Rhino Chasers. ▲ Boîtes en pack de six, bouteilles et étiquettes de la marque de bière Rhino Chasers.

PAGE 156, #319 ART DIRECTORS: John Marota, Thomas Fairclough, Tom Antista DESIGNER: Thomas Fairclough PHOTOGRAPHY: Michael West Photography AGENCY: Antista Fairclough Design CLIENT: Anheuser Busch COUNTRY: USA ■ This packaging was developed from 1800s resource material from the Anheuser Busch archives. These brands was developed to compete with microbreweries. ● Die Verpackung wurde auf der Basis von Archivmaterial der Brauerei aus der Zeit um 1800 entwickelt. Diese Marke wurde lanciert, um den Produkten der kleinen Spezialbrauereien etwas entgegenzusetzen. ▲ Cet emballage a été créé sur la base *des archives de la brasserie qui remontent aux années 1800. Cette marque a été lancée pour concurrencer les produits des petites brasseries.*

PAGE 157, #320 ART DIRECTOR: *Dan Olson* DESIGNERS: *Dan Olson, Todd Bartz, Eden Fahlen* PHOTOGRAPHER: *Lev Tushaus* AGENCY: *Duffy Design* CLIENT: *Flagstone Brewery* COUNTRY: *USA* ■ *The assignment was to brand, package, and promote a Southeastern regional specialty targeting predominantly male, urban, and upscale microbrew consumers.* ● *Der Auftrag erstreckte sich auf die Gestaltung von Logo, Verpackung und Promotionsmaterial für ein Bier, das als Spezialität der Region vermarktet wird. Zielgruppe war vor allem die männliche, urbane Bevölkerung mit hohen Ansprüchen.* ▲ *Ce contrat comprenait la conception du logo, de l'emballage et du matériel de promotion pour une bière lancée sur le marché en tant que spécialité régionale. Le produit s'adresse avant tout à des hommes exigeants vivant en milieu urbain.*

PAGE 157, #321 ART DIRECTOR: *Bill Cahan* DESIGNER: *Kevin Roberson* PRODUCT PHOTOGRAPHER: *Tony Stromberg* AGENCY: *Cahan & Associates* CLIENT: *Boisset USA* TYPEFACE: *Handlettering* COUNTRY: *USA* ■ *This packaging was designed to convey the character of the Prohibition era; many inmates of the Alcatraz penitentiary were arrested for bootlegging alcohol.* ■ *Dieses Bier wurde 'Alcatraz' genannt, weil viele Strafgefangene der berüchtigten Strafanstalt beim Schwarzbrennen erwischt wurden. Die Verpackung sollte dementsprechend an die Prohibitionszeit in den USA erinnern.* ▲ *Le nom de cette bière s'inspire directement du célèbre établissement pénitencier d'Alcatraz. De nombreux prisonniers se sont retrouvés derrière les barreaux parce qu'ils distillaient clandestinement de l'alcool. L'emballage rappelle la période de prohibition aux Etats-Unis.*

PAGE 158, #322 DESIGNER/ILLUSTRATOR: *Jeffrey Caldeway* AGENCY: *Caldeway Design* CLIENT: *Goosecross Cellars* PRINTER: *Gordon Graphics, V&V Metal Fabricators* TYPEFACE: *Garamond, Engravers Gothic* COUNTRY: *USA* ■ *The package design makes use of a metaphorical pun playing off the double entendre "Æros." Forged bronze and nickel wings form a sculptural framework for a cameo of the winged goddess Psyche, lover of Eros.* ● *Bei dieser Packungsgestaltung geht es um den doppelten Sinn des Wortes Æros. Flügel aus Bronze und Nickel bilden den Rahmen für eine Miniatur der Göttin Psyche, der Geliebten von Eros.* ▲ *Cet emballage joue sur le double sens du mot «Æros». Les ailes en nickel et en bronze forment un cadre sculptural pour le camée de la déesse ailée Psyché, amante d'Eros.*

PAGE 158, #323 ART DIRECTOR: *Barrie Tucker* DESIGNERS: *Barrie Tucker, Hans Kohla, Nick Mount* PRODUCT PHOTOGRAPHER: *Simon Vaughn* AGENCY: *Tucker Design* CLIENT: *Spicers Paper* BOTTLE MANUFACTURER: *JAM Factory Adelaide* PRINTER: *Stalley Box Co (gift box), Five Star Press (box sticker)* TYPEFACE: *Gill Sans* PAPER: *Mirrorkote (gift box), Spicers self-adhesive (box sticker)* COUNTRY: *Australia* ■ *This item was created for a paper merchant as a bottle-and-package corporate Christmas gift. Hand blown glass bottles were filled with wood-aged fortified Chardonnay.* ● *Handgefertigte Glasflaschen mit Verpackung als Weihnachtsgeschenk für die Kunden eines Papierherstellers. Der Inhalt: in Holzfässern gereifter Chardonnay.* ▲ *Bouteilles en verre soufflé contenant du chardonnay vieilli en fûts avec emballage comme cadeau de Noël pour les clients d'un fabricant de papier.*

PAGE 158, #324 ART DIRECTOR/ILLUSTRATOR: *Barrie Tucker* DESIGNERS: *Barrie Tucker, Claire Rose* PRODUCT PHOTOGRAPHER: *Simon Vaughn* AGENCY: *Tucker Design* CLIENT: *Lactos* JEWELER/METALSMITH: *Peter Coombs* COUNTRY: *Australia* ■ *This is a limited-edition bottle created as a Christmas gift. The three-dimensional star is gold-coated sterling silver with a moonstone at the center of the eye-graphic, the design firm's symbol.* ● *In limitierter Anzahl hergestellte Flasche, die als Weihnachtsgeschenk gedacht war. Der dreidimensionale Stern besteht aus vergoldetem Sterling-Silber mit einem Mondstein im Zentrum des Auges, dem Symbol der Designfirma.* ▲ *Bouteille en série limitée créée comme cadeau de Noël. L'étoile tridimensionnelle est en argent fin doré avec, au centre de l'œil, une pierre de lune, symbole de l'agence de design.*

PAGE 158, #325 ART DIRECTOR: *Barrie Tucker* DESIGNERS: *Barrie Tucker, Hans Kohla* ILLUSTRATOR: *Hans Kohla* PRODUCT PHOTOGRAPHER: *Simon Vaughn* AGENCY: *Tucker*

Design CLIENT: *Southcorp Wines* PRINTER: *ASAP Adelaide* TYPEFACE: *Bodoni* COUNTRY: *Australia* ■ *Packaging created for Seppelt brand Viva 1 & 2 Liqueur Shiraz and Liqueur Chardonnay products. The design is printed onto the bottles.* ● *Flaschengestaltung für zwei Liköre. Die Flaschen wurden direkt bedruckt.* ▲ *Emballage conçu pour deux liqueurs. Impression directe sur les bouteilles.*

PAGE 158, #326 ART DIRECTOR/DESIGNER: *Barrie Tucker* PRODUCT PHOTOGRAPHER: *Simon Vaughn* AGENCY: *Tucker Design* COUNTRY: *Australia*

PAGE 158, #327 ART DIRECTOR/DESIGNER: *Barrie Tucker* ILLUSTRATOR: *Hans Kohla* PRODUCT PHOTOGRAPHER: *Simon Vaughn* AGENCY: *Tucker Design* CLIENT: *Southcorp Wines* PAPER: *Spicers Paper Mirrokote* COUNTRY: *Australia*

PAGE 159, #328 ART DIRECTOR: *Taku Satoh* AGENCY: *Taku Satoh Design Office Inc.* CLIENT: *Nikka Pure Malt Whiskey* COUNTRY: *Japan*

PAGE 160, #329 ART DIRECTOR: *Charles S. Anderson* DESIGNER: *Todd Piper-Hauswirth* AGENCY: *Charles S. Anderson Design Company* PHOTOGRAPHER: *Darrell Eager* COPYWRITER: *Lisa Pemrick* CLIENT: *French Paper Company* PAPER: *French Construction Pure White* TYPEFACE: *Todder Stencil, Trade Gothic* PRINTER: *Litho Inc.* COUNTRY: *USA* ■ *This paper promotion for T-shirts utilized blueprint typography and imagery of the shirt.* ● *T-Shirt-Promotion eines Papierherstellers mit Blaupausen-Schrift und Photos von den T-Shirts, die man im Austausch gegen bedruckte Baupläne in einer Papierqualität der Firma erhielt.* ▲ *Tee-shirts promotionnels d'un fabricant de papier utilisant la typographie d'une ozalide et une reproduction photographique du tee-shirt.*

PAGE 161, #330 ART DIRECTOR/DESIGNER: *Carter Weitz* COPYWRITER: *Mitch Koch* AGENCY: *Bailey Lauerman & Associates* CLIENT: *Western Paper Compay* PAPER: *60 lb. Cream White Hammerhill Opaque, Vellum* TYPEFACE: *Clarendon Black* COUNTRY: *USA* ■ *This announcement was created for the opening of a new warehouse for a paper company. The design involved conceptually integrated the opening of the new warehouse with the opening of the large piece of paper.* ● *Ankündigung der Eröffnung des neuen Lagerhauses eines Papierherstellers. Das Öffnen eines grossen Papierbogens dient dabei als Symbol für die Öffnung des Lagers.* ▲ *Information sur l'inauguration d'un nouvel entrepôt d'un fabricant de papier. En dépliant ou plutôt «en ouvrant» la feuille de grand format, on est sensé penser à l'ouverture de l'entrepôt.*

PAGE 162, #331 CREATIVE DIRECTORS: *Brad Copeland, George Hirthler* ART DIRECTOR/DESIGNER: *Raquel Corripio Miqueli* COPYWRITERS: *Melissa James Kemmerly, Kim Dickinson* PRODUCTION MANAGER: *Laura Perlee* SENIOR PRODUCTION ARTIST: *Donna Harris* CLIENT: *Neenah Paper* COUNTRY: *USA*

PAGE 162, #332 ART DIRECTOR: *Dana Arnett* DESIGNERS: *Curtis Schreiber, Fletcher Martin* AGENCY: *VSA Partners, Inc.* PHOTOGRAPHER: *Scott Shigley* CLIENT/PAPER MANUFACTURER: *Potlatch Corp.* PAPER: *Vintage Remarque Gloss 80 lb.* TYPEFACE: *Franklin Gothic, Futura* PRINTER: *Bradley Printing Company* COUNTRY: *USA* ■ *The playbill is intended to build audience excitement before viewing a satirical film about the designer Ben Day.* ● *Gestaltung eines Programms, das die Stimmung des Publikums anheizen soll, bevor es sich einen satirischen Film über den Designer Ben Day anschaut.* ▲ *Affiche conçue pour susciter l'envie du public avant la diffusion d'un film satirique sur le designer américain Ben Day.*

PAGE 163, #333 ART DIRECTOR: *Kit Hinrichs* DESIGNERS: *Belle How, Amy Chan* PHOTOGRAPHER: *Gerald Bybee* COPYWRITER: *Delphine Hirasuna* AGENCY: *Pentagram Design* CLIENT: *Simpson Paper Company* COUNTRY: *USA*

PAGE 163, #334 ART DIRECTOR: *Don Sibley* DESIGNERS: *Don Sibley, Donna Aldridge* AGENCY: *Sibley/Peteet Design* CLIENT: *Weyerhaeuser* PRINTER: *A2 Dryography* COUNTRY: *USA* ■ *This brochure promoting a paper company is part of series entitled "American Artifacts," which takes a nostalgic look at America's legendary Route 66.* ● *Die Broschüre für eine Papierfirma gehört zu einer Serie, deren Thema amerikanische Wahrzeichen sind, hier die Route 66, Amerikas legendärer*

Highway. ▲ *Brochure publicitaire d'une papeterie faisait partie d'une série nostalgique sur le thème de la Route 66, autoroute légendaire.*

PAGE 164, #335 ART DIRECTOR: *Michael Bierut* DESIGNERS/EDITORS: *Michael Bierut, Emily Hayes* AGENCY: *Pentagram Design* CLIENT: *Mohawk Paper Mills* PAPER: *Mohawk Vellum 65lb., Jute (cover), Mohawk Satin, 80 lb., cool white recycled (text)* PRINTER: *Diversified Graphics, Inc.* COUNTRY: *USA* ■ *This follow-up to "Rethinking Design" focuses on the so-called Age of Information and the potential "end of paper" in the digital future.* ● *Papierpromotion innerhalb einer Reihe, die sich mit speziellen Themen befasst: Hier das sogenannte Informationszeitalter und das angebliche «Ende des Papiers» in der digitalen Zukunft.* ▲ *Publicité de relance pour un fabricant de papier axée sur l'«ère de l'information» et la «fin du papier» potentielle à l'âge du numérique.*

PAGE 164, #336 CREATIVE DIRECTOR: *James A. Sebastian* ART DIRECTOR: *Michael McGinn* DESIGNERS: *James A. Sebastian, Agnes deBethune, Brian Fingeret* ILLUSTRATOR: *Brian Fingeret* AGENCY: *Designframe Inc.* CLIENT: *Strathmore Papers* PAPER: *Strathmore Writing, Script, Cotton Grades (various weights)* TYPEFACE: *Sabon, Gill Sans* PRINTER: *Diversified Graphics Incorporated* FABRICATOR: *ACGS, Inc.* COUNTRY: *USA* ■ *The product line was redesigned so that all products share a color palette of very subtle shades. The agency created portfolios for each brand featuring an accordion pocket system constructed of papers in the system's colors. Several samples of each item are included in color coordinated pockets. A reply card and a swatchbook are also included.* ● *Für alle Produktes dieses Papierherstellers war eine neue, sanfte Farbpalette kreiert worden. Für jede Sorte wurde daraufhin eine Mappe mit einem harmonikaartigen Taschensystem entworfen, das aus Papieren in den neuen Farben besteht. Mehrere Muster jeder Sorte sind in farblich abgestimmten Taschen enthalten. Ausserdem enthalten die Mappen Musterbücher und Antwortkarten.* ▲ *L'idée était de créer une nouvelle palette de teintes subtiles pour tous les produits de ce fabricant de papier. L'agence conçut pour chaque marque un système en accordéon réalisé avec les nouveaux papiers et contenant des échantillons de chaque qualité présentés dans des pochettes assorties aux différentes couleurs. Une carte-réponse et un jeu d'échantillons complétaient le tout.*

PAGE 164, #337 ART DIRECTORS: *Rik Besser, Douglas Joseph* DESIGNER: *Rik Besser* PHOTOGRAPHER: *Terry Heffernan* COPYWRITER: *Margaret Burger* AGENCY: *Besser Joseph Partners* CLIENT: *Hopper Paper Company* COUNTRY: *USA* ■ *The brochure demonstrates how precious metals print on the client's papers.* ● *Diese Broschüre eines Papierherstellers demonstriert, wie gut sich seine Papierqualitäte für den Druck mit Edelmetallen eignen.* ▲ *L'objectif de cette brochure était d'illustrer l'effet obtenu par l'impression de métaux précieux.*

PAGE 165, #338 ART DIRECTOR/DESIGNER: *Laura Gillespie* ILLUSTRATOR: *Chris Gall* COPYWRITER: *Chris Heile* AGENCY: *Northlich Stolley Lawarre Design Group* CLIENT: *Mead Communication Papers* TYPEFACE: *Schneidler, Berling, Hand Drawn, City, Helvetica* PRINTER: *Mead Carton* COUNTRY: *USA* ■ *The client was creating new opportunities in the small business/home office market, so the packaging had to have impact in the oversaturated consumer market. Each product has a carton and ream wrapper package. Because of budget considerations, the bottom of the carton is consistent throughout the line of products. The illustration style was chosen to convey the hard-working industry with a hero perspective on the customer. The scratchboard technique worked with the limitations of the flexo printing on corrugated board.* ● *Die Verpackung dieser Papierqualitäten musste sich im stark umkämpften Endverbrauchermarkt durchsetzen. Jedes Produkt wird in einem Karton mit Ries-Streifband verpackt. Aus Kostengründen sind die Unterteile der Kartons für alle Papiersorten identisch. Der Stil der Illustrationen ist eine Anspielung auf die harte Arbeit, die in dieser Branche geleistet wird. Die Schabkartontechnik eignete sich für den Anilingummidruck auf Wellkarton.* ▲ *Le packaging de ces papiers devait se démarquer sur le marché déjà saturé du matériel de bureau pour PME/domestique. Chaque produit est présenté comme une rame de papier, avec un carton. Pour des raisons budgétaires, le fond des cartons est le même pour tous les produits de la gamme. Les illustrations évoquent le dur labeur des artisans de l'industrie du papier et élèvent le consommateur au*

rang de héros. Cette technique de la carte à gratter se prêtait à la flexographie sur carton ondulé.

PAGE 165, #339 ART DIRECTOR: *Bill Thorburn* DESIGNER: *Alex Tylevich* AGENCY: *Thorburn Design* PHOTOGRAPHER: *Chuck Smith* COPYWRITER: *Matt Elhardt* CLIENT: *Domtar* TYPEFACE: *Tema Cantanta, Rotis semi serif, Officina sans and serif* PAPER: *Domtar Cornwall Coated Cover* PRINTER: *PPP* COUNTRY: *USA*

PAGE 166, #340 ART DIRECTOR/DESIGNER: *Michael Vanderbyl* AGENCY: *Vanderbyl Design* PHOTOGRAPHER: *Gaby Brink* CLIENT: *Type Directors Club* PAPER: *Warren Dull 80 lb. text* PRINTER: *Quality House of Graphics, Inc.* ■ *This competition announcement discusses the concept of good and bad typography.* ● *Ankündigung eines Wettbewerbs, in der gute und schlechte Typographie diskutiert wird.* ▲ *Annonce d'un concours sur le thème de la bonne et de la mauvaise typographie.*

PAGE 166, #341 ART DIRECTOR: *Barry Shepard* DESIGNER: *Michael Barton* AGENCY: *SHR Perceptual Management* PHOTOGRAPHER: *Rodney Rascona* CLIENT: *Mercruiser* PAPER: *100 lb. Quintessence Gloss Book* TYPEFACE: *Girlfriend, Futura Extra Black* PRINTER: *Graphic Arts Center, Pasadena* COUNTRY: *USA* ■ *The agency wanted to change perceptions in the competitive water-ski market in which brand loyalty is fierce. The agency sought to visually communicate ideas of precision and performance along with power and aggression and to make the product stand out from the competition.* ● *Mit diesem Plakat für eine Wasser-Ski-Marke wollten die Gestalter den Markt erobern, der für die Markentreue der Abnehmer bekannt ist. Dabei ging es um Darstellung von Präzision und Leistung, kombiniert mit dem Ausdruck von Kraft und Aggression, um die Aufmerksamkeit der Verbaucher zu gewinnen.* ▲ *Affiche d'une marque de skis nautiques. Le but de l'agence était d'apporter une nouvelle approche sur un marché réputé difficile en raison de la grande fidélité des consommateurs à des marques bien précises. Pour y arriver, elle communique sur le mode de la précision, de la performance, de la puissance et de l'agressivité de façon à ce que le produit se démarque de la concurrence.*

PAGE 167, #342 ART DIRECTOR/DESIGNER/AGENCY: *Holger Matthies* CLIENT: *Kulturbehörde* COUNTRY: *Germany* ■ *This announcement for an exhibition of the designer's posters utilizes a combination of posters.* ● *Dieses Plakat für eine Austellung von Holger Matthies zeigt verschiedene Plakate des Gestalters.* ▲ *Cette affiche conçue pour une exposition de Holger Matthies présente diverses affiches de l'artiste.*

PAGE 168, #343 ART DIRECTORS/DESIGNERS: *Jacques Koeweiden, Paul Postma* AGENCY: *Koeweiden Postma Associates* PHOTOGRAPHER: *Rob V/d Vet, stock (ladies)* COPYWRITER: *Peter Hansen* CLIENT: *CREATIVE REVIEW MAGAZINE* COUNTRY: *England* ■ *The design presents a vision of Amsterdam as a major European creative city.* ● *Amsterdam, präsentiert als eine bedeutende, kreative europäische Metropole.* ▲ *La ville d'Amsterdam, présentée en tant que grande métropole européenne, bouillonnante de vie et d'idées.*

PAGE 168, #344 ART DIRECTORS: *Hans-Heinrich Sures, Ingo Eulen* DESIGNER: *Hans-Heinrich Sures* CLIENT: *Fachhochschule Dortmund* TYPEFACE: *Meta Caps* PRINTER: *COD Color-Offset-Druck* COUNTRY: *Germany* ■ *This visual identity was created for a symposium on the scope and super 35 movie formats. The strategy was to show the location of the symposium in the scope movie-format. The black "letterbox" is well known from television when broadcasting scope movies.* ● *Auftritt für ein Symposium über Cinemascope und Super-35-Kinofilmformate. Es ging darum, den Ort des Symposiums und das Cinemascope-Format darzustellen. Die schwarzen Streifen sind typisch für TV-Ausstrahlungen solcher Filmformate.* ▲ *Identité visuelle créée pour un symposium consacré au cinémascope et aux films en super 35. L'idée fut de montrer l'endroit où a lieu le symposium en cinémascope. Les bandes noires s'affichent sur le téléviseur lors de la diffusion de film de ce format.*

PAGE 169, #345 ART DIRECTOR: *Antony Redman* CREATIVE DIRECTORS: *Jim Aitchinson, Graham Fink* AGENCY: *Batey Ads Singapore* PHOTOGRAPHER: *Charles Liddall* CLIENT: *Asian Pals of the Planet* PAPER: *Varnished Art* TYPEFACE: *Customized Franklin Gothic* PRINTER: *Columbia Offset* COUNTRY: *Singapore* ■ *Despite monsoonal rainfalls, water is becoming a scarce commodity in Asia due to wastage, lack of controls* and rapid industrialization. The designer wanted to communicate that the water wasted in the home can be reduced if it is treated with respect.● Trotz der mit dem Monsun einsetzenden Regenzeit wird das Wasser in Asien knapp. Die Gründe sind Verschwendung, mangelnde Kontrolle und rapide Industrialisierung. Hier sollte zum Ausdruck gebracht werden, dass der Privatverbrauch von Wasser reduziert werden kann, wenn die Menschen begreifen, wie kostbar es ist.▲ Malgré les moussons, l'eau devient rare en Asie. Cela est dû au gaspillage, aux contrôles déficients et à l'industrialisation rapide. Le message du graphiste: la consommation domestique peut être réduite si l'être humain comprend à quel point l'eau est précieuse.

PAGE 169, #346 ART DIRECTOR/DESIGNER/AGENCY: Le Petit Didier ILLUSTRATOR: O.H. Dancy COPYWRITER: François Noel CLIENT: François Noel PRINTER: Offset

PAGE 170, #347 ART DIRECTOR/DESIGNER/COPYWRITER: Louise Fili AGENCY: Louise Fili Ltd. PHOTOGRAPHER: Ed Spiro CLIENT: Cincinnati Art Directors Club PAPER: Potlatch Millcraft TYPEFACE: Futura Book, Excelsior Script PRINTER: Pepper Printing COUNTRY: USA ■ To announce her speaking engagement at the Art Directors Club of Cincinnati, a city to which the designer had vowed not to return until cappuccino was available, she decided to design the poster as a cappuccino cup. ● Ankündigung eines Vortrags von Louise Fili beim ADC von Cincinnati. Da sie geschworen hatte, diese Stadt zu meiden, bis man dort Cappuccino bekommt, gestaltete sie ihr Plakat als Kaffeetasse. ▲ Tasse à café. Affiche annonçant une conférence de la graphiste américaine Louise Fili à l'ADC de Cincinnati: l'artiste avait déclaré qu'elle ne remettrait plus les pieds dans cette ville tant que l'on ne pourrait y boire de cappuccino.

PAGE 171, #348 ART DIRECTOR/DESIGNER/ILLUSTRATOR: Brian Boyd AGENCY: RBMM/The Richards Group CLIENT: Williamson Printing COUNTRY: USA ■ This poster was created for a printing company. ● Plakat für eine Druckerei. ▲ Affiche pour une imprimerie.

PAGE 172, #349 CREATIVE DIRECTORS: David Young, Jeff Laramore ART DIRECTOR: Carolyn Hadlock TYPOGRAPHER: Scott Montgomery PHOTOGRAPHER: Dale Bernstein SCULPTOR: David Bellamy COPYWRITER: Tim Abare AGENCY: Young & Laramore CLIENT/PRINTER: Kubin-Nicholson TYPEFACE: Montee Licenseplate COUNTRY: USA ■ The poster was created to represent a 6,000 mile road trip. A torch made of old license plates and tail lights seemed appropriate. ● Das Plakat entstand anlässlich einer 9600km weiten Autofahrt. Die Flamme besteht aus alten Nummernschildern und Rücklichtern. ▲ Affiche créée pour un rallye de 6'000 miles. Feux arrière et anciennes plaques minéralogiques forment la lampe.

PAGE 173, #350 ART DIRECTOR: Karl Madcharo COPYWRITER: Bob Cianfrone PHOTOGRAPHER: David Kiesgen AGENCY: Cleveland Clark, Inc. CLIENT: Creative Club of Atlanta TYPEFACE: Attic PRINTER: Graphic Response COUNTRY: USA ■ Problem: Too little time and too little money. Solution: A friendly photographer and a friendly printer. ● Bei wenig Zeit und wenig Geld ist die Lösung des Problems ein freundlicher Photograph und ein freundlicher Drucker. ▲ Pressé par le temps? Petits moyens? La solution: un photographe et un imprimeur sympas

PAGE 174, #351 ART DIRECTORS/DESIGNERS: D. Mark Kingsley, Karen Greenberg AGENCY: Greenberg Kingsley, Inc. CLIENT: Guggenheim Museum TYPEFACE: Wright Normal MANUFACTURER: Global Solutions COUNTRY: USA ■ The project was to produce an inexpensive desk clock utilizing the Frank Lloyd Wright typeface developed exclusively for the museum. ● Hier ging es um die Schaffung einer preisgünstigen Tischuhr mit der Typographie, die Frank Lloyd Wright speziell für das Museum entwickelte. ▲ Le projet consistait à réaliser une pendulette bon marché qui reprenne la typographie de Frank Lloyd Wright, créée en exclusivité pour le musée Guggenheim.

PAGE 174, #352 DESIGNER: Barbie Loesing AGENCY/CLIENT/MANUFACTURER: Hallmark Cards, Inc. MATERIALS: Metal COUNTRY: USA ■ The purpose was to design a product using recycled material. ● Es ging um die Gestaltung eines Produktes unter Verwendung von Recycling-Material. ▲ L'objectif était de fabriquer un produit à partir de matériaux recyclés.

PAGE 175, #353 ART DIRECTOR: Tucker Viemeister DESIGNERS: Debbie Hahn, Stephanie Kim, Nick Graham PRODUCT PHOTOGRAPHER: Peter Medilek AGENCY: Smart Design CLIENT: Timex, Joe Boxer TYPEFACE: Janson COUNTRY: USA ■ The smiley face boxes, which protect the product and provide a souvenir, were designed to promote a line of watches. ● Diese Smiley-Boxen dienen als Souvenir und Werbung für eine Uhrenlinie, der sie gleichzeitig als Verpackung dienen. ▲ Conçues pour lancer une collection de montres, ces boîtes «smiley» font office d'«écrins» et peuvent être conservées en souvenir.

PAGE 175, #354 DESIGNERS: Lella Vignelli, Massimo Vignelli AGENCY: Vignelli Designs, Inc. CLIENT: Pierre Junod Watches MANUFACTURER: Pierre Junod COUNTRY: Switzerland

PAGE 175, #355 ART DIRECTOR: Alan Chan DESIGNERS: Alan Chan, Peter Lo, Phillip Leung AGENCY: Alan Chan Design Company CLIENT: Alan Chan Creations

PAGE 175, #356 DESIGNER: Michael Graves AGENCY: Michael Graves Architect CLIENT: Projects MANUFACTURER: Projects (collaborating with Pierre Junod Swiss Program) COUNTRY: Switzerland

PAGE 176, #357 ART DIRECTOR/DESIGNER/COPYWRITER: Thomas Vasquez AGENCY/CLIENT: Squires & Company PAPER: UV Ultra TYPEFACE: Garamond Italic PRINTER: Colotone COUNTRY: USA ■ The client needed a memorable holiday greeting card that could also be utilized as an invitation to a Christmas party. By using a translucent sheet as the vehicle, the luminaria provided the receiver of the greeting card with a holiday keepsake. ● Hier ging es um die Gestaltung einer Weihnachtskarte, die sich auch als Einladung zu einer Weihnachtsfeier eignen sollte. Durch die Verwendung des transparenten Papiers, erhält der Empfänger ein Art Laterne als Souvenir. ▲ Le client désirait une carte de vœux spéciale, pouvant également servir d'invitation à une fête de Noël. L'utilisation de papier translucide permit de créer une sorte de lampion pouvant être conservé en souvenir.

PAGE 176, #358 ART DIRECTOR: Robin Perkins DESIGNER: Jeff Breidenbach AGENCY: Clifford Selbert Design Collaborative CLIENT: Spinergy, Inc. COUNTRY: USA

PAGE 176, #359 ART DIRECTOR: Charles S. Anderson DESIGNERS: Charles S. Anderson, Paul Howalt, Erik Johnson ILLUSTRATOR: Erik Johnson COPYWRITER: Lisa Pemrick AGENCY: Charles S. Anderson Design Company CLIENT: CSA Archive PRINTER: KEA Inc. COUNTRY: USA ■ These magnet pieces, based on images from the client's archive, interchange to create different faces. The tin package also works as a self-standing display. ● Mit diesen Magneten, die auf Bildern aus dem Archiv der Design-Agentur basierten, lassen sich verschiedene Gesichter bilden. Die Blechdose funktioniert auch als Display. ▲ Puzzle permettant de créer différents visages suivant l'assemblage des aimants qui reprennent des photographies d'archives du client. Le packaging, une boîte en fer blanc, fait aussi office de présentoir.

PAGE 176, #360 ART DIRECTOR: Charles S. Anderson DESIGNERS: Charles S. Anderson, Todd Piper-Hauswirth AGENCY: Charles S. Anderson Design Company COPYWRITER: Lisa Pemrick ILLUSTRATOR/CLIENT: CSA Archive PAPER: French Construction Cement Green TYPEFACE: 20th Century PRINTER: KEA Inc. COUNTRY: USA ■ This novelty product, described as "a light, refreshing, unisex scent just like your dad used to wear," was based on images from the client's archive.● Die Verpackung für dieses neue Produkt, 'ein leichter Unisex-Duft, wie ihn Ihr Vater benutzte', basiert auf Bildern aus dem Archiv des Auftraggebers, einem Design-Studio.▲ Nouveau produit présenté comme «un parfum unisexe léger et frais, qui rappelle celui de papa». Des photos d'archives du client illustrent le packaging.

PAGE 177, #361 DESIGNERS: Bruce Burdick, Susan Burdick, Johnson Chow AGENCY: The Burdick Group PRODUCT PHOTOGRAPHER: Studio Convex CLIENT: Itoki Co. Ltd. MANUFACTURER: Itoki Co. Ltd.■ This seating was developed as a versatile new interpretation of seating for lobbies, reception areas, etc. By utilizing components, the product can be used as a single chair, as a sofa, or as modular seating. ● Eine neue Art von Sitzgelegenheiten, die speziell für Hotel-Lobbys, Empfangsräume etc. bestimmt sind. Das Produkt ist als einzelner Sessel, als Sofa oder als Anbau-

Element erhältlich. ▲ *Nouveau système de sièges destiné à des hôtels, des aires de réception, etc. Le produit peut être utilisé comme chaise unique, comme sofa ou comme élément modulaire.*

PAGE 177, #362 DESIGNER/PRODUCT PHOTOGRAPHER: *Todd Bracher* MATERIALS: *Fiberglass paper with a clear rubber coating, aluminum* COUNTRY: *USA* ■ *Inspiration for this fixture comes from the typical umbrella. The designer created a way of adjusting the amount of light emitted without the use of an electronic dimmer, by raising or lowering the shade. The character of the fixture changes as it displays different levels of lighting.* ● *Leuchte aus Fiberglas-Material mit transparenter Gummibeschichtung und Aluminium. Inspiriert wurde sie durch den klassischen Regenschirm. Die Lichtstärke lässt sich ohne Dimmer durch Verstellen des Schirms variieren, wodurch sich auch die Wirkung der Leuchte selbst verändert.* ▲ *Luminaire en papier de fibres de verre avec revêtement caoutchouc transparent et aluminium, inspiré des parapluies classiques. L'intensité de la lumière ne se règle pas à l'aide d'un variateur, mais en modifiant l'inclinaison de l'abat-jour, l'effet obtenu variant suivant la luminosité.*

PAGE 178, #363 ART DIRECTOR/DESIGNER: *José Serrano* AGENCY: *Mires Design, Inc.* ILLUSTRATOR: *Tracy Sabin* COPYWRITER: *Jeff Lindenthal* CLIENT: *Found Stuff Paperworks* TYPEFACE: *Nuptial Script, Latin Extra Wide, Latina* PRINTER: *Graphics Ink* COUNTRY: *USA* ■ *This piece was designed to place emphasis on the fact that it is made from recycled materials. "Old world" style illustration was used to convey how writing used to be.* ● *Bei diesem Produkt ging es um die Demonstration des Einsatzes wiederverwerteten Materials. Die Illustration im Stil «der alten Welt» sollte zeigen, wie man in früheren Zeiten schrieb.* ▲ *Le but était de mettre en évidence les matériaux recyclés utilisés dans la fabrication. L'illustration rétro montre le style de l'écriture d'antan.*

PAGE 178, #364 ART DIRECTORS: *György Kara, Péter Nagy* DESIGNER/ILLUSTRATOR: *György Kara* PHOTOGRAPHERS: *György Kara, Géza Molnár* AGENCY: *Part Studio* CLIENT: *Egely Research Co. Ltd.* ■ *This package and booklet was created for an "Egely Wheel" vitality meter, the first device in the world by means of which one can measure and feel "life energy" level.* ● *Diese Verpackung und Broschüre entstanden für ein in der Welt einzigartiges Gerät, mit dem sich die Lebensenergie messen und fühlen lässt.* ▲ *Packaging et mode d'emploi d'un appareil unique au monde permettant de mesurer et de sentir l'énergie vitale.*

PAGE 179, #365, 367 DESIGNER: *Jeffrey Milstein* AGENCY: *Paper House Productions* PHOTOGRAPHERS: *Dan Lavoie, Al Seib, Jeffrey Milstein* CLIENT: *Paper House* COUNTRY: *USA*

PAGE 179, #366 DESIGNER: *Olga Browning* AGENCY: *RomeAntics* COUNTRY: *USA* ■ *The designer wanted to elevate the greeting card to the realm of small visual art by transforming a greeting card into an art card.* ● *Eine Glückwunschkarte, die dank ihrer Gestaltung zu einer Kunstkarte wird.* ▲ *Le concepteur a voulu traiter cette carte de vœux comme un véritable objet d'arts plastiques.*

PAGES 180-181, #368 ART DIRECTOR: *Alessandro Franchini* AGENCY/CLIENT: *Crate and Barrel* COUNTRY: *USA* ■ *The designer wanted to create a graphic program to introduce the first Crate and Barrel store to the New York City market. He utilized the equity built up over thirty years in the black and white logotype, with a slight twist for the New York launch.* ● *Hier ging es um die Einführung des ersten Crate & Barrel-Ladens in der Stadt New York. Für die Promotion verwendete der Gestalter das schwarzweisse Logo, mit dem sich die Firma in dreissig Jahren ihren guten Ruf geschaffen hat und wandelte es speziell für die New Yorker Lancierung ab.* ▲ *Pour le lancement du premier magasin Crate & Barrel à New York, le designer reprit le logo noir et blanc de la maison – qui fonctionnait depuis plus de trente ans – en le réinterprétant pour lui donner une touche «new-yorkaise».*

PAGE 182, #369 ART DIRECTORS: *Stan Church, Derek Samuel* DESIGNER/COPYWRITER: *Derek Samuel* AGENCY/CLIENT: *Wallace Church Associates, Inc.* TYPEFACE: *Custom, Trajan* PRINTER: *Silk Screen Industries* COUNTRY: *USA* ■ *This promotional gift was sent to clients during the December holiday season. The agency developed the concept of packaging a t-shirt in a tin, playing on the word "tea." A large ban-*

dlettered 'T' with the company logo was silk-screened onto the t-shirt. ● *Dieses Werbegeschenk eines Design-Studios wurde in der Weihnachtszeit an Kunden verschickt. Das Wort 'Tee' war das Thema, und ein grosses, handgeschriebens 'T' mit Firmenlogo wurde im Siebdruck auf ein T-Shirt appliziert, das dann in einer Dose verpackt wurde.* ▲ *Cadeau promotionnel d'une agence à ses clients à l'occasion des fêtes de fin d'année. L'idée était d'offrir un tee-shirt présenté dans une boîte métallique et de jouer sur le mot «tea». Un grand «T» tracé à la main et accompagné du logo de l'agence a été sérigraphié sur les tee-shirts.*

PAGE 182, #370 ART DIRECTOR: *Joe Schovitz* DESIGNER: *André Seibel* AGENCY: *Reed and Steven* PHOTOGRAPHER/ILLUSTRATOR: *stock, Joe Schovitz* COPYWRITER: *Joe Schovitz* CLIENT: *Reed and Steven* TYPEFACE: *Futura Cond* PRINTER: *Southeast Graphics* COUNTRY: *USA* ■ *To create an inexpensive, unusual direct mail brochure to solicit new advertising clients, the agency utilized a simple, familiar subject everyone recognizes as being "good for you"–milk–as a vehicle and developed the creative art direction, design and copy from there.* ● *Hier ging es um die Produktion einer kostengünstigen, ungewöhnlichen Broschüre, mit der die Werbeagentur neue Kunden ansprechen wollte. Man entschied sich für 'Milch' als Thema für Gestaltung und Text, ein einfaches, vertrautes Produkt, das in der Vorstellung eines jeden 'gut für dich' ist.* ▲ *Brochure originale et peu coûteuse réalisée par une agence de publicité dans le but de prospecter de nouveaux clients par voie de marketing direct. Le thème retenu était le lait, produit simple et familier, associé dans l'esprit de chacun comme un aliment qui «fait du bien».*

PAGE 182, #371 AGENCY: *P.A.K. Planung Architektur Konzeptdesign* PHOTOGRAPHER: *Emanuel Raab* CLIENT: *ZETBE* PAPER: *Self-adhesive* TYPEFACE: *Helvetica* COUNTRY: *Germany*

PAGE 182, #372 ART DIRECTOR: *Michael Stelzer* DESIGNERS: *Michael Stelzer, Bill Mammorella* AGENCY: *The Marlin Company* PHOTOGRAPHER: *Bruce Andrews* COPYWRITER: *J.R. Richardson* CLIENT: *Reckitt and Colman* PAPER: *Warren 120 lb. dull cover* TYPEFACE: *Journal, JR Script* PRINTER: *Constable Hodgins* BINDERY: *My Sisters Book Binding* COUNTRY: *USA* ■ *At the end of a nine month sales promotion period, the client wanted to deliver a dramatic communication piece that would capture the unique aspects of the grand prize trip to the Orient. The agency developed a "coffee table" keepsake to serve as a reminder of this incentive trip. The photos were taken prior to the start of the program and based entirely on the pre-planned itinerary. Book materials, subject matter and journal entries were composed to reinforce the theme, "Mysteries of the Orient."* ● *Am Ende einer neunmonatigen Verkaufspromotionsperiode wollte der Auftraggeber auf dramatische Art auf den Grand Prix, eine Reise in den Orient, aufmerksam machen. Sie war Belohnung für besonders erfolgreiche Arbeit seines Verkaufspersonals gedacht. Die Photos für die luxuriös gestaltete Mappe mit den Reiseunterlagen folgen dem festgelegten Reiseplan. Alles ist auf das Thema «Der geheimnisvolle Orient» ausgerichtet.* ▲ *Au terme d'une période de promotion de neuf mois, le client désira communiquer le caractère exceptionnel du 1er prix de son concours: un voyage en Orient. L'agence a conçu un bel ouvrage souvenir de ce voyage. Les photographies ont été prises avant le départ; les articles et le matériel utilisés ont été sélectionnés de façon à mettre l'emphase sur le thème des «Mystères de l'Orient».*

PAGE 183, #373 ART DIRECTOR: *Jerry Hutchinson* DESIGNERS: *Jerry Hutchinson, David Colley* AGENCY: *Hutchinson Associates, Inc.* CLIENT: *Dupli-Graphic* PAPER: *Star White Vicksburg* PRINTER: *Dupli-Graphic* COUNTRY: *USA* ■ *To promote a printer to the design community in Chicago, the agency needed to create a piece that designers would find interesting and want to keep.* ● *Mit dieser Promotion für eine Druckerei sollte die Graphikbranche in Chicago angesprochen werden.* ▲ *Pour promouvoir une imprimerie dans le monde de la création à Chicago, il fallait éveiller l'intêret des professionnels et leur présenter quelque chose qu'ils aient envie de conserver.*

PAGE 184, #374 ART DIRECTOR: *Dana Arnett* DESIGNERS: *Curtis Schreiber, Joy Panos Stauber* AGENCY: *VSA Partners, Inc.* CLIENT: *Harpo Productions, Inc* PRINTER: *The Etheridge Printing Co.* TYPEFACE: *Caslon* PAPER: *Simpson Teton* COUNTRY: *USA* ■ *This affiliate kit was produced in limited quantities for stations that carry the*

Oprah Winfrey Show. The kit houses literature, video, and radio shots. ● *Dieses Set, zu dem Literatur, Video und Radioaufnahmen gehören, wurde in beschränkter Anzahl für TV-Regionalsender produziert, die die Oprah Winfrey Talk-Show im Programm haben.* ▲ *Produit en quantités limitées pour des chaînes de télévision régionales, ce set contient des extraits radiophoniques, des vidéos et de la littérature.*

PAGE 184, #375 CREATIVE DIRECTOR: *Mike Stewart* DESIGNER/PHOTOGRAPHER/ILLUSTRATOR: *Anna Matulaitis* COPYWRITER: *Betsy Adelmann* AGENCY/CLIENT: *Stewart Holt Advertising* PAPER: *UV Ultra II, Karma Matte Natural (text)* TYPEFACE: *Stone Serif, Folio Light, Palatino, Pepita* PRINTER: *Franklin Press* COUNTRY: *USA* ■ *The kit was designed for businesses that are ready to flourish. Seed packets are labeled by agency function on the front, and describe a client's success story on the back. Inside the packets are slides displaying work created for that client. A viewer is provided to preview the slides.* ● *Promotion einer Werbeagentur. Die Vorderseiten der Samentüten informieren über die Funktion der Agentur, die Rückseite berichtet von der Erfolgsgeschichte eines Kunden. In den Tüten befinden sich Dias, die Beispiele der Arbeiten für den jeweiligen Kunden zeigen. Ein Gucki wird mitgeliefert.* ▲ *Kit créé pour les entreprises en pleine croissance. Sur le recto des paquets de graines: des informations sur l'intervention de l'agence (dont des exemples sous forme de diapositives sont inclus dans le sachet. Au verso, un résumé de l'histoire de la réussite de l'entreprise. Une visionneuse est fournie avec le kit.*

PAGE 184, #376 ART DIRECTOR: *John Meyer* DESIGNER: *Steve Sandstrom* AGENCY: *Sandstrom Design* PHOTOGRAPHER/ILLUSTRATOR: *Leland Burke* CLIENT: *Levi Strauss & Co.* PAPER: *Simpson Evergreen Kraft* TYPEFACE: *Agency Gothic, Bank Gothic, Janson* PRINTER: *Premier Press* COUNTRY: *USA* ■ *This promotion was a direct mail introduction of the client's apparel to retailers and pro golf shops. It included a letter, schedule of advertising, videotape, pin, tin box, golf balls and tees, and an announcement of endorsement by golf pro Tom Lehman. All the components were individually packaged to stand alone as well.* ■ *Eine Promotion für Sportkleidung, die direkt an Einzelhändler und spezielle Golf-Läden versandt wurde. Sie bestand aus einem Brief, einem Anzeigenüberblick, einem Video-Tape, einem Pin, einer Blechdose, Golfbällen und Teesorten sowie aus der Bekanntmachung, dass die Firma den Golf-Profi Tom Lehman für sich gewinnen konnte. Alle Teile waren einzeln verpackt, so dass sie auch ausserhalb des Kits wirkten.* ▲ *Promotion pour des vêtements de sport envoyée à des commerces au détail et à des magasins proposant des articles de golf. Elle comprenait une lettre, un index publicitaire, une cassette vidéo, un pin, une boîte de conserve, des balles de golf et différentes sortes de thé et annonçait également que la société a réussi à s'attacher les services de Tom Lehman, golfeur professionnel.*

PAGE 185, #377 ART DIRECTOR: *Steven Sikora* DESIGNERS: *Richard Boynton, Eddie Hofmeister* AGENCY: *Design Guys* COPYWRITER: *Rachel Eager* CLIENT: *Target Stores* TYPEFACE: *Trade Gothic, Trixie, OCRB* PRINTER: *General Litho Services* COUNTRY: *USA* ■ *The client wanted to issue an invitation to an event celebrating a relationship between a chain of retail pharmacies and the Mayo Clinic. The invitation is in the form of a medical chart diagnosing stress due to intense involvement in the partnership. The treatment is a celebration of a luncheon at which "refreshments will be administered."* ● *Einladung zu einem Fest, mit dem die guten Beziehungen zwischen einer Apothekenkette und der Mayo-Klinik gefeiert werden. Sie erhielt die Form einer Patientenkarte, die Stress aufgrund intensiven Engagements in einer Partnerschaft diagnostiziert. Als Behandlung wird ein Mittagessen verschrieben, an dem «Erfrischungen eingeflösst werden».* ▲ *Carton d'invitation pour une manifestation événementielle organisée pour célébrer les bonnes relations unissant une chaîne de pharmacies et la clinique Mayo. L'invitation se présente sous la forme d'un diagramme médical diagnostiquant un état de stress dû à l'intensité de la collaboration. Le traitement prescrit prévoit un déjeuner au cours duquel des «rafraîchissements seront administrés».*

PAGE 185, #378 ART DIRECTOR/DESIGNER: *George Vogt* AGENCY: *Sandstrom Design* ILLUSTRATORS: *(from top left to bottom right) Greg Clarke, Adam McCauley, Joel Nakamura, Michael Bartalos, Gerald Bustamente, Ward Schumaker, Greg*

Spalenka, Craig Frazier, John Hersey, Vivienne Flesher, Ann Field, Malcolm Tarlofsky COPYWRITER: *Jack Harding* CLIENT: *California Marriott Hotels, Katsin/Loeb Advertising* COUNTRY: *USA* ■ *Five convention hotels pooled their yearly direct mail budget to target top meeting planners. They expected a promotion that would continue to boost bookings for an entire year. A wooden clock was sent to each planner. The face is a removable work of art by a California illustrator. Each month the planner receives a new face, along with seasonal offers. On the back of the clock are five cards which rotate into view with details on each resort. There is no corporate logo on the clock to make sure it had a place on the planners' desks.* ● *Eine gemeinsame Direktwerbeaktion von fünf Hotels, die sich an die Planer von Kongressen richtet. Von der Promotion erhoffte man sich höhere Buchungen während eines ganzen Jahres. Jedem Planer wurde eine hölzerne Tischuhr geschickt. Das Zifferblatt, das austauschbar ist, wurde von einem kalifornischen Illustrator geschaffen. Jeden Monat erhält der Planer zusammen mit den Angeboten der Saison ein neues Zifferblatt. Bei der Uhr wurde auf das Firmenlogo verzichtet, um sicher zu sein, dass die Uhr auch aufgestellt wird.* ▲ *Cinq hôtels se sont associés dans le cadre d'une publicité sous forme de publipostage adressée aux responsables de la planification de congrès. Chaque responsable a reçu une pendule de table en bois. Le cadran interchangeable a été conçu par un illustrateur californien. Chaque mois, en fonction des offres saisonnières, les responsables de la planification reçoivent un nouveau cadran. Aucun logo ne figure sur la pendule afin qu'elle soit réellement exposée.*

PAGE 186, #379 ART DIRECTOR/DESIGNER: *Michael James Wheaton* AGENCY: *Borgardt Scheibel & Wheaton* PHOTOGRAPHER: *Peter Carter* COPYWRITER: *Michael James Wheaton* CLIENT: *Peter Carter Photography* PAPER: *80lb. Karma White* TYPEFACE: *Helvetica* PRINTER: *Color Ink* COUNTRY: *USA* ■ *To announce the birth of his baby, the photographer used a visual analogy between the photographic process and childbirth. It is designed to lead the recipient to assume that the announcement is a promotional piece, but after four panels of photography it is evident that the newborn girl is the real masterpiece.* ● *Um die Geburt seines Kindes bekanntzugeben, bediente sich der Photograph einer visuellen Analogie zwischen dem photographischen Prozess und der Geburt. Der Empfänger sollte glauben, es handle sich um Werbung, aber nach vier Phototafeln wird klar, dass das neugeborene Mädchen das wahre Meisterwerk ist.* ▲ *Pour annoncer la naissance de sa fille, le photographe joua sur l'analogie visuelle entre le processus photographique et la naissance. Le destinataire croit dans un premier temps avoir affaire à une publicité; dès le quatrième panneau, il devient clair que la véritable œuvre d'art, c'est le bébé*

PAGE 186, #380 ART DIRECTOR: *Steven Scheiner* AGENCY: *Ritta & Associates* COPYWRITER: *Victoria List* CLIENT: *BMW of North America* PACKAGE: *Walden Lang* VIDEO: *Dick Clark Coporate Productions* VOICE CHIP FOLDER: *Structural Graphics* PRINTERS: *Digital Color Services, Central Letter Shop, Mid-Atlantic Graphics* ■ *The agency built upon the James Bond theme to introduce the new car to BMW dealers across the US. This promotion features a "spy kit" containing a sound-chip message from the vice-president of marketing and dossiers on target customers. A "top secret," sealed bottom compartment contains a video and CDI disk for showroom kiosks and a cannister containing a 35 mm filmstrip of spy photos. The roadster's first year production was sold out before it reached the showrooms.* ● *Basis für diese an alle BMW-Händler in den USA gerichtete Promotion ist das James-Bond-Thema. Sie kommt in Gestalt eines Spionage-Kits daher, der eine Botschaft des Vice President of Marketing auf einem Ton-Chip enthält sowie Dossiers über die anvisierten Kunden. Ein "Top Secret" markiertes, versiegeltes Geheimfach enthält ein Video und eine CDI Diskette für Showroom-Kioske und einen Behälter mit einem 35mm-Filmstreifen mit Spionage-Photos. Die erste Jahresproduktion des Roadsters war ausverkauft, bevor die Wagen in die Showrooms gelangten.* ▲ *L'agence choisit le thème de «James Bond» pour le lancement d'un nouveau modèle de roadster auprès des concessionnaires BMW à travers les Etats-Unis. La promotion s'articule autour d'une malette du parfait espion comprenant un message électronique du vice-président du marketing ainsi que des dossiers sur le public cible. Un double-fond pourvu de la mention «top secret» contient une vidéo et un CDI pour les stands promotionnels des showrooms ainsi qu'un jerrycan recelant un film 35 mm de photos d'espionnage. La* *première année, tous les véhicules produits ont été vendus avant même d'arriver chez les concessionnaires.*

PAGE 187, #381 ART DIRECTOR: *Charles S. Anderson* DESIGNERS: *Charles S. Anderson, Todd Piper-Hauswirth, Joel Templin* AGENCY: *Charles S. Anderson Design Company* COPYWRITER: *Lisa Pemrick* CLIENT: *CSA Archive* PAPER: *French Dur-O-Tone Newsprint* TYPEFACE: *20th Century* PRINTER: *Litho Inc.* COUNTRY: *USA* ■ *This catalog was created for an extensive collection of 20th century line art illustrations. It was extensively indexed and cross referenced by subject category.* ● *Katalog für eine umfangreiche Sammlung von Illustrationen aus dem 20. Jahrhundert. Er enthält ausführliche Indexe nach verschiedenen Gesichtspunkten.* ▲ *Catalogue présentant une vaste collection d'illustrations du XXᵉ siècle admirablement répertoriées, avec des critères croisés.*

PAGE 187, #382 ART DIRECTOR: *Jack Anderson* DESIGNERS: *Jack Anderson, John Anicker, Cliff Chung* AGENCY: *Hornall Anderson Design Works, Inc.* CLIENT: *Microsoft Corporation* COUNTRY: *USA* ■ *These promotional materials (awards) were designed for the Microsoft World Wide Sales and Marketing Conference.* ● *Promotionsmaterial für eine Verkaufs- und Marketingtagung von Microsoft World Wide Sales.* ▲ *Matériel promotionnel conçu pour une conférence sur les ventes et le marketing de Microsoft World Wide.*

PAGE 187, #383 ART DIRECTOR: *Dan Olson* DESIGNERS: *Dan Olson, Todd Bartz, Eden Fahlen* PHOTOGRAPHER: *Lev Tushaus* AGENCY: *Duffy Design* CLIENT: *Flagstone Brewery* COUNTRY: *USA* ■ *The assignment was to brand, package, and promote a Southeastern regional specialty targeting predominantly male, urban, and upscale microbrew consumers.* ● *Der Auftrag erstreckte sich auf die Gestaltung von Logo, Verpackung und Promotionsmaterial für ein Bier, das als Spezialität der Region vermarktet wird. Zielgruppe war vor allem die männliche, urbane Bevölkerung mit hohen Ansprüchen.* ▲ *Ce contrat comprenait la conception du logo, de l'emballage et du matériel de promotion pour une bière lancée sur le marché en tant que spécialité régionale. Le produit s'adresse avant tout à des hommes exigeants vivant en milieu urbain.*

PAGE 187, #384 ART DIRECTOR/DESIGNER: *Neil Powell* AGENCY: *Duffy Design* PHOTOGRAPHERS: *Mark LaFavor, Hugh Kretschmer* CLIENT: *Wieland Furniture* COUNTRY: *USA*

PAGES 188-189, #385 ART DIRECTOR: *Jeff Weithman* DESIGNER: *Clint Gorthy* AGENCY/CLIENT: *Nike, Inc.* COUNTRY: *USA* ■ *Clean, simple solutions were developed to clearly and consistently communicate the "new" brand identity at retail stores.* ● *Einfache, saubere Lösungen für den Auftritt einer 'neuen' Nike-Marke in Einzelhandelsgeschäften.* ▲ *Solutions propres et simples élaborées dans le but de communiquer de manière claire et cohérente la «nouvelle» identité de marque sur les points de vente.*

PAGE 190, #386 ART DIRECTORS: *John McConnell, Justus Oehler* DESIGNERS: *John McConnell, Justus Oehler, Kristina Langhein* PHOTOGRAPHERS: *Nick Turner, Amanda Clement* COPYWRITER: *Juliet Barclay* AGENCY/CLIENT: *Pentagram Design, Ltd.* PAPER: *Parilux Matte Art White 250 gm. (cover, jacket) Parilux Matte Art White 170 gm (text)* TYPEFACE: *Franklin Gothic* PRINTER: *Gavin Martin* COUNTRY: *England* ■ *This monograph is one in a series of limited edition monographs designed and produced by the agency since its inception in 1975.* ● *Diese Monographie gehört zu einer Reihe, die die Agentur seit ihrer Gründung im Jahre 1975 in limitierter Auflage herausgibt.* ▲ *Une des monographies réalisées et éditées en série limitée par l'agence depuis sa fondation en 1975.*

PAGE 190, #387 ART DIRECTOR/DESIGNER: *David Hillman* AGENCY: *Pentagram Design, Ltd.* CLIENT: *The Hong Kong Management Association* ■ *This lightbulb trophy was awarded for best marketing achievement and was designed to highlight the importance of "inspired ideas." It is made of brown perspex, with a gold, silver, or bronze filament indicating the level of award.* ● *Diese Glühbirne, eine Auszeichnung für die besten Marketing-Leistungen, symbolisiert die Bedeutung grossartiger Ideen. Sie besteht aus braunem Akrylglas mit Gold-, Silber- oder Bronzefaden, je nach Art der Auszeichnung.* ▲ *Cette ampoule, une distinction*

pour les meilleures productions en matière de marketing, fait allusion à l'importance que revêtent inspiration et traits de génie dans le domaine de la créativité. Elle se compose de verre acrylique brun avec un filament en or, en argent ou en bronze selon le rang occupé au classement général.

PAGE 190, #388 ART DIRECTOR: *John McConnell* DESIGNERS: *John McConnell, Alan Dye* PHOTOGRAPHER: *Nick Turner* AGENCY/CLIENT: *Pentagram Design, Ltd.* PAPER: *Somerset, soft white textured finish 250 gm. (cover), Neptune Unique 155 gm (text)* TYPEFACE: *Letterpress Caslon Oldface* COUNTRY: *England* ■ *Each year the agency creates a small book for clients, friends, and colleagues for the holidays. Following this tradition, "The Pressman's Hat" was created.* ● *Jedes Jahr zu Weihnachten entwirft die Agentur ein kleines Buch für Kunden, Freunde und Kollegen. "The Pressman's Hat" entstand im Rahmen dieser Tradition.* ▲ *Chaque année, à l'occasion des fêtes de Noël, l'agence conçoit un petit livre pour ses clients, collaborateurs et amis. C'est dans ce contexte que «The Pressman's Hat» a vu le jour.*

PAGE 191, #389 ART DIRECTORS: *Robert Verhaart, Ron van der Vlugt* AGENCY: *Designers Company* CLIENT: *Hooghoudt Distillers* COUNTRY: *The Netherlands* ■ *This promotion was created for the hundredth anniversary of the Hooghoudt Distillery which is allowed to carry the Royal Coat of Arms. The "promotion" bottles create a link between the hedonism within the Western party scene and are extreme examples from the history of the European Church and royalty.* ● *Promotion zum 100jährigen Bestehen einer Distillerie, die berechtigt ist, das königliche Wappen zu führen. Die Promotions-Flaschen stellen eine Verbindung zwischen dem Hedonismus innerhalb der westlichen Party-Szene her und beziehen sich auf extreme Fälle in der Geschichte der europäischen Kirchen- und Monarchie.* ▲ *Promotion pour le 100ème anniversaire d'une distillerie autorisée à présenter les armoiries royales sur ses produits. Les bouteilles promotionnelles établissent une relation avec l'hédonisme qui régne dans la scène du divertissement occidental et se référent à des cas extrêmes de l'histoire de la royauté et du christianisme en Europe.*

PAGE 191, #390 ART DIRECTOR/DESIGNER/ILLUSTRATOR: *Joel Templin* PHOTOGRAPHER: *Paul Sinkler* COPYWRITER: *Lisa Pemrick* AGENCY: *Templin Design* CLIENT: *Joel Templin* PAPER: *French Dur-O-Tone* COUNTRY: *USA* ■ *To creatively let friends and family know be married, the designer developed the "Official Handbook on Tying the Knot."* ● *Um seine Familie und Freunde über seine bevorstehende Hochzeit zu informieren, kreierte der Designer das «Offizielle Handbuch über das Anfertigen eines Knotens».* ▲ *Le designer a conçu ce «manuel officiel sur la manière de faire des nœuds» pour informer sa famille et ses amis de son mariage. L'anglais joue sur l'expression «tying the knot» signifiant à la fois se marier et faire un nœud.*

PAGE 192, #391 ART DIRECTOR: *Doo H. Kim* DESIGNERS: *Dongil Lee, Seunghee Lee* AGENCY: *DooKim Design* CLIENT: *Samsung Corp., Utoo Zone* COUNTRY: *Korea* ■ *This bag was designed for Utoo Zone, a fashion department store in the core of the fashion district of Seoul. "Have a nice day, you too!," the client's slogan, is utilized.* ● *Tragtasche für Utoo Zone, ein Mode-Kaufhaus im Herzen des Modedistrikts von Seoul, mit dem Slogan des Kunden: «Einen schönen Tag – auch für Sie !»* ▲ *Sac conçu pour Utoo Zone, un grand magasin situé au cœur du quartier de la mode à Séoul, avec pour slogan: «Bonne Journée, à vous aussi!»*

PAGE 193, #392 ART DIRECTOR: *Alan Chan* DESIGNERS: *Alan Chan, Peter Lo* AGENCY: *Alan Chan Design Company* CLIENT: *Davinci Co. Ltd, Kosta Boda* ■ *Kosta Boda is a renowned Swedish manufacturer of high quality glassware. The multi-color, overlapping letters of the client's name enhance the principal characteristics of the product.* ● *Kosta Boda ist eine bekannte schwedische Marke für qualitativ hochwertige Glasartikel. Die mehrfarbigen, überlappenden Buchstaben des Namens des Herstellers entsprechen den Haupteigenschaften des Produktes.* ▲ *Kosta Boda est un fabricant suédois réputé pour ses articles en verre. Les lettres multicolores superposées qui reprennent le nom du client font ressortir les principales caractéristiques du produit.*

PAGE 194, #393 ART DIRECTOR/DESIGNER: *Sibylle Haase* AGENCY: *Atelier Haase & Knels* CLIENT: *Boutique Evelyn* PAPER: *Kraftbraun, Gerippt, 120g/qm* TYPEFACE: *Futura*

Bold PRINTER: *Cabas Verpackung & Design OHG* MANUFACTURER: *Cabas Verpackung & Design OHG* COUNTRY: *Germany* ■ *To create a shopping bag that clients would be able to use several times, the agency made it similar to a typical leather shopping bag and transferred the client's corporate design in an unobtrusive manner.* ● *Tragtasche für eine Boutique, die zur häufigen Wiederverwendung einladen sollte. Die Lösung ist eine an Ledertaschen erinnernde Tüte mit einem unaufdringlichen Aufdruck.* ▲ *Sac conçu pour être réutilisé plusieurs fois. Semblable à un sac en cuir, il est frappé du logo du client qui apparaît discrètement.*

PAGE 195, #394 ART DIRECTOR/DESIGNER: *Yasuo Tanaka* AGENCY/CLIENT: *Package Land Co., Ltd.* COUNTRY: *USA* ■ *3-D gift bag.* ● *Eine für Geschenke bestimmte Tragtasche.* ▲ *Pochette-cadeau tridimensionnelle.*

PAGE 196, #395 CREATIVE DIRECTOR: *Peter Levine* DESIGNER: *Kim Tyska* AGENCY: *Desgrippes Gobé & Associates* PHOTOGRAPHER/ILLUSTRATOR: *Andrew Bordwin* CLIENT: *Ann Taylor Loft* PAPER: *Recycled kraft paper* MANUFACTURER: *Wright Packaging* COUNTRY: *USA* ■ *The identity for a women's retail fashion chain is intended to appeal to young women just beginning their careers. The challenge was to launch a new line without losing the brand's core visual vocabulary. The shopping bag is simple, unpretentious, and natural.* ● *Tragtasche für eine neue Linie einer Modefirma, die junge Frauen am Anfang ihrer beruflichen Karriere ansprechen soll. Die Herausforderung bestand darin, diese neue Linie unter Einbeziehung der wichtigsten visuellen Elemente der bestehenden Marke zu lancieren. Das Resultat ist ein schlichter, natürlicher Auftritt.* ▲ *Graphisme créé pour plaire aux jeunes femmes qui débutent une carrière professionnelle. Le résultat est un sac simple, discret, ayant un côté très «nature».*

PAGE 197, #396 ART DIRECTOR: *Kit Hinrichs* DESIGNER: *Jackie Foshaug* AGENCY: *Pentagram Design* CLIENT: *The Gymboree Corporation* COUNTRY: *USA* ■ *This shopping bag is part of an identity program that includes the design and implementation of a new visual identity for the client. The "new look" replaces traditional primary colors with an updated version.* ● *Packungsgestaltung im Rahmen eines Erscheinungsbildes des Kunden. Zum «neuen Look» gehört eine neue Farbpalette, die die traditionellen Grundfarben ersetzt.* ▲ *Emballage conçu dans le cadre de l'identité visuelle du client. Pour ce «look» revisité, de nouveaux coloris remplacent les traditionnelles couleurs primaires.*

PAGE 198, #397 ART DIRECTOR: *Akio Okumura* DESIGNER: *Katsuji Minami* AGENCY: *Packaging Create Inc.* CLIENT: *New Oji Paper Co., Ltd.* TYPEFACE: *Original* COUNTRY: *Japan*

PAGE 199, #398 ART DIRECTOR: *Lowell Williams* DESIGNER: *Bill Carson* AGENCY: *Pentagram Design* CLIENT: *Gianfranco Lotti* TYPEFACE: *Bodoni* ■ *To create packaging for a new line of Italian leather products, the agency used the gussets of the bags and the buttons of the boxes as a visual field and a famous Italian painting was printed with the products stripped into the scene.* ● *Für die Verpackung einer neuen Linie italienischer Lederwaren wurde ein italienisches Gemälde verwendet, in das die Produkte hineinstrippt wurden.* ▲ *Emballages et sacs d'une nouvelle ligne d'articles en cuir italiens. L'agence utilisa les soufflets des sacs et les systèmes de fermeture comme champ visuel. Le tableau d'un grand maître italien dans lequel des dessins des produits ont été intégrés est reproduit sur le packaging.*

PAGE 199, #399 ART DIRECTOR/DESIGNER: *Kai Mui* AGENCY: *Mui + Gray, Inc.* CLIENT: *AKI S.p.A.* TYPEFACE: *Lubalin* COUNTRY: *Italy* ■ *The agency wanted to create a comprehensive communications package that would make the client's brand stand out from other athletic brands. The clenched fist was used as a focal point, and sophisticated design contrasted with the rough, common materials.* ● *Bei dieser Tragtasche eines Sportartikelherstellers steht das anspruchsvolle Design im Kontrast zu dem rauhen, gewöhnlichen Material. Zentrales Element ist die geballte Faust.* ▲ *L'objectif de l'agence était de concevoir une communication ayant un impact suffisamment fort pour que la marque de son client se distingue de celle des autres fabricants. Le design sophistiqué contraste avec l'aspect brut du matériau choisi. L'élément central est le poing fermé.*

PAGE 199, #400 EXECUTIVE CREATIVE DIRECTOR: *Peter Allen* CREATIVE DIRECTOR: *Amy Knapp* ART DIRECTOR: *Albert Treskin* DESIGNER: *Alan Yu* ILLUSTRATOR: *Daniel Pelavin* AGENCY: *DFS Group Ltd.* CLIENT: *DFS Merchandising Ltd.* TYPEFACE: *Canton Market (custom)* PRINTER: *Sun's Paper Bags* COUNTRY: *Hong Kong* ■ *This carrier was created for a shop-within-a-store which sells a unique collection of Chinese gifts and souvenirs. The agency wanted to create a colorful "traveling billboard" which reinforces the shop identity and continues to advertise the shop on the busy streets of Hong Kong.* ● *Tragtasche für einen speziellen Shop innerhalb eines Ladens mit einem einzigartigen Angebot von Geschenk- und Souvenirartikeln aus China. Ziel der Gestalter war ein farbenfrohes, «wandelndes Plakat», das auf den belebten Strassen Hongkongs auf den Shop aufmerksam macht.* ▲ *Sac destiné à promouvoir le stand d'objets rares chinois d'un magasin de Hongkong. L'objectif était de créer un «panneau publicitaire mobile» qui permette à la boutique de renforcer son image, tout en attirant l'attention dans les rues animées de Hongkong.*

PAGE 200, #401 ART DIRECTOR/DESIGNER: *Todor Vardjiev* CLIENT: *Komitet für Post und Fernverbindung* COUNTRY: *Bulgaria*

PAGE 200, #402 ART DIRECTOR/DESIGNER: *John Spatchurst* AGENCY: *Spatchurst Design Associates* COUNTRY: *Australia*

PAGE 201, #403 ART DIRECTOR: *Pauline Ciamciolo* DESIGNER/ILLUSTRATOR: *Lloyd P. Birmingham* AGENCY: *Birmingham Studios* TYPEFACE: *Hobo, Helvetica* COUNTRY: *Republic of Palau* ■ *To design a unified sheet of postage stamps, the designer eliminated white borders and created a unifying background of undersea terrain.* ● *Um ein homogenes Briefmarkenblatt zu erhalten, verzichtete der Gestalter auf die weissen Ränder und benutzte eine Unterwasserlandschaft als verbindenden Hintergrund.* ▲ *Pour obtenir une feuille de timbres homogène, le graphiste renonça aux bords blancs et s'inspira de paysages sous-marins pour le fond.*

PAGE 201, #404 ART DIRECTOR: *Dick Sheaff* DESIGNER/ILLUSTRATOR: *Mark Hess* AGENCY: *Hess Design Works* CLIENT: *United States Postal Service* COUNTRY: *USA* ■ *This stamp set was created to commemorate the American Civil War. The agency had to design and execute all images in a dignified, historic, serious, yet slightly contemporary style. Four important battles were positioned in the four corners. Images were united through color, style, and graphic balance. The header had to complement these strategies.* ● *Dieses Briefmarken-Set entstand im Gedenken an die Verdienste verschiedener Menschen im amerikanischen Bürgerkrieg. Der Stil der Darstellungen musste würdevoll, historisch, ernsthaft und doch auch ein bisschen zeitgemäss sein. Vier wichtige Schlachten wurden in den vier Ecken untergebracht. Den Bildern wurde durch Farbe, Stil und Gestaltung ein homogenes Aussehen verliehen.* ▲ *Cette série de timbres rend hommage aux acteurs de la guerre de Sécession. Dignité, caractère historique, sérieux et touche moderniste, tels étaient les critères prévalant au style de ces images. Quatre batailles importantes sont représentées dans les quatre coins respectifs. Un effet unitaire a été obtenu en harmonisant les couleurs, le style et la conception graphique.*

PAGE 202, #405 ART DIRECTOR/DESIGNER/ILLUSTRATOR: *Jean Evain* COUNTRY: *France* ■ *Self-promotion of an artist presenting his designs for postal stamps. For his collage he used painting, engraving, and photography. On the envelope, one of his stamps is beside the regular postage stamp.* ● *Eigenwerbung eines Designers, der hier seine Briefmarkenentwürfe präsentiert. Für die Collage verwendete er verschiedene Techniken (Malerei, Radierung, Photographie). Auf den Briefumschlag klebt jeweils einer seiner Markenentwürfe neben der offiziellen Briefmarke.* ■ *Pour sa promotion personnelle, l'artiste a choisi de présenter ses esquisses de timbres-poste. Diverses techniques (peinture, gravure, photo) ont été utilisées pour le collage. Sur chaque enveloppe, il colla un timbre de sa création à côté du timbre officiel.*

PAGE 202, #406 ART DIRECTOR/DESIGNER/ILLUSTRATOR: *Jean Evain* COUNTRY: *France* ■ *Greeting card for the tenth anniversary of the magazine of the Loire region, France. The collage consists of images that appeared in the magazine during the last ten years.* ● *Glückwunschkarte zum 10jährigen Bestehen der Revue der Loire-Regionen. Die Collage besteht aus Bildern, die in den letzten zehn Jahren in* diesem Magazin erschienen sind. ▲ Carte de vœux pour le 10ᴱᴹᴱ anniversaire d'une revue des Pays de Loire. Ce collage est composé d'éléments iconographiques parus dans la revue au cours des dix dernières années.

PAGE 202, #407 ART DIRECTOR/DESIGNER/ILUSTRATOR: *Marie-Christine Ecklin* AGENCY: *MC Ecklin* COUNTRY: *France* ■ *Fictitious stamps on the subject of "censored communication."* ● *Timbres fixtifs sur le theme "communication censuré."*

PAGE 203, #408 ART DIRECTOR/DESIGNER/ILLUSTRATOR/COPYWRITER: *Thomas Vasquez* AGENCY: *Squires & Company* CLIENT: *Deep Ellum Arts Festival* COUNTRY: *USA* ■ *This t-shirt designed for the Deep Ellum Arts Festival in Dallas, Texas is meant to appeal to "Generation X."* ▲ *Das T-Shirt für das Deep Ellum Arts Festival wurde für die «Generation X» entworfen.* ▲ *Tee-shirt créé à l'occasion du Deep Ellum Arts Festival, à l'intention de la «génération X».*

PAGE 203, #409 ART DIRECTOR/DESIGNER/ILLUSTRATOR: *Mark Geer* AGENCY: *Geer Design* CLIENT: *Times 3 Productions* COUNTRY: *USA* ■ *Corporate identity for a film production company.* ● *Firmenzeichen für eine Filmproduktionsfirma.* ▲ *Identitié visuelle d'une société de productions cinématographiques.*

PAGE 204, #410 ART DIRECTOR/DESIGNER/ILLUSTRATOR: *Heward Jue* AGENCY: *Hewardesign* CLIENT: *Java The Hut* TYPEFACE: *Bank Gothic* COUNTRY: *USA* ■ *This souvenir t-shirt for the Greenwich Village espresso bar 'Java The Hut' makes use of the well-liked logo.* ● *Dieses Souvenir-T-Shirt für die Espresso Bar 'Java The Hut' in New Yorks Greenwich Village zeigt das beliebte Logo der Bar.* ▲ *Tee-shirt aux couleurs d'un bar à espresso de Greenwich Village, New York, reprenant son logo très apprécié.*

PAGE 204, #411 ART DIRECTOR: *Joan Donnelly* DESIGNER: *Tim Frame* AGENCY: *FRCH Design Worldwide* CLIENT/MANUFACTURER: *Aca Joe* TYPEFACE: *Copperplate* COUNTRY: *Mexico* ■ *This series of t-shirts was designed to complement the jeans brand; the diamond shape was maintained and the words "slim," "easy," "loose" or "big" were placed within the diamond logo in a series of bold colors.* ● *Diese T-Shirt-*

Serie wurde als Ergängzung zu einerJeans-Marke entworfen. Die Karoform des Jeans-Logos wurde übernommen und durch farbenfrohe Eindrucke der verschiedenen Bezeichnungen wie "slim", "easy", "loose" oder "big" ergänzt. ▲ Gamme de tee-shirts créée par une marque de jeans. Le losange a été systématiquement repris sur les tee-shirts; les mots «slim», «easy», «loose» ou «big» sont imprimés à l'intérieur du losange, dans des couleurs vives.

PAGE 204, #412 ART DIRECTORS: *Charles S. Anderson, Todd Piper-Hauswirth* DESIGNER: *Todd Piper-Hauswirth* AGENCY: *Charles S. Anderson Design Co.* CLIENT: *Chums* COUNTRY: *USA*

PAGE 204, #413 ART DIRECTORS: *Scott MacDonald, David Jemerson Young* DESIGNER: *Chris Beatty* ILLUSTRATOR: *David Jemerson Young* AGENCY/CLIENT: *Second Globe* COUNTRY: *USA* ■ *This shirt was created for fishing and fish aficionados. Since every t-shirt has a head coming out of it, the agency turned the predator/prey rules around.* ● *Dieses T-Shirt ist für Angel- bzw. Fischliebhaber gedacht. Da aus aus jedem T-Shirt ein Kopf herausschauen wird, wird das Jäger-Opfer-Verhältnis hier umgekehrt.* ▲ *Tee-shirt destiné aux mordus de pêche. Partant du fait qu'une tête sort de chaque tee-shirt, le rapport entre le prédateur et sa proie a été inversé.*

PAGE 205, #414 ART DIRECTOR/DESIGNER: *José Serrano* ILLUSTRATOR: *Tracy Sabin* AGENCY: *Mires Design, Inc.* CLIENT: *Boy Scout Troop # 260* TYPEFACE: *Custom* PRINTER: *Ship Shape Silkscreen* COUNTRY: *USA* ■ *This T-shirt was created to celebrate an annual event coordinated by the Boy Scouts of America.* ● *T-Shirt für einen jährlichen Anlass der Pfadfinderorganisation Amerikas.* ▲ *Tee-shirt célébrant une manifestation annuelle organisée par les boy-scouts d'Amerique.*

PAGE 206, #415 ART DIRECTOR: *Kit Hinrichs* DESIGNER: *Jackie Foshaug* AGENCY: *Pentagram Design* CLIENT: *Columbus Salame* COUNTRY: *USA*

PAGE 206, #416 ART DIRECTOR: *Alan Disparte* DESIGNERS: *Alan Disparte, Lucia Matioli* AGENCY: *The Gap, Inc.* CLIENT: *Old Navy Clothing Co.* TYPEFACE: *Franklin Gothic, Coronet* COUNTRY: *USA*

INDICES

VERZEICHNISSE

INDEX

EDITORS · COPYWRITERS · PROGRAMMERS

DESIGN FIRMS · ADVERTISING AGENCIES

CLIENTS·PUBLISHERS·RECORD COMPANIES

GRAPHIS BOOKS

BOOK ORDER FORM: USA, CANADA, SOUTH AMERICA, ASIA, PACIFIC

BOOKS		ALL REGIONS
☐ BLACK & WHITE BLUES (HARDCOVER)	US$	69.95
☐ BLACK & WHITE BLUES (PAPERBACK)	US$	45.95
☐ GRAPHIS ADVERTISING 97	US$	69.95
☐ GRAPHIS ALTERNATIVE PHOTOGRAPHY 95	US$	69.95
☐ GRAPHIS ANNUAL REPORTS 5	US$	69.95
☐ GRAPHIS BOOK DESIGN	US$	75.95
☐ GRAPHIS BROCHURES 2	US$	75.00
☐ GRAPHIS CORPORATE IDENTITY 2	US$	75.95
☐ GRAPHIS DESIGN 97	US$	69.95
☐ GRAPHIS EPHEMERA	US$	75.95
☐ GRAPHIS FINE ART PHOTOGRAPHY	US$	85.00
☐ GRAPHIS INFORMATION ARCHITECTS	US$	49.95
☐ GRAPHIS MUSIC CDS	US$	75.95
☐ GRAPHIS NUDES (PAPERBACK)	US$	39.95
☐ GRAPHIS PACKAGING 7	US$	75.00
☐ GRAPHIS PHOTO 96	US$	69.95
☐ GRAPHIS POSTER 96	US$	69.95
☐ GRAPHIS PRODUCTS BY DESIGN	US$	69.95
☐ GRAPHIS SHOPPING BAGS	US$	69.95
☐ GRAPHIS TYPOGRAPHY 1	US$	69.95
☐ GRAPHIS TYPE SPECIMENS	US$	49.95
☐ **GRAPHIS PAPER SPECIFIER SYSTEM (GPS)**	US$	495.00
** ADD $30 SHIPPING/HANDLING FOR GPS		
☐ HUMAN CONDITION	US$	49.95
☐ SHORELINE	US$	85.95
☐ WATERDANCE (PAPERBACK)	US$	24.95
☐ WORLD TRADE MARKS 1OO YRS.(2 VOL. SET)	US$	250.00

NOTE! NY RESIDENTS ADD 8.25% SALES TAX

☐ CHECK ENCLOSED (PAYABLE TO GRAPHIS)
(US$ ONLY, DRAWN ON A BANK IN THE USA)

USE CREDIT CARDS (DEBITED IN US DOLLARS)

☐ AMERICAN EXPRESS   ☐ MASTERCARD   ☐ VISA

CARD NO.   EXP. DATE

CARDHOLDER NAME

SIGNATURE

(PLEASE PRINT)

NAME

TITLE

COMPANY

ADDRESS

CITY

STATE/PROVINCE   ZIP CODE

COUNTRY

SEND ORDER FORM AND MAKE CHECK PAYABLE TO:
GRAPHIS INC.,
141 LEXINGTON AVENUE, NEW YORK, NY 10016-8193, USA

GRAPHIS MAGAZINE

SUBSCRIBE TO GRAPHIS: USA, CANADA, SOUTH AMERICA, ASIA, PACIFIC

MAGAZINE	USA	CANADA	SOUTHAMERICA/ ASIA/PACIFIC
☐ ONE YEAR (6 ISSUES)	US$ 89.00	US$ 99.00	US$ 125.00
☐ TWO YEARS (12 ISSUES)	US$ 159.00	US$ 179.00	US$ 235.00
☐ AIRMAIL SURCHARGE (6 ISSUES)	US$ 59.00	US$ 59.00	US$ 59.00

☐ ONE YEAR (6 ISSUES)   US$ 59.00
FOR STUDENTS WITH COPY OF VALID STUDENT ID AND
PAYMENT WITH ORDER

☐ CHECK ENCLOSED   ☐ PLEASE BILL ME

USE CREDIT CARDS (DEBITED IN US DOLLARS)

☐ AMERICAN EXPRESS

☐ MASTERCARD

☐ VISA

CARD NO.   EXP. DATE

CARDHOLDER NAME

SIGNATURE

(PLEASE PRINT)

NAME

TITLE

COMPANY

ADDRESS

CITY

STATE/PROVINCE   ZIP CODE

COUNTRY

SERVICE BEGINS WITH ISSUE THAT IS CURRENT WHEN
ORDER IS PROCESSED.

SEND ORDER FORM AND MAKE CHECK PAYABLE TO:
GRAPHIS INC.,
141 LEXINGTON AVENUE, NEW YORK, NY 10016-8193, USA

(C9B0A)

Graphis Design 99 (Entry Deadline: November 15, 1997)

■ Eligibility: All work produced between December 1996 and November 1997. Annual reports, books, brochures, calendars, corporate identity/signage, currency, diagrams, editorial, ephemera, games, illustration, letterhead, logos, menus, music, new media, packaging, paper companies, posters, products, promotion, shopping bags, stamps, t-shirts, typography. ● In Frage kommen: Arbeiten, die zwischen Dezember 1996 und November 1997 entstanden sind. Jahresberichte, Bücher, Broschüren, Kalender, Corporate Identity/Beschilderungen, Geldnoten, Münzen, Diagramme, redaktionelles Design, Ephemera (kurzlebige Graphik), Spiele, Illustrationen, Briefschaften, Logos, Menus, CD Design, neue Medien, Packungen, Promotionen für Papierhersteller, Plakate, Produktdesign, Promotionsmateriel, Tragtaschen, Briefmarken, T-Shirts, Typographie. ▲ Seront admis: les travaux réalisés entre décembre 1996 et novembre 1997. Rapports annuels, livres, brochures, calendriers, identité institutionnelle, billets de banque, monnaies, diagrammes, design rédactionnel, graphisme éphémère, jeux, illustrations, lettres, logos, menus, musique, nouveau médias, promotions des fabricants de papier, affiches, design de produits, matériel promotionnel, sacs, timbres, T-Shirts, typographie.

Graphis Products by Design (Entry Deadline: December 15, 1996)

■ All products designed or launched since January, 1994 are eligible. Cameras, electronics, exhibition displays, fashion, furniture, games, home, industrial, lighting, luggage, medical, office, sports, transportation, varia. ● Zugelassen sind alle Produkte, die nach Januar 1994 auf den Markt gekommen sind bzw. entworfen wurden: Kameras, elektronische Geräte, Ausstellungs-Displays, Uhren und Schmuck, Mode-Accessoires, Möbel und Einrichtungsgegenstände, Spiele, Werkzeuge, Leuchten, Gepäck, Medizinalgeräte, Büro- und Sportartikel, Fahrzeuge. ▲ Sont susceptibles d'être sélectionnés tous les produits créés ou lancés sur le marché après janvier 1994 qui entrent dans les catégories suivantes: appareils-photo, électronique, présentoirs d'exposition, horlogerie-bijouterie et accessoires de mode, meubles, jeux, maison et décoration, outillage, luminaires, bagages, appareils médicaux, articles de sport et de bureau, véhicules.

Graphis Advertising 99 (Entry Deadline: October 31, 1997)

■ Eligibility: All work produced between December 1996 and October 1997. Automotive, bank, beverages, broadcast, camera/film, computer/electronics, credit cards, delivery service, education, events, fashion, food, insurance, outdoor, paper company, printer, products, promotion, publishing, retail, social, sports, travel. ● In Frage kommen: Arbeiten, die zwischen Dezember 1996 und Oktober 1997 entstanden sind. Automobile, Banken, Getränke, Rundfunk/Fernsehen, Kameras/Film, Computer/Elektronik, Kreditkarten, Kurierdienste, Ausbildung, Veranstaltungen, Mode, Nahrungsmittel, Versicherungen, Aussenwerbung, Papierhersteller, Druckereien, Produkte, Promotionen, Verlage, Einzelhandel, soziale Anliegen, Sport, Reisen. ▲ Seront admis: les travaux réalisés entre décembre 1996 et octobre 1997. Automobiles, banques, boissons, radiodiffusion/télévision, appareils, photo/film, ordinateurs/électronique, cartes de crédit, courriers rapides, formation, manifestations, mode, alimentation, assurances, publicité extérieure, fabricants de papier, imprimeurs, produits, promotions, éditions, commerce de détail, social, sports, voyage.

■ **What to send:** Reproduction-quality duplicate transparencies (4″x5″ or 35mm), printed piece, or both. Transparencies are required for large, bulky or valuable pieces. ALL 35MM SLIDES MUST BE CARDBOARD-MOUNTED. NO GLASS SLIDE MOUNTS! *All transparencies must be clearly marked with the name of the agency (entrant) and client.* If you send printed pieces, they should be unmounted. WE REGRET THAT ENTRIES CANNOT BE RETURNED. ● **Was einsenden:** Wenn immer möglich, schicken Sie uns bitte reproduktionsfähige Duplikatdias. *Bitte Dias mit Ihrem Namen versehen.* Bitte schicken Sie auf keinen Fall Originaldias. KLEINBILDDIAS BITTE IM KARTONRAHMEN, KEIN GLAS! Falls Sie uns das gedruckte Beispiel schicken, bitten wir Sie, dieses gut geschützt aber nicht aufgezogen zu senden. WIR BEDAUERN, DASS EINSENDUNGEN NICHT ZURÜCKGESCHICKT WERDEN KÖNNEN. ▲**Que nous envoyer:** Nous vous recommandons de nous faire parvenir de préférence des duplicata de diapositives 4x5″ ou 35mm. N'oubliez pas d'inscrire votre nom dessus). NE PAS ENVOYER DE DIAPOSITIVES SOUS VERRE! Si vous désirez envoyer des travaux imprimés, protégez-les, mais ne les montez pas sur carton. NOUS VOUS SIGNALONS QUE LES ENVOIS QUE VOUS NOUS AUREZ FAIT PARVENIR NE POURRONT VOUS ÊTRE RETOURNÉS.

■ **How to package your entry:** Please tape (do not glue) the completed entry form (or a copy) to the back of each printed piece. For transparencies, enclose forms loose and make sure transparencies are labelled. Also enclose an extra photocopy of the entry form with each entry. Do not send anything by air freight. Write "No Commercial Value" on the package, and label it "Art for Contest." ● Wie und wohin senden: Bitte befestigen Sie das ausgefüllte Einsendeetikett (oder eine Kopie davon) mit Klebstreifen auf jeder Arbeit und legen Sie noch ein Doppel davon lose bei. Bitte auf keinen Fall per Luftfracht senden. Deklarieren Sie «Ohne jeden Handelswert» und «Arbeitsproben für Wettbewerb». ▲Comment préparer votre envoi: Veuillez scotcher (ne pas coller) au dos de chaque spécimen les étiquettes dûment remplies. Nous vous prions également de faire un double de chaque étiquette, que vous joindrez à votre envoi, mais sans le coller ou le fixer. Ne nous expédiez rien en fret aérien. Indiquez «Sans aucune valeur commerciale» et «Echantillons pour concours».

■ **Entry fees:** Make check or money order payable to Graphis Inc. Single entries: US $25, £ 23, DM 52, FFR 175 CHF 42. Series entered in a single contest category: US $65, £ 49, DM 110, FFR 375, CHF 90. To pay by Visa, Mastercard or American Express, include your card number, expiration date, and signature of approval; the entry fee will be debited in US$. ● **Einsendegebühren:** Für jede einzelne Arbeit: US $25, £ 23, DM 52, FFR 175 CHF 42. Für jede Kampagne oder Serie von drei oder mehr Stück: US $65, £ 49, DM 110, FFR 375, CHF 90. Für die Bezahlung mit Visa, Mastercard oder American Express fügen Sie die Kartennummer, das Verfalldatum sowie Ihre Unterschrift als Zeichen der Genehmigung hinzu; die Einsendegebühr wird Ihrer Karte in US-Dollar belastet. ▲ **Droits d'admission:** Envoi d'un seul travail: US $25, £ 23, DM 52, FFR 175 CHF 42. Campagne ou série de trois travaux ou plus pour un seul concours: US $65, £ 49, DM 110, FFR 375, CHF 90. Pour régler par carte Visa, Mastercard ou American Express, veuillez inclure le numéro de votre carte, sa date d'expiration et votre signature d'approbation. Le droit d'inscription sera débité en dollars US.

COMPLETE FORM, TAPE IT TO ENTRY, ENCLOSE A PHOTOCOPY AND PAYMENT. SEND TO CLOSEST ADDRESS:
GRAPHIS BOOK CONTEST, C/O AMERICAN BOOK CENTER, BROOKLYN NAVY YARD, BLDG. #3, BROOKLYN, NY 11205 USA
GRAPHIS BOOK CONTEST, C/O CRONAT, PARC 3, F-68870 BARTENHEIM FRANCE

ENTRY FORM

GRAPHIS **PRODUCTS BY DESIGN**
ENTRY DEADLINE: DECEMBER 15, 1996

GRAPHIS **ADVERTISING** 99
ENTRY DEADLINE: OCTOBER 31, 1997

GRAPHIS **DESIGN** 99
ENTRY DEADLINE: NOVEMBER 15, 1997

☐ **GRAPHIS PRODUCTS BY DESIGN**
(DECEMBER 15, 1996)
CATEGORY CODES

☐ PR1 CONSUMER PRODUCTS
☐ PR2 COMMERCIAL PRODUCTS
☐ PR3 ELECTRONICS
☐ PR4 FURNITURE
☐ PR5 VARIA

☐ **ADVERTISING** 99
(OCTOBER 31, 1997)
CATEGORY CODES
☐ AD1 AUTOMOTIVE
☐ AD2 BANK
☐ AD3 BEVERAGES
☐ AD4 BROADCAST
☐ AD5 CAMERA/FILM
☐ AD6 COMPUTER/ELECT.
☐ AD7 CREDIT CARDS
☐ AD8 DELIVERY SERVICE
☐ AD9 EDUCATION
☐ AD10 EVENTS

☐ AD11 FASHION
☐ AD12 FOOD
☐ AD13 INSURANCE
☐ AD14 OUTDOOR
☐ AD15 PAPER COMPANY
☐ AD16 PRINTER
☐ AD17 PRODUCTS
☐ AD18 PROMOTION
☐ AD19 PUBLISHING
☐ AD20 RETAIL
☐ AD21 SOCIAL
☐ AD22 SPORTS
☐ AD23 TRAVEL

☐ **GRAPHIS DESIGN** 99
(NOVEMBER 15, 1997)
CATEGORY CODES
☐ DE1 ANNUAL REPORTS
☐ DE2 BOOKS
☐ DE3 BROCHURES
☐ DE4 CALENDARS
☐ DE5 CORP. ID
☐ DE6 CURRENCY/STAMPS
☐ DE7 DIAGRAMS
☐ DE8 EDITORIAL
☐ DE9 EPHEMERA
☐ DE10 GAMES

☐ DE11 ILLUSTRATION
☐ DE12 LETTERHEAD
☐ DE13 LOGOS
☐ DE14 MENUS
☐ DE15 MUSIC (CD DESIGN)
☐ DE16 NEW MEDIA
☐ DE17 PACKAGING
☐ DE18 PAPER COMPANIES
☐ DE19 POSTERS
☐ DE20 PRODUCTS
☐ DE21 PROMOTION
☐ DE22 SHOPPING BAGS
☐ DE24 T-SHIRTS

SENDER _____ ENTRY NAME _____

TELEPHONE _____ FAX _____

COMPANY _____

STREET ADDRESS _____

CITY/STATE _____ ZIP/COUNTRY _____

ART DIRECTOR _____

MAILING ADDRESS _____ E-MAIL ADDRESS _____

CITY/STATE _____ ZIP/COUNTRY _____

TELEPHONE _____

DESIGNER _____

MAILING ADDRESS _____ E-MAIL ADDRESS _____

CITY/STATE _____ ZIP/COUNTRY _____

TELEPHONE _____

ILLUSTRATOR _____ MEDIUM _____

MAILING ADDRESS _____

CITY/STATE _____ ZIP/COUNTRY _____

TELEPHONE _____

PHOTOGRAPHER /PRODUCT PHOTOGRAPHER / AGENCY (PLEASE CIRCLE)

MAILING ADDRESS _____

CITY/STATE _____ ZIP/COUNTRY _____

TELEPHONE _____

AUTHOR / COPYWRITER /EDITOR (PLEASE CIRCLE)

MAILING ADDRESS _____

CITY/STATE _____ ZIP/COUNTRY _____

TELEPHONE _____ FAX _____

PRINTER/MANUFACTURER _____

PAPER _____ TYPEFACE _____

CLIENT/PUBLISHER _____ CITY/STATE/COUNTRY _____

PROVIDE A BRIEF DESCRIPTION (100 WORDS OR LESS) OF THE DESIGN OR ADVERTISING STRATEGY:

SIGNATURE _____ DATE _____

COMPLETE FORM, TAPE IT TO ENTRY, ENCLOSE A PHOTOCOPY AND PAYMENT. SEND TO CLOSEST ADDRESS:
☐ PAYMENT ENCLOSED   ☐ PAYMENT BY CREDIT CARD # _____ EXP. DATE _____
GRAPHIS BOOK CONTEST, C/O AMERICAN BOOK CENTER, BROOKLYN NAVY YARD, BLDG. #3, BROOKLYN, NY 11205 USA
GRAPHIS BOOK CONTEST, C/O CRONAT, PARC 3, F-68870 BARTENHEIM FRANCE